ST PAUL

THE MAN AND HIS WORK

BY

H. WEINEL
PROFESSOR EXTRAORDINARY OF THEOLOGY IN THE UNIVERSITY OF JENA

Translated by

THE REV. G. A. BIENEMANN, M.A.

And edited by

THE REV. W. D. MORRISON, LL.D.

Wipf and Stock Publishers
199 W 8th Ave, Suite 3
Eugene, OR 97401

St. Paul
The Man and His Work
By Weinel, H.
ISBN: 1-59752-156-6
Publication date 4/25/2005
Previously published by G. P. Putnam's Sons, 1906

PREFACE

THE greater part of this book appeared last year as a series of articles in the "*Christliche Welt.*" In answer to repeated requests, I have determined to recast these articles and publish them as a book. There is scarcely a page which has not been changed more or less, and two entire chapters, "The Theologian" and "The Man," have been added. I was more especially inclined to undertake this work because this book forms a necessary supplement to my *Jesus in the Nineteenth Century*, for it shows how the Gospel came to make that concordat with the "world," *i.e.* with the ancient state and its religion and morality which we call "church." I have tried to show how necessary and how salutary this compromise was, by what pure motives it was animated, but also with what dangers it was pregnant for the Gospel itself.

One other object I have had in writing: I have wanted to make our people understand and love Paul. And so nothing has pleased me more than when schoolmasters and other teachers of religion urged me to publish the articles in book form. I should be more than rewarded if it should help in making our educated classes realise the great discovery of the theology of the nineteenth century which is called "Paul." Most people still distrust Paul, the "fanatic" and the "dogmatist"; and no wonder: he whose fiery spirit could brook no bonds, on the rock of whose truthfulness and absoluteness the law made shipwreck, has himself become a bond and a yoke; a new law has been formed out of the husks of his religion, and the kernel has been laid on one side as un-essential. The boy was plagued at home with Paul's dogmas. Can we wonder that the man should detest this unendurable compulsion put upon his thoughts and conscience, together with its supposed cause? Or, at best, by dint of mechanical drill there remained an unintelligible, lifeless acceptation of formulæ. That is why Paul is so little known. And yet we are at least as much indebted to him as we are to Luther, whom he resembles the most nearly in all points, and for whom he paved the way to the religion of the Divine Fatherhood by his unwearied wrestling till he had found God.

Two things may perhaps be looked for in this book and sought in vain, and there may be some who will miss them. First, that the external features of the apostle's journeys have been passed by in silence. Schoolmasters especially may be sorry not to have the material wherewith to add a little realistic interest to their lessons. Secondly, there are possibly many who would like to have a fuller examination of the question of authenticity; they would like to know on what grounds only Romans, first and second Corinthians, Galatians, Philippians, and first Epistle to Thessalonians have been used as genuine Pauline epistles, and what reasons there are for upholding their authenticity against the attacks of Bruno Bauer, Loman, Steck, Kalthoff, etc.

As for the first omission, I would say that I do not consider it to be in the slightest degree necessary to discuss the harbour of Seleucia and the long walls of Athens and the Areopagus in order to understand the apostle Paul. And I think that, amid all the details about the apostle's journeys which schoolboys have to learn out of the Acts of the Apostles, they often entirely lose sight of the apostle himself; they can sometimes recite whole lists of perfectly useless names which have been drilled into them, but of the great missionary's spirit they have learnt next to nothing. This book was not written to perpetuate this mischievous system. Some of my readers, however, may with good reason wish to know rather more of the external setting of St. Paul's life; they may be referred to the excellent account which is given in the recently published life of Paul by C. Clemen Giessen, 1904, two vols. The writings of Renan (1869) and Hausrath (*The Apostle Paul*, 2nd edition, 1872), which are there referred to, may still be consulted with advantage; L. Schneller, *In alle Welt*, 1897, contains a good deal of modern material presented in a vivid manner.

We should have needed a volume of about the same length as the one we have written in order to discuss the question of authenticity in a satisfactory manner for those who are not professional theologians. It is especially difficult to convey to those who are not acquainted with the whole field of ancient Christian literature any satisfactory idea why it is an altogether hopeless undertaking to call in question the genuineness of all the letters that are written in the name of Paul. The facility, not to say the facile superficiality, with which Kalthoff fancies that he can decide this question in a few pages, I confess I do not possess. I have therefore determined to employ for my sketch of the personality of Paul and of his work only those letters which are recognised as genuine by almost all critics. The picture which I have first endeavoured to present will best speak for itself, and every reader can put the question to himself whether the man and the circumstances which are mirrored in the letters here employed really do or do not belong to the first age of Christianity.

The letters in the New Testament bearing the name of Paul, of which I have made no use, may be divided into four groups.

I. The Epistle to the Hebrews is only ascribed to Paul in later MSS. The Church always hesitated whether to ascribe it to the apostle or not: it was certainly not written by Paul.

II. The letters to Timothy and Titus (the so-called Pastoral epistles) are not to be attributed to Paul either. The majority of critics are agreed on this point: they are led to this conclusion, first, by the altogether different style of these letters; secondly, by the complete change of circumstances in the Church, which has reached a considerably later stage of development, and which the "Paul" of these letters prophesies for a later age (*e.g.* 1 Tim. iv.). Thus B. Weiss, who is one of the chief champions of the genuineness of these letters, no longer ventures to maintain that they are anything more than a further development of Paul's earlier standpoint, and of the circumstances of the Church, composed by the apostle himself. But even this compromise falls to the ground. Other critics consider small portions of these letters containing personal directions to be notes by the apostle which a later writer has incorporated into these letters which he wrote for his own time.

III. The genuineness of the Epistle to the Ephesians is upheld even by such critics as work according to the historical method without any dogmatic prepossessions. But the contrary opinion appears gradually to be gaining ground. The whole tenor of the letter, as well as some of the views there maintained, do not favour the opinion of a Pauline authorship. If we turn to this epistle after reading the Epistles to the Corinthians, it cannot fail to strike us as strange that in this letter (Cor. ii. 20) " Paul " speaks of the apostles (including himself therefore) as the foundation of the Church (no longer Christ, as in 1 Cor. iii. 11): nay, more, that he calls them (including himself) the holy apostles (iii. 5). This is the language of a later age. There are other considerations which invalidate the genuineness of the second Epistle to Thessalonians, which is upheld by practically the same critics who ascribe the Epistle to the Ephesians to the apostle himself.

IV. The vast majority of critics consider the Epistle to the Colossians and the short note to Philemon to be genuine, *i.e.* written by the same author as Romans and first and second Corinthians. Some few passages in the Epistle to the Colossians, which are strongly antignostic, are considered by some of these critics to be later insertions, while they acknowledge the Pauline authorship of the letter as a whole. Objections have also been raised against the letter to the Philippians, but scarcely anyone upholds them any longer.

There are besides, of course, isolated passages and chapters, the authenticity of which is contested; for an instance of such a case, the reader may be referred to page 277.

The first volume of Clemen's work is the best and most succinct book of reference for anyone who wishes to know the most recent opinions on all these questions. It contains, besides, complete indications of the literature of the subject. We may also refer to Pfleiderer, *Das Urchristentum*, Berlin, 2nd edition, 1902, 2 vols., for an examination of the question, written in a clear and beautiful style, and from a standpoint which is very nearly that of the present book, or to Jülicher's Introduction to the New Testament.

I trust that no essential feature will be found to be missing in the picture which I have attempted to draw of St Paul, although I have strictly confined myself to those letters the authenticity of which is acknowledged by the great majority of critics, including myself. Whoever wishes to know more about the first age of Christianity, should read the great and important work of C. Weizsäcker, *The Apostolic Age*, Tübingen, 3rd edition, 1902; and the smaller but very able book of Wernle, *The Beginnings of Christianity*, Tübingen, 2nd edition, 1903, English trans., Williams & Norgate, 1904, 2 vols.

The present work is intended to be read, and not used as a book of reference. But by combining the table of contents with the index of passages quoted, it will be easily possible to find a text in the particular connection in which it has been used.

We lay the surest foundation of all true goodness in man when we train him to gratitude and to reverence. Our forefathers, who, in the stress of circumstances, so often swept paganism out of the Church in the wrong place, have robbed us of one great source of reverence and of gratitude when they banished from the Church our great ancestors, the true saints, along with all the intruder crew, the Florians and Sebastians. Surely, since Carlyle has once more prepared us for a real hero-worship, we might make the attempt to restore true saint's-day celebrations in our Evangelical Church, and thus secure the great men of our religion their right place in divine service. Till this is possible, the school and the lecture-room are the places where Paul, as well as our other heroes, must be made to live again.

The more this book is used for such a purpose, the more will the author's dearest wish be realised.

TABLE OF CONTENTS

CHAP.		PAGES
I.	INTRODUCTION	i–13

THE PHARISEE.

II.	HOME AND PARENTAGE	14–20
III.	THE HERITAGE OF THE SCHOOL	21–35
IV.	THE HERITAGE OF THE SCHOOL—*continued*	36–52
V.	THE HERITAGE OF THE SCHOOL—*continued*	53–61

THE SEEKER AFTER GOD.

VI.	SAUL THE PATRIOT. THE FIGHT FOR THE LAW	62–76
VII.	THE DAY OF DAMASCUS. NIETZSCHE'S ACCUSATION	77–93

THE PROPHET.

VIII.	THE NEW MAN. THE NEW GOD	94–111
IX.	MAN'S COMMUNION. THE NEW FELLOWSHIP	112–133
X.	THE NEW MORALITY. ORIGIN OF CHRISTIANITY AND NIETZSCHE'S CRITICISMS	134–150

THE APOSTLE.

XI.	THE CALL OF THE MASTER. THE SOIL OF THE MISSION FIELD. THE MISSION FIELD	151–172
XII.	THE LIFE OF THE MISSIONARY. THE MISSION PREACHING	173–191
XIII.	THE PREACHER. THE ORGANISATION OF THE MISSION	192–207

CONTENTS

CHAP.		PAGES

THE FOUNDER OF THE CHURCH.

XIV. The Founder of the Church 208–217
XV. The Struggle for Freedom from the Law and for the Independence of Christianity . . 218–237
XVI. Freedom and Scrupulosity 238–248
XVII. Enthusiasm and Apostolical Worship . . 249–262
XVIII. The Faith and the World . . . 263–285

THE THEOLOGIAN.

XIX. The Beginning of Dogma. Justification by Faith 286–299
XX. The Significance of the Death of Christ . 300–312
XXI. The Christ and the Jesus 313–328
XXII. The Pauline Ethics. Foundation of Ethics . 329–352

THE MAN.

XXIII. Dross. The Apostle's Human Greatness. Winning Love 353–373
XXIV. The Friend. Contrasts. In the Presence of Death 374–386

INDEX 387–399

ST PAUL

INTRODUCTION.

CHAPTER I.

PAUL once said of Moses, "To this day a veil lies on their hearts when he is read," and at present the words may be applied to the apostle himself. To some he has become a great authority, a marvel, or even a canonised saint; to others a mere name, a mass of shadowy recollections and of half-forgotten texts, which they learned as children with much toil and trouble. Few, very few, really know him, and these few are for the most part scholars or theologians.

But for those that do know him, the form of this tentmaker and divine looms ever higher and higher in the world's history. They feel that they are in the presence of one who, having suffered, struggled, and prevailed, has left the impress of his character upon many centuries; one with whose individuality we of to-day have still to reckon, as did those who saw him face to face, and were carried away by the mighty words that proceeded out of his mouth.

Just as during his lifetime he was loved and hated as scarce any other man has been, so he fares to this day amongst those that know him. Here we have the proof of his imperishable greatness. Nor should we be astonished to find that he was hated as bitterly as he was loved. Every active, independent mind excites hatred and love at once. Even He who was Incarnate Love was compelled to give utterance to the sad and painful words: " I come to set at variance a man with his father, a daughter with her mother; and a man's foes will be they of his own household." But He knew too what that man was worth who never made a foe: "Woe unto you when all men speak well of you." So He spake who loved His enemies even unto His death.

Let us listen to two of St Paul's adversaries of our own day—two men in whom an accurate acquaintance with the facts of the case was combined with a bold, intrepid spirit and a clear sense of truth, and who for all that hated the apostle as only one of those great personalities can be hated that sin against humanity.

Lagarde (see the *Deutsche Schriften*, 1886, pp. 71 fol.) conceives himself justified in presenting the following picture of St Paul to the German people:—

"It was only owing to the fact that the disciples chosen by Jesus Himself were able to form but an extremely inadequate, one-sided conception—it was almost a caricature—of the great picture that their eyes had gazed upon, that a complete stranger, an outsider, came to exercise influence upon the Church.

"Paul—for so this outsider was called—was a true child of Abraham, a Pharisee from top to toe even after he became a Christian. He persecuted the Nazarenes with all his might for a while, and was then convinced—it was some eight or ten years after

INTRODUCTION

Jesus' death—by a vision on a journey to Damascus that he was persecuting the truth in showing himself hostile to Jesus' teaching. This may be found to be psychologically conceivable, and I do not doubt in the very least that so fanatical a character was converted (in consequence of a hallucination) into the very opposite of that which he had been some time previously. But it is monstrous that men of any historical training should attach any importance whatever to this Paul. . . .

"It was Paul who introduced the Old Testament into the Church, through the influence of which book the Gospel has perished as far as it could perish: it was Paul who conferred upon us the priceless boon of the Pharisaic exegesis which proves everything from whatever you like, inserting the contents ready-made into the text which are supposed to be found therein, and then pluming itself on a faithful adherence to the very words of Scripture: it was Paul who popularised the Jewish sacrificial theory pregnant with so many consequences: it is he .... who saddled us with the Jewish view of history. All this he did in spite of the energetic protests of the early Christian Church, which, Jewish as it was, was less Jewish than Paul in its opinions, and at least did not hold a refined form of the Israelite faith to be a gospel sent by God. Paul was impervious to all criticism. The book of Exodus furnished him with a defence proof against all arguments. 'Pharaoh's heart was hardened.' With such a theory it is as easy to dispute as it is easy to send a man about his business if he comes to you with arguments and wishes to hear your answer. You have only to say: 'His heart was hardened.'"

In Lagarde you have the theologian, the man who feels that heavy yoke of dogma which Paul more than all others has laid upon us—for Paul has become the law and canon of our faith.

Nietzsche, on the other hand, hates in Paul the man, his struggles and his redemption. A passage in the *Morgenröte*, in which the author sums up his judgment upon Paul, will be sufficient to show this:—

"The majority of people still believe in the work of the Holy Ghost as author, or are under the after-effects of this belief: if they open their Bibles it is to 'get some good,' to find some indication of comfort in their own personal need, be it great or small—in a word, they find in the Bible what they put into it. But who knows, with the exception of a few scholars, that in the Bible there also stands recorded the history of one of the most ambitious of men, a past master in importunacy whose superstition was only equalled by his cunning? That is the history of the apostle Paul. But if it had not been for this strange story, if it had not been for the aberrations of his mind and the waves of emotion that passed over his soul, there would be no Christianity. . . . Of course, if the story had been understood in time, if Paul's writings had been read, really read, not as revelations of 'the Holy Ghost,' but with an honest, unfettered, independent mind and without thinking of all our personal needs—there were no such readers for fifteen centuries—then Christianity would also have come to an end long ago. It is this same story—the story of this much tortured, much to be pitied man, an exceedingly unpleasant personage both to himself and others—which shows us how the ship of Christianity threw a good portion of its Jewish ballast overboard, so that it was enabled to go out among the heathen."

Much against their will, Lagarde and Nietzsche are alike compelled to recognise the importance of the man while condemning him and his work. But we shall have something more to say as to this severe condemnation. For, however severe and unhistorical it may be, it must be based upon certain facts and certain features in the apostle's character. And that is the very reason why it is all the more dangerous, for it has rightly been observed that half a truth is more dangerous than a lie.

Another and a very difficult problem has arisen, however, for those who, while accepting the apostle's every word as their authority, have acquired some insight into his individuality, his work, and his greatness. Schell has very clearly and rightly defined it in the introduction to his *Christus* when he asks : " Who has the greater claim to be called the founder of the world-religion, Jesus or Paul? Who has the right to be counted the originator of ecclesiastical Christianity with its belief in original sin, vicarious sacrifice, the atonement, the sacraments, and the Christian ministry?"

There can be no doubt that we should give the answer "Paul" to the latter question, even though the organisation of the Christian ministry was not his work but that of his successors. Even the first question may be answered with "Paul" if by Christianity we understand belief in dogmas as to the person of Christ and His propitiatory death. For of all the Christians of the first generation Paul was the first, as far as we know, to attempt a theoretical explanation of His death.

It is all the more regrettable that Paul is so little known, for what Schell says of Roman Catholic Christianity can be applied, *mutatis mutandis*, to our Protestant people: " And yet St Paul, a saint if ever there was one, who has fanned into flame the fire of devotion in so many a heart in search of its God, has never become an object of religious worship—in the real sense of the word—as the Virgin Mary, as St Joseph, as St Anthony, as St Aloysius. St Paul has always remained a stranger to the soul of the people."

We are not surprised that Paul has never become a popular Roman Catholic saint, in spite of all official ecclesiastical honour that is paid to him; for there is nothing whatever Catholic in the rugged, sharply outlined features of this soldier of the Cross. But it is all the more remarkable that Paul *our* apostle still remains, on the whole, a sealed book to our Protestant people, a book of which a few words are known by heart, but which otherwise is never disturbed in its place on the bookshelf. St Paul, however, was something more than a collection of aphorisms on the subjects of sin and grace. Of all the Christians of the first generation he is by far the most conspicuous, in very truth a man of genius. When Jesus and the faith of His first disciples had won their victory over this man—their greatest adversary—then Christianity triumphed as it never did before or since.

It was an event of world-historic importance as well. For it is a great deal more than a mere fanciful comparison when it is said that the apostle's great missionary journeys from Antioch to Rome were a repetition of Alexander the Great's conquests, only in the opposite direction. The very first of historians, Herodotus, "the father of history," saw that the chief subject in the many chapters of the history of humanity was that never-ending exchange, that great struggle between the civilisations of East and West, in which Alexander's expedition marks the first decisive battle wherein the West scores an apparent victory. Now St Paul's mission, with which Christianity enters upon its triumphant progress, forms the introduction to the last and most important epoch in this same struggle.

The great mission of Christianity is in reality mainly St Paul's work, the work of a man who knew not fear, and whose pride was to be called by one title, and one alone: an apostle of Jesus the Christ. To Him he sacrificed in true manliness all the strength he possessed, and for Him he won the victory. At his death the new faith stretched from one end of the empire to the other, as far as Rome, in a chain of flourishing congregations. When he was won over to the cause of Jesus, Christianity was an insignificant Jewish sect. Though the disciples had found life and salvation in their faith in Jesus, the Messiah who had died for sinners and had been raised up by God, they did not know all that they had in Him. Jesus of Nazareth had given them much, but after all they could not quite efface the impression that they had looked upon a pious Jew who had fought and who had suffered for the right exposition of the law and for the purity of the

Temple. So they sat at Jerusalem and preached and waited for Him to descend upon the clouds of heaven with the New Jerusalem and His many mansions for the poor and devout children of God. They were, it is true, hated and persecuted by many of their fellow-countrymen. They were dispersed to Samaria and as far as Antioch; but they did not know that a new religion had started on its progress throughout the world, and that all the peoples of the earth were destined to find therein their blessedness and their salvation. Paul was the first to experience Christianity as a new religion in his own life, in fightings without, in fears within; and it was he who saved it when the Twelve could scarcely keep it from sinking down into Judaism again, so heavily were they oppressed by the weight of ancient Jewish tradition.

These external effects are but the manifestation of the all-compelling power that resided within him. St Paul is a hero in the domain of the will, a born leader of men. He is also a hero in the domain of thought. We have grown accustomed to look upon the history of thought as the history of philosophy, and to look for its chief exponents among the constructors of great systems of thought — men who renounce every form of activity. We are mistaken, however, for decisive action rests upon decisive insight. And this we find in its original power just as frequently among great poets and prophets and men of great force of will as amongst thinkers in the narrower sense of the word. St Paul has impressed for ever a whole series of fundamental ideas, above all, a new outline of history, and certain ethical conceptions and observations, on the thought of the

Western world. Millions of men to-day think with his thoughts and speak with his words, who have but the vaguest notion of his personal life.

St Paul is also epoch-making in the history of religion. Whilst Jesus falls out of the line of development of the Judaism of His time as much as He belongs to it, Paul forms the natural reaction against the theology of the Scribes, which was an attempt to organise the people according to the prophetic ideal by a codified string of laws. Here, as ever, the means became an end, and the organisation came finally to be the sworn foe of every prophetic element in the people: John the Baptist and Jesus are opposed to the Scribes and Pharisees. Now, Paul is the Pharisee, in whom the weight of the law upon a true and genuine soul was so oppressive that it finally burst all fetters, and turned in its destructive energy against the law—against all law, in every religion. Paul is the great discoverer of the fact that God and the law are contrary the one to the other, and that the only way in which the law can lead to God is by becoming our torment and awaking in us a longing for escape. Paul could only attain after sore struggles, in the hardest hour of his life, to that goal which for Jesus was the natural childlike life of love felt for the heavenly Father. But the position thus gained was, moreover, maintained; triumphantly Paul repelled all attacks, and so rescued this priceless possession for all mankind. Yet once again it was recaptured by the old religion in the shape of Roman Catholicism, until Martin Luther, having passed through a crisis like that of Paul, recovered it with Paul's words for his weapons.

There are, however, other reasons for the important position which Paul occupies in the religious history of the West. In the West, the soul of man has ever yearned to obtain two blessings by means of religion — holiness and immortality. In scarcely any man in ancient times has this yearning been manifested as clearly and as loudly as in Paul; no one has ever believed with such intensity that his yearning had been satisfied, and in no one has this belief been transformed into as great a capacity for ethical volition and courageous action. That is why he has kindled this same inner life in so many others; and the flame of his enthusiasm still burns throughout the centuries, in spite of the dross still visible in his personality, after all that the ecclesiastical refiners and purifiers have done.

There was yet another factor in St Paul's nature, which rendered him especially capable of influencing the age in which he lived, and of satisfying the particular way in which it sought for holiness and immortality. In Paul two currents meet: that flowing from all religions of antiquity in so far as they had been re-cast in mysteries and Hellenistic philosophy of religion, and that proceeding from the unique religious life of Israel. Just as St Paul is the first Protestant if we look at his religion, so he is the first Catholic if we think of his theology and ecclesiastical activity. Jesus is a far more solitary figure in His time, however much He belonged to it; and to this day His position in history is far more isolated than that of Paul, who had absorbed a great deal more of the general knowledge and culture of his day. That is why Paul's influence was greater than that of Jesus, who could only be apprehended by the Gentile world, with its longing for mysteries, sacraments, and philosophy, through and by means of Paul. And here we come to the last and greatest question which Paul raises for us. Is the Christianity which Paul preached, and which still lives to-day in Church and dogma, another religion than the gospel which Jesus proclaimed? What is the significance of dogma and of Church for the history of Christianity? But with these questions the problem presented by St Paul's life becomes a present-day problem of the most immediate interest.

For at the present day the very existence of Christianity is at stake, and the struggle is concentrated upon two positions. The first question round which the tide of battle surges is this: Can Christianity be separated from the conceptions of the fall, original sin, the blood-bought atonement of God, and the sacraments which it owed to Paul above all others when it entered with him on the great stage of the world's history? Those who answer this question in the negative are either people who stifle the claims of reason for the sake of Christianity, for reason is for ever repeating to them that the modern conception of the world is the right one; or, again, they are men who doubt their religion because of the claims of reason, and in this state they either cling to the morality of Christianity, or cast even that overboard into the sea of doubt. And this brings us to the second position round which the contest is being waged. Men are realising more and more clearly that the ethics of the Christian Church are a weak compromise between the stern morality of

Jesus, with its note of hostility to the world, and the claims of the State and civilisation, or even the demands of human convenience and the love of domination. And the question as to its truth has come upon Christianity like the thief in the night.

Here, too, St Paul plays an important part, for it is he who laid the foundations of the Church and paved the way for its reconciliation with the "world" —that is, with the life of the ancient state and civilisation. Nor can anyone pretend to solve these problems, either for himself or for others, who has not obtained some insight into their historical origin. This insight he will obtain from none better than St Paul.

Such are the considerations that have guided the author in the following pages. The reader will look in vain for the externals of Paul's life, for the description of the peculiarities of his missionary work, for any discussions as to the date and authorship of the letters. Great and learned books have been written on these subjects. Our task is to get to understand a character of the first century in and for this our twentieth century, to represent the everlasting questions that assail the human heart in the apostle's features of human weakness and human greatness, and guided by this, its "second founder," to obtain some preliminary grasp of the fundamental problems of Christianity. The more the historian attempts to go beyond the mere narration of events and description of conditions, the more he essays the delineation of character, the greater the danger of error. He is not, however, to be deterred by this danger from undertaking this most precious task, if only he can honestly say to himself that he has done

INTRODUCTION

all that lay in his power to base his description upon a solid foundation, even if he must forego the pleasure of showing some of the results of this preliminary work in the shape of notes or excursus. The second danger, that of adapting the history to the practical needs of our own day, is considerably diminished by the mere fact that it is clearly realised. Those historians who imagine that they are writing without being influenced by contemporary events, really encounter a far greater peril: more than once they have fallen unconscious victims to the problems of their age.

THE PHARISEE.

CHAPTER II.

HOME AND PARENTAGE.

RIGHTLY do biographers, both in old and new times, attach the greatest importance to a description of the soil in which their heroes have grown up. Guided by them, we set out on a journey to the hero's home; directed by them, we knock at the door of his father's house, we look in his parents' face and we get to know them, and they tell us the old tales that have been handed down from one generation to another. But such good fortune has never fallen to the lot of those who have written the lives of the great men in the history of religion in ancient times. All that we know of them is really but the one brilliant period in which they stand out from the mass of their contemporaries with the light of their love and their hatred beating upon them, while they struggle bravely forward and scatter blessings far and wide. And yet it is just in their case that we would give so much to know what kind of a mother it was that folded the hands of the boy that was the father of the man and taught him his first prayer, and how the special features of his ancestors, their inmost characters, their outward manners, their

HOME AND PARENTAGE

inclinations and their sins, their gentleness and their strength, their faith and their longing, are all reflected in the famous son of the family.

Of Paul, too, we know very little directly concerning his youth, his parentage, and his relations. He has told us himself that his parents were strict Hebrews of purely Jewish extraction, of the tribe of Benjamin. This he asserted more than once, with eager vehemence, in his letters, when his enemies taunted him with being no real Jew.

"Whereinsoever any one is daring (I speak in folly), I am daring also. Are they Hebrews? So am I. Are they Israelites? So am I. Are they the seed of Abraham? So am I."[1]

He can lay claim to these old and honourable titles of his people. He can claim them for himself and for his ancestry. They are of pure descent; there has been no intermixture of foreign blood.

But when we go on to seek for more definite information as to his parents, all our sources fail us. We cannot even state with certainty which was his native town, or where he spent his youth. The author of the Acts places the following statement in St Paul's mouth: "I am a Jew, a native of Tarsus in Cilicia, brought up in the city, trained at the feet of Gamaliel[2] in the strict system of our ancestral law. I was as zealous in God's service as you are all to-day."[3] Perhaps, if we bear another passage[4] in mind, where mention is made of his nephew in Jerusalem, we are meant to suppose that he grew up in the house of an elder sister who was married there.

[1] 2 Cor. xi. 22; *cp.* Rom. xi. 1, Phil. iii. 5.
[2] *Cp.* Phil. iii. 5.   [3] Acts xxii. 3 *seq.*   [4] Acts xxiii. 16.

We may assume, then, according to the Acts, that St Paul found a second, his real, home in Jerusalem.

It is still possible for us, even at the present day, to prove the correctness of this assumption. For there is a way whereby we can trace the mysterious growth of a personality. We can reason *a posteriori* from the character of the grown man to the traces of his development. In St Paul's case, the facts that he is a man who has been converted, that we are fairly well acquainted with the period after his conversion, and that he himself gives us a very detailed account of all the phenomena of his conversion, make the reasoning to be a comparatively easy matter. If you eliminate in a converted man all the new factors that have come into his life through his conversion, the transformation which this decisive occurrence has effected in his emotional life and in the processes of volition and of thought, then you can form a distinct picture of the man's character, of what he had already acquired and possessed in the period of development before his conversion. Caution must, of course, be exercised, and we must impartially weigh all the attendant circumstances if we would guard against error; but we need by no means despair of attaining to certain and definite results.

Unless a man's true self has been overlaid by a literary education, the very pictures in which he clothes his thoughts accurately reflect his surroundings, especially that first environment which met his soul's clear eyes on its first voyage of discovery in the world without. The Gospel of Jesus is the offspring of village life. In His pictures we breathe wafts of Nature, ever fresh and wholesome. Nature spoke to

HOME AND PARENTAGE

Him in her still, clear voice. In the quiet evening hour, when the cool wind blows softly down from the mountains, He leaves house and tools to go forth into the open air and commune with His Father. There He sees the people standing in the street and speaking of the red sky and to-morrow's weather. He sees the children playing in the streets, and He smiles at their childish self-will. Soon He learns that older children also play in like manner. Out He goes, through the gates and far up on the hillside, where the bright anemones grow, the flowers which gladden the inmost heart. What are Solomon's purple robes compared with their living sheen as each sways its calyx in the evening breeze? He sees the sower in the field, the mustard tree in the garden. He sees the shepherd and his flock and the sparrow that has fallen from the roof and is lying dead on the ground. And all speaks to Him in living tones, tells Him that His Father is ever working, heralds the coming of the kingdom, holds converse with Him in the thousand still, small voices that only He can hear.

Paul, too, employs pictures from Nature. No man is so impoverished, so town-bred, as not to have some such, at least, at his command. Paul, too, knows that God's divine character and the Eternal powers may be recognised in God's creation.[1] He speaks of the grain of wheat as a picture of the resurrection,[2] of the beauty of the stars;[3] he compares himself and others to gardeners,[4] and his are those beautiful words of "creation's distrest, expectant gaze awaiting the un-

[1] Rom. i. 20 *seq.*   [2] 1 Cor. xv. 37.
[3] 1 Cor. xv. 40.   [4] 1 Cor. iii. 6–9.

veiling of the sons of God."[1] But these same words also reveal the great difference that exists between the apostle and his Master. St Paul's view of Nature is pessimistic, and, as he wrote, he had before his mind's eye the weary, heavy-laden, hardly-used beasts of burden of a great city.

It is the mood of the decaying year, not the young and vigorous faith of spring, which we meet with in Jesus' pictures, to whom even the sparrow that falls from the roof speaks, not of universal decay, but of the almighty will of His heavenly Father. We seem to detect in the apostle's character something of that weariness, that longing, which marks the city-dweller of the ancient world. His pictures, too, are for the most part taken from urban life. Whether it was ignorance of Nature or the forced illustration of a thought that produced his defective simile of the grafting of a wild olive on a cultivated plant,[2] can no longer be established with certainty, but the great majority of his comparisons clearly show him to have lived, as a rule, in a town.

Metaphors derived from building and "edification" are employed by Paul very frequently, far more frequently than by Jesus "the young masterbuilder." He knows all the houses of the city, from the palaces with their gold and silver to the workman's thatched cottage in the suburbs.[3] He leads us into the room where the mother is feeding the child with milk,[4] whence the leaven is purged out before Easter.[5] The earthenware vessels on the bench,[6] the

---

[1] Rom. viii. 18–23.
[2] Rom. xi. 16 *seq.*
[3] 1 Cor. iii. 12 *seq.*
[4] 1 Cor. iii. 2 ; 1 Thess. ii. 7 *seq.*
[5] 1 Cor. v. 6–8 ; Gal. v. 9
[6] 2 Cor. iv. 7.

HOME AND PARENTAGE 19

mirror on the wall,[1] the letter on the table,[2] all alike serve to illustrate his thoughts. He shows us the busy town life with its rows of shops[3] past which the "schoolmaster" leads his pupil to school,[4] and the street through which the glorious triumphal procession wends it way.[5] He frequently takes his images from the soldier's life[6]—even the trumpets[7] are impressed into his service; and the life of the legal world,[8] the theatre,[9] and the racecourse[10] also furnish him with metaphors. All these figures come to him so naturally that it is extremely probable he was acquainted with these things before he started on his missionary journeys, that these pictures from the life of a Hellenistic city impressed themselves on his soul while he was still a child, and therefore that Tarsus was not only his birthplace but also his home.

Tarsus was a populous city, situated on one of the principal lines of commerce of the world, just on the frontier of the two most important languages of the time—Greek and Aramaic. It was the seat of one of the most important schools of philosophy, a genuinely Hellenistic town, exactly reproducing the mixed civilisation of the age.

There St Paul's soul was filled with all those influences which made the man capable of becoming the apostle of the whole Roman empire, of becoming a Jew unto the Jews and a Gentile to the Gentiles,

[1] 1 Cor xiii. 12; 2 Cor. iii. 18.　　[2] 2 Cor. iii. 2 *seq.*
[3] 2 Cor. ii. 17.　　[4] Gal. iii. 25.
[5] 2 Cor. ii. 14.　　[6] 2 Cor. x. 3–5.　　[7] 1 Cor. xiv. 8.
[8] Gal. iii. and iv. 1–6; Rom. ix. 4, viii. 15, vii. 1 *seq.*, etc.
[9] 1 Cor. iv. 9; vii. 31.　　[10] 1 Cor. ix. 24, etc.

to win both unto his Master, for in his inmost soul he understood them both.

Of his father's house we can only say one thing. Trained as he was in the severe Pharisaic discipline,[1] the time of his childhood was probably a hard and certainly a serious one. For his tender, delicate conscience, for his strong and resolute will, he was probably indebted, as was Luther, to his father's strict education. Such a youth is, in the case of richly dowered, strong natures, the earnest of a manhood that accomplishes great things.

[1] Phil. iii. 3; Acts xxiii. 6.

THE PHARISEE.

CHAPTER III.

The Heritage of the School.

MANY and varied are the influences which combine to fashion the man out of the boy. The friendly atmosphere of home imprints its pictures on his mind; all that he sees in the streets, his games and his intercourse with his playmates, help silently to mould his character; but greater and more lasting than all these is the effect of the school, with its established traditions and the penetrating power with which it takes possession of the youthful memory.

What the boy Saul learned in the school of the Pharisees, that determined Paul the Christian's thoughts and feelings in decisive hours, although to himself he seemed to have become "a new creature." As certainly as he was *that*, so certainly it was no new birth he had experienced, but simply the transforming of his innermost life. If, then, we wish to understand Paul, we must get as clear a grasp as possible of the man Saul. I do not mean to reproduce the external setting of his life. That would, after all, be but to draw in very general terms a historical picture setting forth the social life of a Jew's quarters in a Hellenist town. I shall rather endeavour to present the Pharisee's inner life—his intellectual and religious property, in so far as this is open to inspection. And this can really be done even to-day; first, because we can draw the above-mentioned inferences from a later period in his life, and then, also, because it is possible to verify our conclusions by comparison with contemporary Jewish literature, both Pharisaic and non-Pharisaic. And so we shall see that a large proportion of what is traditionally known as "Paulinism" no more specifically belongs to Paul than does much of the rest of the stock inherited from previous generations. It is contemporary Jewish theology.

The best and most valuable heritage Jesus and Paul received from their fathers was their belief in God. Although God revealed Himself to each of them in their life in a new way—and it was just at this vital point of piety that each experienced that which was convincingly new for himself and for humanity—yet the experience was alone possible by reason of the belief in God which each inherited from their people. It is one God in whom their people believes, one God to whom it offers its sacrifices and its prayers; one God, however many so-called gods there may be [1]—for there are no gods, but angels or demons. One will there is that rules, almighty, over the world; not a summary of blind natural forces, not the indivisible Divinity of ancient philosophy, but a powerful, holy Person. He is indeed the Creator of the heavens and the earth,[2] but He is not merely immanent in this creation. He rules over it with a strong hand and an outstretched arm.

[1] 1 Cor. viii. 6.   [2] 1 Cor. viii. 6; x. 26.

THE HERITAGE OF THE SCHOOL

He has a history with humanity on earth. He is the God of Abraham, Isaac, and Jacob, the God of His people ; a living God, Spirit and Will, not wood and stone like the popular gods of the heathen.[1] And He has made Himself known to His people, and through them to all nations by the prophets; there needs not to seek Him in vain disputes of rhetorician and philosopher, in the wisdom of this world. And we know He works not blindly like the brute forces of Nature, nor capriciously like the gods and goddesses of Greece, the spoiled children of fortune: He is a God who will make manifest in tremendous judgment, that in His sight nothing stands higher than Righteousness.[2]

This same belief in God, inherited from Judaism, inherent in the Old Testament, constituted a most substantial factor in the eagerness with which the Gentile world laid hold of Christianity, completely accepting the Old Testament into the bargain, in spite of the heavy stumbling-blocks it presented, alike in æsthetic and moral aspects. For such belief brought with it just what the noblest spirits of the dying old world yearned for: the certainty of an almighty, holy, and just will, and of a goal towards which the world was travelling. Paul had indeed this treasure too, in earthen vessels. The particular way in which the people of Israel were brought into connection with this God, became untenable after a time, and was by degrees discarded among the Gentiles ; we are passing through the final stage in this process to-day, while we are exchanging the thought of a special revelation of God to His people

[1] 2 Cor. iii. 6, vi. 18 ; Rom. ix. 26.   [2] Rom. iii. 25.

for that of the great history of religion throughout all humanity. The evolution of thought has also long since outstripped the conceptions which one used to form of the personality of the Deity. I do not mean to discuss how far we may or may not apply a literal interpretation to the New Testament passages about God sitting on a throne, God's eye, God's right hand, and so forth. The one circumstance, that Paul seriously conceives God under the image of a man as distinct from a woman—and thus admits the man to a superior position with regard to her[1]—this is in itself sufficient to show under what human conceptions people at this time still thought of God, and how even a "scholar" like Paul lived in the ideas of his time.

We notice the same thing when we consider the conception of the universe that forms the basis of his whole outlook. To him as to his people the world appears as a three-storied building: the lowest story is the realm of the dead;[2] above this, the terrestrial world; and over it, heaven with its inhabitants.[3] Heaven is a space, an arched dome, from the midst of which Christ appears,[4] within which God dwells, surrounded by angels and spirits.[5] There are several heavenly domes one above another, with "many mansions," in which even the glorified bodies of the Redeemed are already at rest.[6] Paul himself has once been in the third heaven and in Paradise,[7] which latter,

---

[1] 1 Cor. xi. 7. [2] Rom. xiv. 9.
[3] Phil. ii. 10. [4] Gal. iv. 4.
[5] Rom. i. 18 and 1 Cor. viii. 5; 1 Thess. i. 10 and iv. 16; 1 Cor. xv. 47; Gal. i. 8.
[6] 2 Cor. v. 1. [7] 2 Cor. xii. 2, etc.

THE HERITAGE OF THE SCHOOL

according to the passage in question and according to other contemporary indications, must have been conceived as situated in one of the various heavens. This heavenly world is the eternal world; all that pertains to it is eternal;[1] and therefore it is the object of longing to all those who feel themselves delivered over to the bondage of corruption here on earth.[2]

The earth is a small place. Paul's unresting missionary zeal is fired by the ardent wish to preach the gospel to the whole world. This Paul considers quite possible within his lifetime,[3] for his outlook is bounded by the borders of the Roman empire; for him, they are the ends of the habitable earth.

Between the pillars of Hercules and the Indies are contained all that on earth shall bow the knee before the Lord.

It is the same with regard to Paul's conception of Nature. God created the world, when He said, Light shall shine out of darkness![4] The creation often becomes for Paul, as here, an image of man's transformation through faith. The Firstborn, the Messiah, took part in the creation, for "through Him are all things, and we through Him";[5] we, the new creation. The first creation proceeded in appointed stages: God, the Christ, man, woman; the Christ out of God, the man out of Christ, the woman out of the man, and thus each to the glory of the other[6] and for the other.[7]

But perhaps what strikes us as most strange is

[1] 2 Cor. iv. 18. [2] Rom. viii. 21. [3] Rom. x. 18.
[4] 2 Cor. iv. 6.   [5] 1 Cor. viii. 6. [6] 1 Cor. xi. 3 *seq.*
[7] 1 Cor. xi. 9; *cp.* 1 Cor. iii. 23.

Paul's notion of the heavenly bodies; what we see of these is their "bodies" merely:—

"All flesh is not the same flesh; but there is one flesh of man, and another flesh of beasts, and another flesh of birds, and another of fishes. There are also celestial bodies, and bodies terrestrial; but the glory of the celestial is one, and the glory of the terrestrial is another. There is one glory of the sun, and another glory of the moon, and another glory of the stars, for one star differeth from another star in glory."[1]

Evidently Paul thought of himself and his contemporaries, Jew as well as Greek, dwelling in the glorious celestial bodies of the stars, call them Helios or Semele, Azazel or Uriel. In the Hebrew literature of the time, angel and star are very often synonyms for the same being.

No detail of ancient cosmography appears more incongruous to us than the ideas about a world of spirits, which was behind and above our world. Familiar as we are from our schooldays with this world of angels and devils, and denuded as it has become for us alike of bliss and terror, we yet fancy we understand such a conception. When we are brought, however, face to face with the Oriental imagination as presented in form and colour, we instinctively feel that to our eye, trained by the contemplation of the Greek ideal of beauty, and accustomed to imagine fair golden-winged cherubs, such Oriental colours are too crass. And we consider the picture as giving an exaggerated impression of the influence such conceptions may have had on the antique mind. Let us not forget, however, that

[1] 1 Cor. xv. 39 *seq.*

THE HERITAGE OF THE SCHOOL 27

to the Oriental of Paul's day all these things were not mere representations and images of fancy, but rather a terrible reality, and, as was supposed, matters of actual experience.

The idea of a kingdom of good and a kingdom of bad spirits, of angels of light, and angels of darkness with Satan at their head, was probably transferred to the Jewish religion from the Persian. At the same time the personages of the old popular belief, night spectres and demons that roamed in waste places, came into increasing prominence. Both these conceptions were strengthened in proportion as the notion of God gradually became purer and nobler, under the influence of the prophets. Under this influence one no longer ventured to derive from God certain "supernatural" evil effects, as had unhesitatingly been done hitherto. Then came the influence of the dominion of the foreigner, with his belief in demons and gods, whose oracles and miracles were not called in question, but simply interpreted as the work of evil spirits. So it came about that in the last centuries before Jesus, Judaism, and especially Pharisaism, began to believe in a host of spirits, and to connect certain ideas with them, which up till then were either non-existent or quite subordinate. The Apocryphal books, and still more the Apocalyptic literature, such as the books of Daniel and Enoch, are full of angels and spirits of all kinds. And in many passages of Paul's epistles we get indications that there was no portion of the doctrine of his school which he made more emphatically his own, and that none influenced the peculiar nature of his piety more powerfully.

God is ruler of the world He created, and we can see Him in His creation to this day in so far as it has remained Nature. But the history of man is ruled by another, and lies under his will till Christ shall make His enemies God's footstool. This other is Satan. He is the god of this age.[1]

When the Greek says "Zeus" we should rightly say "Satan." He has blinded men's eyes by false wisdom and sinful living—he and his fellows—the "rulers of this age."[2] Apollo, Athene, and the Muses, whom poets and philosophers adore, and all the gods of the Gentiles, though they be called gods, are in reality spiritual powers, demons, whom Christ will abolish,[3] "which are coming to nought."[4] Paul's words do not refer to the Roman dominion or other authority, not to Pilate or to Herod:—

"We speak wisdom among the perfect, yet a wisdom not of this world, nor of the rulers of this world, which are coming to nought; but we speak God's wisdom . . . . which none of the rulers of this world knoweth; for had they known it, they would not have crucified the Lord of Glory."[5]

True, the earthly potentates are the instruments by means of which the real powers work, yet to the apostle this world of spirits is the chief thing, and on this the human instruments depend. What has Pilate, what has Herod, to do with wisdom? Would Paul speak of them as "coming to nought"? That would be a commonplace.

Why does he teach, "they have not known the Lord of Glory"? All this is only clear to us if we

[1] 2 Cor. iv. 4.   [2] 1 Cor. ii. 6-8.   [3] 1 Cor. xv. 24.
[4] 1 Cor. ii. 6.   [5] 1 Cor. ii. 6-8.

THE HERITAGE OF THE SCHOOL 29

take "the rulers of this world" to mean spiritual powers, who did not recognise the Christ who, like them, came from the spirit world. Hebrew " Apocalypse" and gnostic " Revelation" alike have long detailed accounts how that Christ, unrecognised, passed through the various heavens, and descended to earth; and how it was only as risen Lord that He was seen of angels.[1]

The spirit powers that now rule the world have fallen away from God. God had set them as "shepherds" and "watchmen" over the people, as Daniel and Enoch witness. Paul, too, refers to them for purposes of warning. There is no power except it be ordained by God : where there is power, it has been ordered and established by God. And as such, man may submit to it. But the great hope, both of Jew and of Christian, is, that God will soon overturn this Roman rule, and inaugurate His own kingdom upon earth—that God will shortly bruise Satan under the Christians' feet![2] For what concord hath Christ with Belial (= "Evil")?[3]

In this one passage Paul calls the devil, not Satan, but Belial, so that it has been assumed, perhaps rightly, that the Antichrist, or man of sin of the latter days, is here intended:[4] a demonic being whose coming brings about the rule of all evil, whom Christ, on His return, shall slay with the breath of His mouth. In the genuine Pauline epistles the Devil is never called διάβολος, the slanderer, the false accuser, the enemy of men—the English word comes straight from the Greek. Paul always

[1] 1 Tim. iii. 16. [2] Rom. xvi. 20.
[3] 2 Cor. vi. 15. [4] 2 Thess. ii. 7-12.

gives him the corresponding Hebrew and Aramaic name of Satan, of which διάβολος is the translation.

According to Paul's presentment, the devil is "black": for if he wants to play the part of an angel of light, he must first "fashion himself."[1] This he does in his subtlest temptation; deceit and temptation being his means to gain power over men's hearts. So he is called "*the*" Tempter.[2] But he has means yet more mighty to win men for himself and to hinder God's work in them. When Paul wanted to visit the Thessalonians, "Satan placed an external hindrance"[3] in his way: a messenger of Satan was given him to buffet the apostle, to prevent his exulting in the sense of power inspired by his mighty missionary activity.[4] Thus does Paul, in the spirit of his time, interpret the mysterious nervous malady, the strange outbreaks of which oppressed him so sorely, and sometimes hampered his activity—as the indwelling mischief of a bad spirit—a demon. At that time, persons afflicted with such nervous complaints were classed with the "possessed of devils," as is very easy to understand when we consider the awful impression often made on others by the insane, the epileptic, the hysteric.

The sphere of these devilish, mighty spirits extends also to healthy normal men and women. Are not all the chief transactions of state and home consecrated by sacrifices, and are not these sacrifices offered to devils? Do we not enter into a mysterious and yet real communion, at once sensual and

---

[1] 2 Cor. xi. 14.
[2] 1 Thess. iii. 5; *cp.* 2 Cor. ii. 10 *seq.*, 1 Cor. vii. 5.
[3] 1 Thess. ii. 18; *cp.* iii. 11.   [4] 2 Cor. xii. 7.

supersensual, with the devils, if we partake of the flesh offered to them? Paul believed this as firmly as he believed that in the Lord's Supper he partook of the very Body and Blood of Christ.[1]

We are accustomed to imagine a sharp line of distinction between the angels of light and devils, placing man open to influences good and evil midway between them as their field of action. But Paul and his contemporaries draw no such marked line between the different hosts in the spirit world. Just as Satan is a fallen angel who himself sends "angels," so the angels generally, according to a widespread impression then obtaining, are still open to temptation, as, for example, from the beauty of women. On this account, the women present at public worship, where spirits may be hovering, curious, are to be veiled.[2] An angel from heaven may preach another gospel than that which Paul preached. Angels, as well as men, may be spectators of the spectacle given by the apostles to the world.[3] And so they too, if they fall into sin, will be judged, and that by Christians themselves.[4] The Jews believed that Enoch was translated to heaven to announce their judgment to the angels. And just as the gnostic and apocalyptic writers hail the Christ as their refuge from the spirit powers, since He brought to earth the keys of heaven and opened a way through all the tracts of heaven up to the Father of light, so that the upward flight of aspiring souls is no longer impeded by angels and spirits, so Paul triumphs: "I am persuaded, that neither death, nor

[1] 1 Cor. x. 20 *seq*. [2] 1 Cor. xi. 10; *cp*. Gen. vi. 1–4.
[3] Gal. i. 8; 1 Cor. iv. 9. [4] 1 Cor. vi. 3.

life, nor angels, nor principalities, nor things present, nor things to come, nor powers, nor height, nor depth, nor any other creature, shall be able to separate us from the love of God which is in Christ Jesus our Lord."[1]

Here we have three categories of angelic beings: angels, principalities, and powers; *principalities* ἀρχαί, probably superior beings, their name forming the first part of the word archangel ἀρχάγγελοι[2]—the powers, subordinate servants of God. Other categories, too, are mentioned,[3] namely, powers ἐξουσίαι and lords. Some of these names are abstractions; the ancients already employed this mode of address for exalted persons and we still speak of "majesty." There may, however, be another ground for this abstract denomination: these very beings, of a singularly indefinite nature, were already beginning to hover between real personality and mere personification. They are still, indeed, in most cases considered to be actual spirit beings; they certainly are so with Paul: and we must bear in mind that even the Evil One, conceived of as so positively personal, is once called by the abstract name of "evil."

Like human beings, all these spiritual beings hover, as already remarked, between good and evil: they are capable of sinning, and will be judged. Throughout the Pauline epistles we find no actual angels of light,[4] no pure servants of God—his angels are not friendly companions, ministering spirits to serve men. Men, indeed, would welcome such a divine messenger if he came to them;[5] the angels are

[1] Rom. viii. 38 *seq.*   [2] 1 Thess. iv. 16.
[3] 1 Cor. xv. 24; viii. 5.   [4] 2 Cor. xi. 14.   [5] Gal. iv. 14.

THE HERITAGE OF THE SCHOOL 33

great and sublime, and he who could speak their language would be accounted great upon earth.[1] Paul heard it once,[2] when in a trance he was caught up into heaven: yet the angels do not completely and absolutely serve God's will. Even when Paul refers to the legend of angels having transmitted the law to Moses, he does so only the more to emphasise the fact that the law is no perfect expression of the will of God.[3]

In Paul's personal religion, bad angels, or angels as powers, always played a very important part. From his youth upwards the apostle believed himself to be placed in the midst of some such awful contest between two worlds, the devils fighting with God for men's souls. What that meant for him, we, at the present day, can only conceive with an effort. To know that these demons, who hold men ensnared in sin and ruin, in ignorance and death, must themselves pass away—that God summons man to a mighty battle against death and devil, against suffering and sin, against the powers of darkness in the air—to know this was to possess a firmness and resoluteness on the side of God such as we of a wiser and milder age no longer possess. The drawback was a great intolerance even against much that was really great and beautiful—the intolerance of the iconoclast. We readily accept the statement of the Acts, that, surrounded by the marvels of Greek art in Athens, Paul had only the one impression: he was provoked to indignation when he beheld the city full of idols.[4] Yet such indignation and such

[1] 1 Cor. xiii. 1. [2] 2 Cor. xii. 4.
[3] Gal. iii. 19. [4] Acts xvii. 16.

intolerance are, from time to time, necessary, that goodness may not be swallowed up in beauty and the enjoyment of beauty. It was not that "one man might be enriched," as Schiller says, but that a higher bliss might become possible for all men, and that they might be led to a higher degree of human development —it was for this the world of the old heathen gods had to pass away—nay, more, had to undergo a worse thing first, to be transformed into a world of demons.

This, in its general outlines, was the world that gradually opened to the youthful Saul in the school of the Pharisees. Nor did Paul the Christian ever deem it necessary on account of his belief to modify anything in these inherited ideas of heaven and earth, nature and history—a plain proof that neither this conception of the universe nor any other has anything to do with faith. We will not, then, be of those who burden men's hearts and minds with such old-world conceptions of hell, earth and heaven, spirits, angels, and demons, whether altogether or in part, whether in the old-fashioned realistic sense or in refined modern fashion, as articles of the faith. These are not things which have to be "believed"; they are out-of-date scientific or pre-scientific views of the universe.

But just as little will we be of those who consider themselves superior to Paul, because he still "believed" these things and "did not even stand abreast of the classical enlightenment of his time." For then every modern schoolboy might be pronounced Paul's superior.

But the positive gains, of religious and moral nature, which were won by the great men of the past, lose none of their value on account of such mistaken notions. Those regions of spiritual life which depend on a man's temperament and the attitude of his will, are but very faintly influenced by mistaken scientific notions. Above all, the goodness and greatness of a man's character has nothing to do with the individual's idea of a universe. So the apostle shines radiant across the centuries; while the world-idea, which the youthful Saul imbibed in the school of the Pharisees, has long since been left out of sight, and the precious heritage of his fathers, his belief in one God and in an eternal world beyond this visible one, has long since been freed from the narrow form in which Paul received it.

THE PHARISEE.

CHAPTER IV.

The Heritage of the School—*continued*.

Not only the universe, but also man and the history of man, were regarded by Paul from the standpoint of a Jew of his time. The temporal course of the world for the Pharisee comprises two epochs, which are separated by an awful catastrophe— the present æon, the present world,[1] and the future æon, the age to come.[2] The Jew lives in the present age for that which is to come, in this age which is evil,[3] a world of sin and suffering.[4] It is night now— but the night is far spent, the day is at hand.[5] Darkness covers men's minds. They do the deeds of darkness. The heathen are blind.[6]

It is the feeling of a dying humanity, of a world that is perishing, and the longing of an enslaved people for liberty, that is here heard through Paul's life. But on this dark background there stands out the luminous hope of the breaking day, of a new creation of earth and man, by virtue of which the old

---

[1] 1 Cor. ii. 6; Rom. xii. 2; Rom. viii. 18, iii. 26, xi. 5; 2 Cor. iv. 4, viii. 13.
[2] 1 Thess. i. 10, v. 3; Rom. v. 14.   [3] Gal. i. 4.
[4] Rom. viii. 18.   [5] Rom. xiii. 11.   [6] Rom. ii. 19.

THE HERITAGE OF THE SCHOOL

earth with all its corruption of sin is to be transformed in radiant beauty.

In the beginning of time man was made pure and immortal; but the serpent with cunning deceived Eve, and man, unlike Christ, aimed at being equal with God, through robbery.[1]

"Through one man sin entered into the world, and death through sin. And so death passed unto all men, for that all sinned."[2] "By the trespass of the one," death reigned master upon earth, and "the many died" because they all fell into sin.[3] Possibly this fate is conceived as heredity, for Paul always speaks of Adam as being he through whom sin and sin's condemnation came into the world, and he does not mention Eve further in this connection. Adam, as the Pharisees say, bequeathed the "evil principle" to all posterity. Or Paul may mean, the whole of humanity was represented in Adam—just as in the second Adam, in Christ, the new-created humanity. "For since by man came death, by man came also the resurrection of the dead. For as in Adam all die, so also in Christ shall all be made alive."[4] Thus Paul, after conversion. But, without doubt, he already thought so as Pharisee, for he refers to this doctrine of original sin as a familiar thing.[5] Besides, in the Apocalypses of Ezra and Baruch we have statements very like those of St Paul. "By reason of his evil heart the first Adam fell into sin and guilt, and also all who came after him. So the evil became continual: the law verily dwelt in the hearts of men, but beside it, the evil principle. So what was good died out, but the bad remained.

---
[1] Phil. ii. 6; Ezec. xxviii. 4–17. [2] Rom. v. 12.
[3] Rom. v. 15, 17.   [4] 1 Cor. xv. 21 *seq.*   [5] Rom. v. 12.

> " An evil heart has grown up within us,
> Making us exiles from the other world,
> Bringing us near to destruction:
> Showing us the ways of death,
> Pointing the path of ruin,
> It has led us farther and farther away from life.

And this is the same, not for a few only—no, for nearly all who are born into the world."[1]

"Nearly all"; such will probably have been the belief of the Pharisee already: but "all, all," was the conclusion only of the converted Christian after having felt within himself the full power of "the evil principle."

As soon as a man has learned to think about his being, he makes the experience that evil clings to him as a heritage. This stage in the history of mankind is marked in Greece by the rise of the great tragic writers: almost at the same time, there was living in Israel the man who first dared to pronounce the awful doctrine about God, that God "visits the sins of the fathers upon the children to the third and fourth generation." But the doctrine first appears in all its might and terror in Judaism. That age conceived of evil in its own peculiar way: just as in bodily illness, the inward condition was interpreted as depending on the workings of powers foreign to a man; just as the spirit beings, the demons, fall upon a man, so do "sin" and "death" as two living half personal or entirely personal beings who themselves will be "destroyed"[2]—death bearing a form very like the destroying angel.[3]

The world has two aspects: so has man. "I

---

[1] 4 Ezra iii. 20 *seq.*; vii. 48.
[2] 1 Cor. xv. 26.
[3] 1 Cor. x. 10.

was born in iniquity," and "If ye become not as a little child," are the two corresponding expressions of these for us. Both contain truth. But it all depends which of them we allow to gain the upper hand; whether we look for the forbidden fruit of the tree of knowledge in everything human, or whether we are willing to read in the pure glad eyes of a little child: "Your heavenly Father made the human heart capable of confiding trust and communion with Himself, and able to will and to do what is good and noble."

In Paul's time it had long been customary to speak of a doom that weighed upon mankind. For two centuries the story of the Fall had been thus interpreted. Explaining in the first instance, as it does, why work became toil and why childbearing became a labour of sorrow, the story was now used to meet the problem of how sin entered the world and how all men came under its dominion. To Paul, as to us, this doctrine came as inheritance.

"From a woman was the beginning of sin, and because of her we all die."[1]

"God created man for incorruption and made him an image of his own proper being; but by the envy of the devil death entered into the world, and they that are of his portion make trial thereof."[2]

Everything the apostle had to contend against within him, and everything he observed around him, helped to confirm this belief, and we very seldom find in his letters even a single word to prove that he too was not altogether blind to the nobler aspect of human nature. He, too, knew he wanted to do right,

[1] Eccles. xxv. 24. [2] Wisd. ii. 24 *seq.*

that he delighted in the law of God after the inward man,[1] but in the law of spiritual struggle the Pharisee in him saw only the other side of Nature. And what he saw going on around him could but strengthen that impression.

In his letter to the Romans[2] the apostle has drawn us a picture of how the beautiful world of Gentile gods appeared from the standpoint of a strict morality, and we understand how he could there see nothing but downright corruption. Yet even here he cannot overlook the fact that Gentiles, too, have a conscience, and that in them, too, their thoughts one with another accuse or else excuse them.[3]

This, however, did not open his eyes for a different contemplation of the universe: it merely affirmed for him that God would judge the Gentiles justly, according to their conscience.

From amidst the heathen world which has become a prey to sin, to delusion and demons, one nation arises, "to whom were entrusted the oracles of God."[4] True, the Pharisee, too, knew that the principle of evil reigned and worked even here; but in contrast to heathendom as a whole, this people might well boast of a higher morality. But above all, the mighty past of his people was encircled for the Pharisee by the brightest halo of pious romance. The Christian convert still has a Jew's tone of suffering, quivering pride in his people, when he glories in the privileges of his nation: he closes their enumeration with thanksgiving:—

"I say the truth in Christ; I lie not, my conscience

---

[1] Rom. vii. 21. [2] Rom. i. 20–32.
[3] Rom. ii. 14–16. [4] Rom. iii. 2.

bearing witness with me in the Holy Ghost, that I have great sorrow and unceasing pain in my heart. For I could wish that I myself were anathema from Christ for my brethren's sake, my kinsmen according to the flesh: who are Israelites, whose is the adoption, and the glory, and the covenants, and the giving of the law, and the service of God and the promises, whose are the Fathers, and of whom is Christ as concerning the flesh, who is over all, God blessed for ever. Amen."[1]

The adoption and the glory! God is the Father of the people of Israel, whom He has adopted as His child. Out of Egypt He has called His Son, to Him He has promised the inheritance in the glorious future kingdom: for, "if a son, then an heir through God."[2] Yea more, God Himself in the light of the pillar of fire has sojourned with the people. His glory was in the Shekinah; His glory led them out of Egypt, rested over their mercy seat. And the hope that their glory would once more dwell among them, that all might, like Moses of old,[3] be clothed upon therewith, this most precious hope Saul cherished in his heart until he saw that all had sinned—all, himself included, and come short of the glory of God.[4] God had made the covenants with promises of inheritance unto the Fathers, and the sonship of Abraham was a guarantee to the Jews for their own future bliss. Afterwards, Paul strove with all the acumen of his dialectic to prove that Christians are children of Abraham, just because the promise depended on this relationship. Here was one of the beating pulses

[1] Rom. ix. 1–5. [2] Gal. iv. 7.
[3] 2 Cor. iii. 15. [4] Rom. iii. 23.

of Hebrew piety. The other was the law. Even later, when, as a Christian, Paul stood in quite a new relation to the law, he called it spiritual (*i.e.* inspired, heavenly, divine),[1] holy, just, and good; how much more will he have appreciated it as a Pharisee; and in speaking of it being "ordained through angels," he must have rejoiced greatly.

By the side of the natural approach to the promises —the sonship of Abraham—comes the moral approach: the doers of the law will be justified, *i.e.* they will be acquitted at the final judgment day.[2] The law is the way of salvation, along which the will of the individual moves forward. Such is the belief which imparts consistence and an aim to the whole of a Pharisee's life. All his cavils of the jot and tittle in the interpretation of the law bring him by so much nearer to the future glory. Thus Israel pursues after a law of righteousness:[3] "they are those that are after the law," "under the law." And this way of salvation has, for the pious feeling of the Pharisee, completely superseded the other, the natural one, by the seed of Abraham. In his letter to the Romans, Paul again[4] develops this his Pharisaical standpoint fully, attacking the Jew on his own grounds. "O man, after thy hardness and impenitent heart, thou treasurest up for thyself wrath in the day of wrath, and revelation of the righteous judgment of God, who will render to every man according to his works: to them that by patience in well-doing seek for glory and honour and incorruption, eternal life: but unto them that are factious and obey not the truth, but

[1] Rom. vii. 12, 14.   [2] Rom. ii. 13.
[3] Rom. ix. 31.   [4] Rom. ii. 5–10.

obey unrighteousness, shall be wrath and indignation, tribulation and anguish, upon every soul of man that worketh evil . . . . but glory and honour and peace to every man that worketh good." . . . These words are the typical expression of the Pharisee's point of view, and this conception of the way of salvation, which positively contradicts the theory of the seed of Abraham, is the more recent one, introduced by the prophets. John the Baptist contrasted it with the traditional confidence in the Fathers quite as sharply as Paul the Pharisee.

For long the importance of *public worship* as a practice of piety had been diminishing. Judaism is indeed that epoch in the Hebrew religion in which religious aspiration no longer contented itself with the mere observance of the old-established popular form of a religion of altar sacrifices—although indeed the exaggerated emphasis of the idea of expiation lent a new attraction to the yearning for salvation which was a feature of that age. What men wanted was an inward, spiritual redemption from sin and guilt—and in those dark days men clung to the letter of Scripture. And then something more was added. Since the sacerdotal dynasty which had been in office for the two last centuries before Christ had profaned public worship in the eyes of the rigid Jews by political strife and by disgraceful cruelties, pious fervour addressed itself with greater zeal to the synagogue and the written word. It is perhaps to be regarded as a characteristic note of the foreigner, that Paul here mentions the public worship of God at all. The longing for a day in the courts of the Lord lay deep down in the soul of the Jew among the Gentiles; that yearning for home and that deep piety that breathes throughout the gradual psalms,[1] impelled him ever and anon to go up to the city set upon a hill, to the Passover feasts. And it was with a glow of veneration and divinity that this same longing hovered even round that altar in Jerusalem, reeking with fat and blood—which had become to the popular belief, as it were, a relic of an uncivilised past.

But of all that had been vouchsafed to the "chosen people" the most precious possession were *the promises*, that amazing drama of the world's end, the final doom and the coming splendour of the heavens — which, ever since it was fully developed by Hebrew saints, just before the Christian era, has, with its terrifying might, overwhelmed millions of human hearts, and still overwhelms us when we hear it in the requiem service, and this although our reason no longer admits it as possible.

The heart of the youthful Saul had felt it too. His imagination was filled with the stupendous images of the latter days, when heaven and earth should pass away in the fires of Jehovah. His conversion altered scarcely a single point in this picture: everywhere we recognise the Jewish expectation of the future. This is perhaps how it presented itself in the heart of the youthful Saul: there will come times of great and dire distress, days of tribulation when evil shall prevail upon earth.[2] Even the apostle preaches this dogma as prophet to his converts,[3] and comforts them, if they suffer persecution, with the old idea, here in its Messianic dress: when the night is darkest, God is nighest! For to the

[1] Ps. 120-134.   [2] 1 Cor. vii. 26-28.   [3] 1 Thess. iii. 3 *seq.*

THE HERITAGE OF THE SCHOOL 45

triumph of the wicked, as to the tribulation of the saints, God will make a sudden end in the day of Christ's appearing.

This coming of Christ [1] is the great hope that lifts men over all tribulation. The apostle, although he considers the man Jesus as the Christ, still speaks, like all early Christians, of His "presence" (not "return") and of His "coming" (not "coming again"),[2] so firmly set in their minds was the Jewish habit of speech. Even as a Jew, Saul believed the Messiah to be already in existence—needing only to be "revealed"[3] (referred later to a second coming). He is living in heaven with God, whence God will send Him forth, when the time is fulfilled—that is, accomplished.[4] To the faith of the youthful Saul, the Messiah was not only the anointed King of the realm of glory, but also the Son of God. The Messianic interpretation of Psalm ii. was certainly familiar to Judaism. The Messiah is the accepted "shoot out of the stock of Jesse," declared as the Son of God. Paul appears to have known, too, the third title for the heavenly Messiah—the Man (the Son of Man), who plays so important a part in the apocalyptic books and in the gospels. For the apostle's idea about the two Adams, "the first of the earth, earthy; the second of heaven, a life-giving spirit,"[5] clearly refer to this Messianic title. This heavenly being is in "the form of God," filled with glory.[6] He was present at the creation of the world, and "through him are all things."[7]

[1] 1 Thess. ii. 19, iii. 13; 1 Cor. xv. 23.   [2] 1 Cor. iv. 5.
[3] 1 Cor. i. 7.   [4] Gal. iv. 4; Rom. viii. 3.
[5] 1 Cor. xv. 45-49.   [6] Phil. ii. 7.   [7] 1 Cor. viii. 6; xi. 3.

Before He tabernacled in the man of the seed of David, He came forth from heaven and appeared on earth; He revealed Himself to the patriarchs. "That rock" which Moses smote, from which "water came out" which "followed" the people of Israel through the wilderness, "was Christ." Just as, according to the old belief in spirits, God's angels could transform themselves into fiery flames,[1] just as God Himself could appear as fire in the burning bush, so too the Messiah is a being who can change His form at will. So He made Himself rock, and "went with" the people. In Paul's time many people, and possibly he too, believed that every manifestation of God to Israel was a manifestation of the Messiah (or of an angel), for they began to consider God as so infinitely sublime and remote, that they no longer believed He could become visible to the bodily eye. However fantastic the idea of Christ in the form of a rock may appear to us—however curious the notion that it was "spiritual water," some supernatural matter, that flowed from this rock—all this agrees perfectly with the contemporary Jewish conception of the universe.[2]

As already mentioned, however, another category of Messianic ideas, connected with the ancient hope of a crowned, triumphant Son of David, was also familiar to Paul. We cannot now determine how as a Jew, he conceived of the two forms as united in one person. In the Hebrew apocalypses we find the most contradictory notions on this point, and nearly all the different Christological views and disputes which agitated Christendom later on, were already extant in Judaism, either potentially or actually.

[1] Heb. i. 7. [2] 1 Cor. x. 4.

THE HERITAGE OF THE SCHOOL

When Christ shall appear at the sound of the "last trump,"[1] "with all His saints,"[2] the judgment day breaks. Then all depends on having lived "unreprovable, pure, sincere, void of offence"; on "being filled with the perfect fruits of righteousness" so as to be "saved"—"saved" from the wrath of God, which shall be revealed in tremendous doom.[3] This is the salvation that Luther calls "Heil" = healing—according to which Jesus is the "Heiland" = healer—a name which in German has a far sweeter, tenderer sound than was originally in the word, exactly corresponding to the Greek as it does. The "Healer" is originally He who "saves your life" in that tremendous doom, who "plucks" you out of the general destruction, delivers from the wrath of God, so terribly "made known to the vessels of wrath fitted unto destruction."[4]

This awful catastrophe is presented to our view under three cycles of pictures. However variously the expressions may differ, we may refer all allusions to the end of the world to these three cycles. We must not attempt to include the types all under one head; this would mean endless confusion. The first type is lurid—the image of the hurricane: "the day shall be revealed by fire";[5] a downpour of flame from heaven shall destroy whatever is not heavenly.[6] One escape there is: according to the belief of the time a "seal" secures immunity from the destroying fire.[7] To Paul, too, this idea was familiar, and as a Chris-

[1] 1 Cor. xv. 52; 1 Thess. iv. 16.   [2] 1 Thess. iii. 13.
[3] 1 Cor. i. 8; Phil. i. 10; 1 Cor. v. 5; Rom. v. 9.
[4] *E.g.* 1 Thess. i. 9 *seq.*; Rom. ix. 22; Rom. v. 9.
[5] 1 Cor. iii. 13.   [6] 1 Cor. iii. 14 *seq.*   [7] Rev. vii. 3.

tian he recognised this "seal" in the Holy Spirit:[1] he is aware that the term is in reality incongruous in this connection, and he only thus applies it to avoid the introduction of other "seals": the Spirit is an invisible sign. As a Jew, Paul recognised the saving "seal" in the rite of circumcision, which is so called in other primitive Christian literature. This explains his interpretation of circumcision in his letter to the Romans.[2] Not only the wicked, but also all the powers at enmity with God, sin, Satan, death, the "weak and beggarly elements,"[3] will be destroyed;[4] and the same hope is expressed in the Revelation: "death and Hades were thrown into the lake of fire,"[5] which is the second, the final death. The downpour of flame from heaven of which Paul speaks is not this burning lake, but is more probably adapted from the idea of a flash of lightning. This agrees with the way in which Paul handles his figure, and the thunderstorm is a well-known image for the world's end (compare Ps. xviii. and xxix.). Possibly the flash of lightning is but the heavenly glory radiating downwards and consuming in its glow all that is merely carnal, earthly.

Much less frequent is the type of *struggle, victory, and rule* of God, Christ, and the Redeemed. The "kingdom" which Christ has, so to speak, won, is "inherited," "taken possession of."[6] This rule prevails until Christ shall have put all God's enemies under His feet.[7]

The figure generally employed is finally that of a

[1] 1 Cor. i. 22. [2] Rom. iv. 11. [3] Gal. iv. 9.
[4] 1 Cor. ii. 6; xv. 26. [5] Rev. xx. 14. [6] 1 Cor. vi. 9.
[7] 1 Cor. xv. 25, cp. iv. 8; Rom. xvi. 20.

THE HERITAGE OF THE SCHOOL 49

judgment. A solemn, heavenly scene : God enthroned on His judgment seat,[1] before which each one must appear to give an account to Him who knows our secret actions.[2] The book of life, wide open,[3] contains the names of those who have lived pure and blameless lives. An accuser stands on one side of God's throne—Paul does not mention, but clearly refers to him[4]—and on the other side, the advocate, as he is called in the Johannine writings, who intercedes for us, " who stands on God's right hand,"[5] the heavenly Christ. Beside this picture there is another, not only in Paul's writings, but also throughout Judaism: *Christ* the Judge.[6] We must keep the two categories of passages together without attempting any artificial reconciliation of apparent discrepancies, in order to attribute to the apostle a complete system of eschatology, not to speak of any Trinitarian ideas. Only once did he himself connect the two categories of ideas; and then he eludes the difficulty very simply by saying, God judges " through Christ Jesus," a turn of phrase which, exactly as is the case to-day in its ecclesiastical use, represents no distinct idea.

On the judgment day the dead shall arise and each receive his judgment,[7] either a judgment of punishment unto death[8] or a sentence of acquittal unto life.[9] This sentence of acquittal is the " justification " which plays such an important part in Paul and Luther.

[1] Rom. xiv. 10.   [2] Rom. ii. 16.   [3] Phil. iv. 3.
[4] Rom. viii. 33.   [5] Rom. viii. 33.
[6] 1 Thess. ii. 19, and 1 Cor. iv. 4 ; 2 Cor. v. 10.
[7] Gal. v. 10 ; Rom. xiii. 2.
[8] Rom. v. 16, 18 ; Rom. viii. 1, vii. 24.
[9] Rom. v. 16, 17, and viii. 4.

Both found the formula for the fundamental question of religion here; that question which, in the Acts of the Apostles, is thus expressed in terms derived from the first cycle of types: What must I do to be saved? Luther has also stated it in the words, How shall I propitiate God? To this fundamental question the Pharisee Saul answers: he is acquitted, justified in God's sight, who has righteousness, and who has done enough good works. These just ones, the saints of God, now have a part, not alone in the ruling of God's kingdom, but also in God's judgment, and will judge men and angels.[1]

The great heavenly "day" of judgment must not be measured by our human measurements. A long time will pass before all are judged, before all enemies are conquered. Meanwhile the fashion of the world changes:[2] Jerusalem from above, the heavenly city, appears;[3] everything temporal vanishes, only the Eternal is left. Then comes the end, when the Son shall deliver everything up to the Father, making Himself subject unto Him, that God may be All in All.[4] Paul does not mean a general absorption into divinity, nor the return of all created beings, including the wicked, to the Godhead, but he means that after the destruction of all evil the will of God shall reign absolutely over all things created that deserve eternity.

Those who are elected to this life in the kingdom of God "enter into the inheritance,"[5] they inherit the promises, the "land," as the patriarchs of old did Canaan, the kingdom of God,[6] "incorruption."[7]

---

[1] 1 Cor. vi. 2 *seq*. [2] 1 Cor. vii. 31. [3] Gal. iv. 26.
[4] 1 Cor. xv. 28. [5] Gal. iii. 29 and iv. 7.
[6] 1 Cor. vi. 9 *seq*.; Gal. v. 21. [7] 1 Cor. xv. 50.

"Eternal life" is the possession they receive, a life in honour,[1] power,[2] and radiant heavenly glory.[3]

Seldom as Paul describes the punishments of the wicked—he nowhere dwells on the subject—he knows how to stir the soul with moving words about this heavenly life. Yet he does not speak of joys in heavenly places as being like the bliss of Paradise. And that is why he afterwards succeeded in implanting his belief in the eternal world in countless hearts, for it was a power in his own that nothing could uproot: though our outward man is decaying, yet our inward man is renewed day by day. "For our light affliction, which is for the moment, worketh for us more and more exceedingly an eternal weight of glory, while we look not at the things which are seen, but at the things which are not seen; for the things which are seen are temporal, but the things which are not seen are eternal."[4]

Paul could speak of these things calmly, with a settled conviction; he must therefore needs have already reconciled all such things to his mind as make the Jewish inheritance distasteful to us to-day, however much the revelation of St John and a large proportion of our own hymns have familiarised us later Christians with the idea. It is not only our modern attitude of thought with regard to the universe that refuses to accept the figures of a judgment day, a hell fire and a world's end, and forbids to paint the pangs of the damned with an evident satisfaction —it is our moral instinct and our faith in a heavenly Father who gathers His lost sons in His arms. Yet

[1] Rom. ii. 7, ix. 21 ; 1 Cor. xv. 43.　[2] 1 Thess. ii. 12.
[3] Rom. viii. 17; ix. 23, etc.　[4] 2 Cor. iv. 16 *seq.*

however thorough the transformation of such old Bible images may be, the longing for a pure and blessed life in an eternal world beyond and above this our world of phenomena will never die in mankind—the kernel will not, must not, be lost with the discarded shell,—the faith that sees heaven open at the edge of the tomb.

And the faith that believes in the near approach of the world's end, this, too, has its kernel which is imperishable. Every man who wills and works righteousness aims at helping the men of his own time. It is to them that he wishes to impart whatever he recognises as good; it is they whom he strives to fashion to the standard which he considers the pattern of perfection. Thus his efforts will always be strenuous and his hope urgent, even though he may no longer believe that heaven and earth must pass away before "the light shall shine for the righteous."

THE PHARISEE.

CHAPTER V.

THE HERITAGE OF THE SCHOOL—*continued*.

GOD did not leave Himself without a witness among other nations, but to the Jews only did He deliver the promises in a sacred book. He had pronounced them to the patriarchs, and for the later generations who were to see their fulfilment. He had caused them to be written down.[1] Such was the belief Saul shared with his people. Judaism was a book religion in the strictest sense of the term, almost as much as were the post-Reformation churches. God had indeed spoken of old at sundry times and in divers manners unto the fathers, to the holy patriarchs, "by Himself," but all that was left now was a sacred book and theologians—that is to say, expounders of the sacred book. Such was the idea which lay at the root of Judaism.

This sacred book had been of slow growth, and it had been slow to slay the prophets. In the year 621 B.C., when the first fragment of the book of the law was "found," it was thought necessary to "commune" with a prophetess about its validity.[2] Slowly the book increased: the "law" was made up of relics of bygone popular traditions and sacred customs, and this was the

[1] 1 Cor. ix. 10.   [2] 2 Kings xxii. *seq.*

Pentateuch, always regarded by the Jews as peculiarly sacred and absolutely binding. In Paul's time, and even up to the present day, *Tora*, the name for the law, has remained in Hebrew as a term denoting Holy Scripture in general. It embraces all that later collection of scriptures which gradually grew up under the shadow of the sacredness of the book of the law. In this sense Paul (1st Cor. xiv. 21, and Rom. iii. 19) speaks of the law when he quotes passages from the prophets and the Psalms. The prophets by whose efforts the law had once been established and had become *the* sacred book, were the first to benefit by its sacred character, and composed the second portion of holy scripture writings by the side of the *Tora*. The law and the prophets [1] now became the expression for the Bible, and this it remained again for centuries, even after a new class of books, the Psalms, Proverbs, Job, Canticles, Ruth, Lamentations, Ecclesiastes, and Esther, had been attached. These were called briefly "the Scriptures," or, as the introduction to Ecclesiasticus has it, "the other books of our fathers," "the rest of the books," "the others that have followed in their steps" (*i.e.* of the law and the prophets). Judaism in Palestine was narrower in the matter of accepting further scriptures than were the Jews of the Dispersion. The latter handed down to us in their Greek translation of the Old Testament a whole additional series of writings called afterwards the "Apocrypha." These books are mostly Greek, but even that part of them which was originally written in Hebrew was no longer included in the Hebrew Bible. Now Paul, as a Jew of the

[1] Rom. iii. 21.

Dispersion—later, as missionary to the Gentiles—is accustomed to quote from the Greek version, he must have known the apocryphal books; it only remains doubtful if he had read them all. As we have already seen, there are several distinct reminiscences of the wisdom of Solomon in his writings.

The formation of sacred books did not cease with the conclusion of the sacred canon. This book religion could after all not entirely quench the "spirit," *i.e.* prophecy. There were still always men who derived the certainty from their personal religious experience that God Himself or an angel had spoken to them. But the book religion with its dogma of prophets being a thing entirely of the past, forced them, as it were, to wear a mask. So they wrote under the name of some old saint what was in reality the experience of contemporary souls, and, as such, was intended for contemporaries. And thus arose a pseud-epigraphic class of literature in the form of apocalypses, in which such old-time saints as Daniel, Enoch, Ezra, spoke to their descendants. The authors of these writings vindicated their claim to speak for the past, by really transmitting a mass of material of a cosmographical nature, fantastic doctrines of spirits and heavens, of sun, moon, and stars, dew, snow, hail, etc., just as they themselves had heard these things from their forefathers. That Paul was familiar with this class of writings, also that he considered it sacred and that he applied its teaching, is proved plainly first of all by the fact, that his eschatology in its leading details agrees exactly with the accounts found in these Jewish apocalypses. Yet there are but few direct quotations from them in Paul's epistles. According to one of the fathers of the Church, the passage "Neither circumcision availeth anything, nor uncircumcision, but a new creature,"[1] is taken from an apocalypse of Moses. It occurs indeed repeatedly in similarly plain terms, yet it appears to me to be only a genuine quotation in this form: "but the keeping of the commandments of God."[2] Certainly the passage (1 Cor. ii. 9), "Eye hath not seen," etc., which Paul introduces as a passage of Scripture with the solemn formula "as it is written," is such a quotation. It is not found in any of the books of the Old Testament, but according to several of the Church fathers it occurs in an "apocalypse of Elijah."

All the learning of the youthful Saul was interpretation of Scripture. His teachers were nothing if not expounders of the sacred text, and what they did, over and above this, was to "build a hedge round the law," to protect and cherish it by means of a casuistical application of its meaning to all possible and impossible circumstances of life. The whole wisdom of the Pharisee was to learn how to expound Scripture. And Paul practised the methods of exegesis which he learned as Saul with rigid consistency. He shares the belief of his teachers as to inspiration. Not alone the contents are holy, but also the letter—all is alike the word of God. Whenever we understand the apostle's words, "the letter killeth, but the spirit giveth life," in the sense of a more liberal interpretation of Scripture, we do so without his authority. Paul meant something very different (2 Cor. iii. 6). True, Paul once introduces a quotation with the words,

[1] 1 Cor. vii. 19; *cp.* Gal. v. 6; Rom. ii. 25.   [2] Gal. vi. 15.

THE HERITAGE OF THE SCHOOL 57

"Isaiah is very bold and saith" (Rom. x. 20). But we must not read this passage in the light of a broader idea of inspiration, as though emphasis were put upon the fact that Isaiah was something more than a mere machine. For in another passage Paul concludes from a single letter that salvation is not for the Jew but for the Christian. Gal. iii. 16 runs: "Now to Abraham were the promises spoken and to his seed. He saith not, "and to seeds," as of many; but as of one. "And to thy seed, which is Christ." In the Hebrew a single vowel distinguishes in this case the singular from the plural. Where everything, even the minutest detail, was inspired, and everything "was written for our sakes," the interpreters of Scripture had recourse to the most singular expedients, in order to find the fitting meaning for this collection of oracles. The above-mentioned example is characteristic. "Seed" in the Hebrew is a collective, like our word "progeny," and is therefore constantly used in the singular to imply the numerous descendants. Paul as a Jew must have known this just as well as any Bible reader to-day. Yet he makes the most of the letter, the grammatical sense of the word, as opposed to the spirit, the real meaning, in order to have his "proof" from Scripture.

Three methods of interpretation were employed to adapt to present needs books written of old in quite a different sense. The first and most usual method was to take the words as a prophecy of the present, whenever any allusion in the passage made this apparently possible; just as in the word "seed" of the passage alluded to. This method of exposition was largely practised. A further example (Rom. ix. 25): the prophet Hosea had prophesied to his people that God would "put it away for a time, and call it 'not my people,' but then, when it should turn unto Him, He would have mercy on it":

> "And to her that is not loved will I show love,
> And to 'not my people' will I say, Thou art my people,
> And they shall say, Thou art my God." [1]

Yet Paul interprets the "not my people" as the heathen, and so gets a prophetic allusion to his mission, of course in downright contradiction to the historical sense of the words. All the Messianic prophecies of the Old Testament arose more or less in this way: they are naïve, forced interpretations of passages charged with quite different meanings, in the strength of the dogma that all Scripture bears interpretation for the present time. Historical science in its progressive development has therefore once for all made an end of this method of exegesis. In our own time it lingers only in pietistic circles, and—unfortunately—in the schoolroom.

The second method of interpretation was through types. It is founded on convictions, which Paul himself has formulated in one striking passage, and illustrated by an example: "For I would not, brethren, have you ignorant, how that our fathers were all under the cloud, and all passed through the sea; and were all baptized unto Moses in the cloud and in the sea; and did all eat the same spiritual meat, and did all drink the same spiritual (supernatural, heavenly) drink. Howbeit with most of them God was not well pleased; for they were overthrown in the wilder-

[1] Hosea ii. 25.

ness . . . . now these things happened unto them by way of type (τυπικῶs), and they were written for our admonition, upon whom the ends of the ages are come."[1] What happened beforetime in the exodus is a type, an example for the latter-day times in which Paul lived. The historical reality of the circumstances and their significance remains undisturbed, but that they were "written" carried, according to Divine intention, an admonishing and instructive lesson for the generation of these same latter days—which was Paul's present.

Typology is the method pursued by our present practical exegesis, and is quite justifiable: only we certainly are a little more prudent in the matter of asserting that such past events were written only "for our sakes."

Allegory is a third and different way of proceeding, which Paul also used like his contemporaries. Here, finally, the belief in the plenary inspiration of a sacred book is completely developed in all its elements. For only allegory can wring a sense out of such passages as are inapplicable, nay, offensive to the present. Allegory asserts something more, and deeper, is meant than the bare words of the book convey. In employing this method, it is always, of course, necessary to show why a deeper meaning is sought for. But the reason for thus substituting a deeper sense is often merely some æsthetic or moral offensiveness in the literal sense of the passage to be explained. So in 1 Cor. ix. 8 Paul proceeds : " For it is written in the law of Moses, thou shalt not muzzle the ox when he treadeth out the corn." Now follows the

[1] 1 Cor. x. 1–11.

argument to prove that the passage must be understood allegorically, not literally: "Is it for the oxen that God careth, or saith He it altogether for our sake?" And so Paul concludes the meaning of the words to be: the apostles are to be maintained by their congregations. (In reality, the commandment in the Old Testament is intended quite literally as a humane ordinance for the protection of animals.) The explanations in 2 Cor. iii. 13 are similar, in which Paul attributes an exactly opposite meaning to the passage, in flat contradiction to its original plain intention: Exodus xxxiv. 33-35. So too Gal. iv. 24, etc., the well-known passage about Hagar. Abraham had two wives, the one free, Sarah; the other a slave, the Arab woman Hagar. The latter, according to Paul, signifies Sinai, and her marriage the covenant of Sinai, "for Mount Sinai is in Arabia." Therefore the Jews, who received their law at Sinai, are children of the handmaid, not children of Sarah, and heirs of the promise: to be the seed of Abraham is the Christian's portion. And these things are an "allegory—these two women are the covenants."

With such a method of interpretation anything may be "proved." The Reformers, trained in the school of the humanists, recognised this clearly. Therefore they insisted on the historical, the plain, evident sense of the written word. And so they set on foot the whole modern system of Biblical criticism, and made the first breaches in the old doctrine of verbal inspiration — now gone for ever, however desperately our more conservative laymen may still cling to it, and with whatever disguises our orthodox theologians may hide their true convictions on the

THE HERITAGE OF THE SCHOOL 61

subject of inspiration in order to maintain it. Only lately has some effort been made — starting from textual criticism—to introduce a deeper and a truer view of the real essence of the Bible amongst people of this tendency.

On the other hand, in our own day again, men like Richard Wagner, Tolstoi, the theosophists, Wolfgang Kirchbach, and many others, have begun to allegorise the New Testament in behalf of their modern or Buddhist theories—just as formerly the Alexandrines allegorised Homer or Philo Moses. The danger is great nowadays, that by such allegorising a strange religion may take the place of the Gospel—but this danger will pass, for we are armed against it by our historical work. What these men are doing is just the opposite method to that of the traditional Christianity which they attack.

Historical research, the genuine offspring of the Reformation, saves us from both extremes. It does, indeed, destroy the old theory of inspiration absolutely, and teaches us to take the Bible as a collection of documents of the religious history of the people of Israel. But it also quickens this history and its great protagonists the prophets. They live for us as they never did before. By this means it shows us the process of the spiritualising and deepening of a popular religion, until it is completely transformed and exalted into the Gospel—thus giving us the courage to believe that this great history of the spiritual life of a people has been a history of God with mankind, and that its protagonists were actually sent by God to man.

CHAPTER VI.

SAUL THE PATRIOT. THE FIGHT FOR THE LAW.

THE outlook on the universe which the youthful Saul inherited from his fathers, and learned from his teachers, has been presented to us. Even now, there are thousands of people who consider such an outlook the Christian one, who are unable to imagine for themselves any other setting for their Christian faith than the one which the old mythologies have woven around earth, heaven, good and evil, the present and the future. Yet this whole view of things is, after all, only setting, just like any other "views" from that time to our own: a setting for the real life, for inmost personal religion. How little this theology really has to do with the essential life of the spirit, is clear, when we consider that thousands of Paul's contemporaries had the same training, yet one alone, Saul of Tarsus, had his Damascus.

Where are those others, the thousands? They lived and died happily, doing their daily work, pious Jews after the pattern of their fathers; many of them followed perchance in the footsteps of their great fellow-countryman, after he had shown the way. Why did Paul become a pioneer? Why did not his soul, too, remain on the beaten track that was traced for him by his origin and by his education?

It is certainly not ours to fathom the mystery that every new-born human soul brings with it. Yet if we know a man's outward environment and the leading traits of his nature, we may venture to penetrate a little further into the life of his soul, and none may gainsay when we refuse to stop short at the outward and visible life as it appears in the man's words. Those who pretend that the higher task of sympathising with and revealing the inner life is the poet's function, and that to meddle with such problems is not the student's work, take the very breath out of historic research, and lower the historian to the level of an archivist and antiquary. Whoever does not feel something akin to the poet, to the artist, in himself, will never attain the highest aim of the historian. We must have the courage to admit so much, if we only are conscientious enough not to romance, and not to hanker after the satisfaction of our own spiritual needs, in undertaking to give an account of the inmost life of other men.

Saul the Patriot.

Saul the Rabbi had inherited a great soul. His love was warmer than that of other men; his hate too. In the letters of the full-grown man glows the fire of an ardent soul, to whom the whole of life presents itself in violent contrasts. Heaven and earth, light and darkness, day and night, spirit and flesh, God and devil, truth and falsehood: just as his people lived among these contrasts, so he entered into them all with whole-hearted fervour. Effort and conflict was his portion: he fought first for, then against, the law, with his very life constantly at stake; voluntarily giving up every single hour of pleasure and the sleep of his nights, renouncing the joys of marriage, the love of children, the peace of home. He fought even unto blood for the glory of God. Even as Christian he "delivered the fornicator unto Satàn for the destruction of the flesh, that the spirit may be saved."[1] Even as an apostle he launched his anathema against all who should "preach another gospel," even were it an angel from heaven![2] Wherever fire is, there are dross and ashes too. Now and then we see in Paul something of that mysterious demoniacal greatness which awes and terrifies us more than it elevates. To get nearer to him, we must perforce remind ourselves that he wrote the beautiful chapter on love, that he lived a life of loving renunciation, and that he could wish himself accursed and for ever severed from his Lord if only thereby he might save "his brethren and kinsmen according to the flesh."[3]

This lofty soul lived in the great hopes of his people with a more glowing flame; he strove after the great things to be awaited more ardently than the meaner souls who can more or less be filled with the joys and sorrows of this world. His fight for spiritual purity was closer and intenser than theirs, but his hope of glory and eternal bliss, of the triumphing of his nation and the casting down of the heathen and all other adversaries to be God's footstool, was more fervent and more jubilant too. The defiance and bitterness that filled every noble Jewish soul of the time, before the nation had learned from the brutal persecutions

[1] 1 Cor. v. 5. [2] Gal. i. 8. [3] Rom. ix. 3.

of the Middle Ages to fly to stratagems of wily ambition and mean revenge—this defiance fed a force of resistance and of indifference in Paul, that could ignore everything merely external, and fix itself on the hidden essentials. This defiance it was, too, that helped Paul to paint the splendours of that coming time when the enslaved children of his people should be crowned in freedom with honour and heavenly glory. That hope was always uppermost even with Paul the Christian, that treasure was evermore his hidden source of strength: he felt his spiritual liberty within; the earnest of celestial glory, the Holy Ghost, spoke to him in groanings that cannot be uttered. A man's ideal heaven must be the counterpart of his life's sufferings. And the sentence to be passed on the soul is the expression of that soul's hope.

To a soul like that of Paul the Pharisee, no hope, however bright—no book, however sacred—can bring satisfaction. As the hart panteth after the water brooks, so the soul thirsts for God, the living God. In all prophet-souls it is the same—whether the voice of the living God says, "Thou art my beloved Son, in whom I am well pleased"—or whether the voice of the tortured conscience cries, "Saul, Saul, why persecutest thou me?" or whether it speaks with children's lips to a St Augustine, or in Bible texts to a Luther. The longing of a true prophet is to hear God's voice, and the prophet's ear waits upon the heavens till the heavens open, and to his ravished sight in that highest hour his way of life shines clear. In such an hour all traditions vanish, all minor ministrations fall away through which even master spirits sought to recognise their God's will, treading in their fathers' steps.

Saul's hour had not yet struck; he still was treading the path his fathers had trod, and his soul still clung to their sacred traditions. Whole-hearted everywhere, throwing himself body and soul into everything that appeared to him to be right, he outvied many of his Jewish contemporaries in zeal for the national traditions. To him these furnished ever new grounds for delight in his people, and for grateful love to the God of his fathers. With this delight, this love in his heart, he had travelled up from Tarsus to Jerusalem. Here stood God's house, here celebrated doctors guarded and studied the traditions of the fathers; here earnest men were striving unweariedly to rear a holy and just nation, worthy of the fulfilment of the divine promises. Here Paul met the new sect of those who acknowledged as the Messiah a man who had been condemned by the Sanhedrim and crucified by the Romans as a criminal: this sect claimed allegiance for Him, and daily won new souls among the people for their mad fancy. A mad fancy it must surely be, that these men had taken up. Saul burst out into vehement and indignant protest. To him, this was making a farce of the holy of holies. Were the great hopes of his people to become a by-word? Were these Christians to go on proclaiming as Messiah a criminal whom the hated Roman had nailed to the cross, who had worn the purple robe as "king of the Jews," amid the jeers and mockery of the soldier rabble, from whose shameful cross the scoffing inscription I.N.R.I. had proclaimed to the faithful Jews what the unclean and lawless thought of the great promises? A man who had thus dragged down into the dust what was the holy of holies to his people? Were the promises to be yea and amen in such a one? No, a thousand times no; the cross, the gallows, was an " offence " that wormed the very heart of the pious Jew! This was the offence of the cross of which the apostle afterwards has so much to say.[1] The fact that the law attached a curse to one hanged (Deut. xxi. 27), certainly added strength to the argument; yet the worst of all was the shock to the soul, and this Saul could not overcome. So he became a persecutor. Henceforth he had but one aim: destruction and annihilation for all these madmen and blasphemers. With what deep pain did the apostle in later life look back on this period of his experience! when the vehemence of his nature, united with all he thought holy, burst out into the flame of a fanaticism which shrank from no means of violence.[2] But then he thought it was a red-letter day in his life when he saw the bleeding body of a Christian lying at his feet, mangled by the stone-throwing mob. Murder for the glory of God is at once the blackest and the greatest thing that men can do for God and the salvation of their fellows, as they understand it. It is a long, a seemingly endless road till we come to the complete surrender of the whole life in the service of God—to the words that baffle even the readiest fanatic: "And if I bestow all my goods to feed the poor, and if I give my

[1] Gal. i. 13.
[2] Gal. v. 11; 1 Cor. i. 23; cp. Rom. ix. 33; 1 Cor. xv. 9; Phil. iii. 6.

body to be burned, but have not love, it profiteth me nothing!"

An abyss lies between these words and Saul the persecutor. And yet, a little while after the stoning of Stephen, the "wonder" happened. A persecutor started from Jerusalem with letters from the Sanhedrim—a converted Christian, an apostle of the new faith, arrived at Damascus. To understand this, we must first examine the other aspect of his religious life, his life under the law.

The Fight for the Law.

The law was everything to the young Pharisee. Alike fountain of mercy and aim of life, it opened for him the gate of heaven and showed him the moral ideal for the man whose "delight is in the law of the Lord, and in his law doth he meditate day and night; who is like a tree planted by the rivers of water, and whatsoever he doeth shall prosper." The altar had long ceased to be considered a means of propitiating Jehovah's favour by the fat of sacrifice or of securing His pleasure by "sweet savours," or of insuring a man's bodily and spiritual sanctification by the sprinkling of the sacred blood. The sacrifices had for long been nothing more than a portion of the law, carried out because Jehovah had commanded them. Even prayer, the oldest yet ever new approach to God, had in Judaism to suffer itself to be almost entirely relegated within the limits of what was ordained in the law. Its duration and its contents were subjected to the most rigid prescription, and so it had become merely a pious function required by God, for which you expected your reward before

God and men just as you did for fasting and alms-giving. Associate religion with law, and the latter will gain ground with the swiftness of an infectious disease. Nothing is safe from its grasp, not even a man's innermost holy of holies, the intercourse of his heart with God. This is to be seen constantly: the legal religion we witness around us now, Romanism, has allowed the mechanical and the merely ritual to encroach upon prayer. Is not prayer here lowered to the rank of an ecclesiastical punishment?

Yet the legal stage through which every religion must painfully pass from its primitive beginnings, is not without its blessing too. It remained a lifelong power for good to the apostle, that his fiery, passionate nature had passed through the school of the law. His inherent force of energy was thereby increased a hundredfold and his soul acquired a discipline such as no other "taskmaster" could have given. Pharisaism with its painfully precise zeal in keeping all the commandments—nay, even multiplying them endlessly—bred a life as strictly regulated as in any conceivable monastic order. How much time and attention this anxious carefulness for self and care for one's environment demands! How admirably the system of the law teaches the lesson of faithfulness in little things! Above all, it is a preservative against every kind of loose living—the supposed prerogative of men of genius—to which some greatly gifted saints with passionate temperaments have been prone. Under such training was Saul the Pharisee's anxiously delicate, extremely sensitive conscience developed and the deep earnestness fostered which attended him throughout his career.

But in spite of the blessing which he derived from the law, Saul and the law could not remain at peace with each other. One of them had to be the undoing of the other. For when the law in any form meets with a nature so sincere, so energetic, so powerful, a terrible conflict ensues. Nothing better can be conceived for feeble, crippled, half-developed natures than a religion of law. The immense power of the Romish Church over the masses is not without its grounds, and monasteries will always find inmates in thousands who do not experience what Luther had to in the cell. Why? This stupendous system of isolated "pious" deeds, this medley of unintelligible yet sacred rites— the accumulation of centuries—occupies the minds of those to whom the system in itself has become repugnant, with external objects, and bids them do good works for God. The religion of the law offers to such a thousand minor indulgences, encourages a naïve belief that they are doing great things for God, diverts attention from the inner spiritual life, and thus affords satisfaction and comfort—just what they want. The system places sin, real sin, on the same level as the thousandfold transgressions in matters of Sabbath-keeping and fasting and rules of the Order, while it pronounces with an apparently superior profoundness that all sins are alike transgressions of the divine law; thus affording fresh comfort to the easy-going superficial mind, by encouraging the impression that what is downright bad may be made good again through the observance of innumerable ceremonies. Now the laws may be liturgical, or they may be regulations for public worship, moral rules of conduct or dogmas—as long as such a legal religion deals with average men and women, with their innate laziness and superficiality, their longing for slight alterations and compromises and their dislike of absolute truth, all goes smoothly. But the sunken reef is there: the smoothness is only on the surface. For every legal religion must needs diverge into two varieties of piety, the compromise of the masses, the "laymen" and the absolute of the adept, the monk, and the Pharisee. In Judaism the adepts of the legal religion were called Pharisees, which means the "separated ones." They called themselves the "Associates," by contrast to the people. For the masses have never, in Judaism nor in Romanism, in the West nor in India, had time, taste, and money enough to lead an exceptional life of piety. The exceptionally pious have had to be maintained, either as teachers or mendicant friars, by others, for otherwise how could they fulfil all the commandments of God?

Paul had to learn this painful lesson too. According to the promise, the hope of a glorious kingdom was the portion of a holy and just people. Yet the people as a whole were never able really to fulfil the law. Then what availed all their zeal for the traditions of the fathers, all the pious activity of the "Associates"? The people as a whole were lost and remained lost. A heart full of love for his nation as Paul's was, must needs suffer keenly at this thought. While it was the glad tidings of Jesus boldly and unconditionally to open the kingdom of heaven to poor, anxious, suffering, God-seeking souls, it rent the very heart of Saul the Pharisee that his kinsmen according to the flesh were not able to keep the law.

Souls like Saul and Luther coming face to face with the law, draw an inference which is fatal to it. They recognise by an instinct of unerring sincerity that the law offers man no real aim in life, but rather an artificially elaborated something that is powerless to stir any genuine satisfaction and enthusiasm in doing good. To Paul the law was as a taskmaster who constrains the would-be truant youth to follow him to school,[1] as a prison in which he was shut up and under restraint[2]—not as an ideal that liberates and makes for goodness. Honest, loyal natures look for ideals; they gladly submit themselves, feeling that such submission confers an inward freedom and creates an ennobling and harmonious vitality. The law had nothing of this kind to offer; it never will have, let its inner constitution be what it may.

Lastly, there was something else, and *that* decided the issue. He only can be happy under the dispensation of law who can live a lifelong "lie." And, since it is no mere pessimistic notion of our poets, but a bitter fact, that most people live a lifelong lie and that they "worship a lie," the religion of legality is likely to endure long enough. But proud, downright, consistent natures cannot be put off with a lie. If they are unable to resist, they die of the lie: if they are strong it is the lie that dies. The lie inherent in the law was the presumption that it could be fulfilled. Everyone of Paul's associates understood that the commandment could not be kept, but

[1] Gal. iii. 24.   [2] Gal. iii. 23.

they did not own it to themselves. The elder behaved in presence of the younger men as if it could be kept: one believed it on the strength of another, and did not acknowledge the impossibility to himself. They blinded themselves to their own sin by comparing themselves with other just men and had recourse to remote ages, to Enoch, Noah, and Daniel, in order to produce "advocates" for their souls. They hoped God would allow the good works of the saints to cover their own deficiencies, and they did not forget occasionally to beg for mercy —yet, on the whole, they kept up the lie and went on as if all were well.

At the price of tremendous inward conflicts Paul rent the veil of lies which the training of his family and his teachers had woven round his youthful conscience. He had had an experience quite different from that which the good Psalmist had exalted: he was not like a tree planted by rivers of waters; his soul did not dwell in peace and quietness—no, he had to face this terrible thing: the law, holy, just, and good, was changed for him into a demoniacal temptation to sin. He has told us of his experience in terms which recall the story of Eden: "What shall we say then? Is the law sin? God forbid. Howbeit, I had not known sin except through the law: for I had not known coveting, except the law had said, Thou shalt not covet: but sin, finding occasion, wrought in me through the commandment all manner of coveting: for apart from the law sin is dead. And I was alive apart from the law once: but when the commandment came, sin revived, and I died; and the commandment, which was unto life, this

I found to be unto death: for sin, finding occasion, through the commandment beguiled me, and through it slew me."[1]

There was one of the dangers lawgivers are apt to ignore, yet which every law brings with it for proud strong natures. Our religious instruction is not free from this risk: let us see to it that it may not become a school of sin, an invitation to evil. The knowledge of evil may in itself imperil innocence. The youthful Saul felt this with horror, and the law that others blessed, that he himself honoured above everything, became to him ruin, sin, and death. "Did, then, that which is good become death unto me? God forbid. But sin, that it might [according to God's intention] be shown to be sin, by working death to me through that which is good."[2] Sin which dwelt in him—the principle of evil, as his teachers had taught him—made the good for him an instrument of death.

It is an experience common to us all, only not with such profoundness and power—an experience we are not always ready to avow with Paul, when he goes on to speak of his conflict with the law: "For that which I do I know not: for not what I would, that do I practise; but what I hate, that I do. . . . I find then the law, that, to me who would do good, evil is present. For I delight in the law of God after the inward man; but I see a different law in my members, warring against the law of my mind, and bringing me into captivity under the law of sin which is in my members."[3]

In this conflict Saul lived, as Pharisee and perse-

[1] Rom. vii. 7–11.   [2] Rom. vii. 13.   [3] Rom. vii. 15, 21 *seq.*

THE FIGHT FOR THE LAW

cutor. Heavier and heavier did the curse of the law become to him, the more he studied it and the more exactly he tried to keep the commandment. The "principle of evil" of which he had heard, and which he had fancied was easy to overcome, became for him a visible personal reality; and it was just his vehement, proud and fiery temperament that longed after good so passionately, just this rushed him headlong into manifold sins that separated him farther and farther from God. What struggles must have raged through his conscience, until, conquered at last, he breaks out in the despairing cry: " I know that in me, that is, in my flesh, dwelleth no good thing. For to will is present with me, but to do that which is good is not. So now it is no more I that do it, but sin which dwelleth in me!"[1] Terrible hours of anguish for the faithful Pharisee till at last he sees: "It is all in vain! Thou too art lost, art reprobate. If it were not so, then all thy zeal for the commandment, for the sacred ordinances of the Fathers, had not brought thee into sin; sin, the flesh, is all-powerful in thee as in other men. Thou, too, as Adam's son, art subject to the law of death. No man can ever escape this fate."

So he pronounced sentence of death upon himself as a loyal man. None of the paltry consolations that others cling to, could help him here. He was too strong, too proud, too loyal for such. He pleaded guilty. For him the holy law of the fathers had become a law of sin and death.[2] In such a dark hour he hated himself, his body, his flesh—hated them mortally in agonised fear of everlasting damna-

[1] Rom. vii. 18, 20.   [2] Rom. viii. 2.

tion. But he sent up to heaven his cry for help. a clear call amidst the rush and noise of men, a cry of despair: "O wretched man that I am! who shall deliver me from this body of death?"[1]

And this cry of despair was heard.

[1] Rom. vii. 24.

CHAPTER VII.

THE DAY OF DAMASCUS. NIETZSCHE'S ACCUSATION.

SAUL set out from Jerusalem for Damascus as a persecutor of Christians. When he got to Damascus the Pharisee had become a believing Christian, the persecutor an apostle of Jesus. What had happened?

From our youth we know the story in the Acts, where it appears not less than three times, each version containing slightly varying details. The substantial difference between them is this: in chapter ix. there is no mention of a call to apostleship; in chapter xxii. 17, *seq.*, the call comes with a second vision at Jerusalem; in chapter xxvi. 16 it comes immediately with the first. Further, there is no agreement in the three accounts of what was heard or seen by the apostle's companions. Yet in the essential point there is the same impression throughout: Saul, bathed in supernatural light brighter than the sun, hears a voice which says: " Saul, Saul, why persecutest thou me?"

What is implied by St Paul himself, when here and there in his epistles he refers to this capital hour of his life, can be harmonised indeed with the outline of the story in the Acts, yet if we took the apostle's literal words in their simplest sense, we could and should constitute a different picture.

Paul always very strongly emphasises two experiences, which, however, do not in every case stand out with equal clearness in the Acts: he has seen the Lord and has at the same time received his apostle's calling: the new creation of his whole inner man has been sealed by his vocation.

"Am I not free? Am I not an apostle? Have I not seen the Lord?"[1] "He appeared to Cephas, then to the twelve .... then he appeared to James, then to all the apostles, and last of all, as unto one born out of due time, he appeared to me also."[2] "I make known to you, brethren, as touching the gospel which was preached by me, that it is not after man. For neither did I receive it from man, nor was I taught it, but it came to me through revelation of Jesus Christ. Ye have heard of my manner of life in time past in the Jews' religion, how that beyond measure I persecuted the church of God and made havock of it; and I advanced in the Jews' religion beyond many of mine own age among my countrymen, being more exceedingly zealous for the traditions of my fathers. But when it was the good pleasure of God, who separated me even from my mother's womb and called me through his grace, to reveal his Son in me, that I might preach him among the Gentiles, immediately I conferred not with flesh and blood, neither went I up to Jerusalem."[3]

These are the chief passages in which Paul tells of his conversion, not for its own sake, but compelled to

[1] 1 Cor. ix. 1.   [2] 1 Cor. xv. 5–8.   [3] Gal. i. 12–17.

THE DAY OF DAMASCUS

bring it forward as a proof of other things. Elsewhere we only find allusions to it, generally when the apostle is referring to the momentous change in his life. Particularly fine is the great passage Phil. iii. 4-12, where Paul describes the sudden break with Judaism and exalts the power of Christ's resurrection, which has "taken hold" of him. God leads him in triumph as His prisoner everywhere.[1] Since that great day, necessity is laid upon him to preach the gospel.[2] God that said, "Light shall shine out of darkness," has shined in his heart to give the light of the knowledge of the glory of God in the face of Jesus Christ.[3] Perhaps Saul really only saw a radiant light, and concluded from the voice he heard that this was the radiance of the heavenly glory of the risen Christ. Thus the accounts in Acts might possibly be harmonised with Paul's words. Yet according to these latter it is more natural to suppose that he saw, not a mere radiance, but the heavenly form and countenance of the risen Lord Himself.

Paul *saw*: here is the crux for those who desire to substantiate the actual experience of which the apostle was conscious. Men see in two ways. Both these ways appear to the person who sees equally to be the transmission of realities which exist outside himself. The two are in fact exactly opposed to each other: our normal vision and visionary sight. The former rests on retina pictures transmitted physically from without, the latter on retina pictures communicated from within in states of extreme psychical emotion. The scientific standards by which the two are distinguished are not quite simple, for there are col-

[1] 2 Cor. ii. 14.   [2] 1 Cor. ix. 16.   [3] 2 Cor. iv. 6.

lective visions too, in which the appearance is shared by many at once; and besides, most people are open to the visionary spell, either through intentional or unintentional suggestive influence. Yet the two ways of seeing are distinct for outsiders, even if they are not so for those concerned.

What sort of vision was it in which Paul beheld the Son of God in the light out of heaven on the way to Damascus? The answer to the question will vary according to a man's conception of the universe; I say conception of the universe, meaning nothing about faith or religion. The question has no existence for faith. Faith knows that what happened, happened in any case because God chose to work it then—whether Paul really beheld Jesus in the light, or whether it was merely a visionary sight. It is a question of our conception of the universe, in so far as it brings us face to face with the problem: Do we admit the possibility of appearances of persons from another world to the sensual vision? or do we uphold the theory of a world in unbroken conformity to law? Do we refuse to the Maid of Orleans, who, in the same celestial radiance as Paul, beheld the saints of her native village, what we grant as a possibility in the apostle's case? Do we regard only this particular radiance of Damascus as supernatural, or also the radiance of which the pious Greek hermit tells us wherein he saw and held converse with his Lord? May we in the one case call it a natural experience, in harmony with our general point of view, and yet in Paul's case, and in opposition to that point of view, consider it a supernatural event? All these three cases are reported verbally

THE DAY OF DAMASCUS 81

by those who themselves saw the visions and believed them to be verily the impression of objective reality.

With Paul, however, we can see a little further. We know, besides, that he "had visions" in decisive hours of his life, and that in supreme moments he acted in obedience to dreams. Thus in the Acts one of his companions tells of the vision at Troas, when Paul saw the Macedonian who said, " Come over and help us!"[1] Thus Paul himself tells us, he went the second time up to Jerusalem " by revelation."[2] And lastly,[3] he uses the same expressions " revelations " and " visions " for experiences which everyone nowadays would call " visions," such as being " caught up to the third heaven," and " into Paradise," where he " heard unspeakable words which it is not lawful for a man to utter." But why does not the apostle go on to refer in this connection to the appearance before Damascus? Some have answered: Because that belongs to quite a different category; the real reason is, however, because Paul had already told the Corinthians of his Damascus experience—it invariably formed a portion of his missionary addresses.[4] We should, on the contrary, emphasise the fact that Paul reckoned that " being caught up into heaven " as one of his supreme experiences, that he uses the identical expressions about it, and treats it with the same entire faith in its objective reality as he uses with regard to the Damascus scene. If, therefore, in agreement with our conception of the universe which no longer admits of a material heaven, we consider those flights to heaven as purely visionary, we should have the bold-

[1] Acts xvi. 9.   [2] Gal. ii. 2.
[3] 2 Cor. xii. 2 *seq*.   [4] 1 Cor. xv. 1–11.

ness to draw the same conclusion with regard to the occurrence on the road to Damascus.

But how shall we account for the temporary blindness which befell the apostle? Surely that proves the reality of some outwardly visible, dazzling effect on his eyes? On the one hand, the story in the Acts of the healing and directing of Paul by Ananias is hardly tenable, considering the apostle's own solemn assertion that he "conferred not with flesh and blood";[1] on the other hand, it must not be forgotten that, just as hair may whiten in a sudden fright, so the eye may be disorganised by a psychical commotion. And finally, if it is objected that the apostle's statement about not "receiving his message from man," and not being "taught it," necessarily excludes all idea of a previous heart-searching, of an inward conflict—we must answer: This would be an unjustifiable application of words intended to refer solely to the subject of instruction in Christian doctrine.

Accordingly, we must take the inward experience of the apostle, the vision, to be really that which effected the change in his life. Or rather it accompanied, it did not effect, that change. Struggles which proceed in our own souls much less vehemently are condensed into visions in the souls of prophets. They shake body and soul, until in the end it is rather the issue that overtakes the man in a "mysterious" event, than it is the man who goes to meet the issue. Paul's uneasy conscience cries: "Saul, Saul, why persecutest thou me?" He, half a renegade, a frequent backslider, to whom the law was sin, was

[1] Gal. i. 16.

going to Damascus to slaughter more Christians. He was going to bind and slay in behalf of that same law that oppressed him, whose claim he doubted, the law that sentenced him to death! Deeper and deeper the iron goad entered into his soul: What if the law were not given as a savour of life unto life? What if after all *they* were right, in whose torture-twisted faces he had seen the great triumphant joy he himself lacked, and which was evidently the fruit of faith in the risen Lord? Yes—he had experienced the "power of His resurrection" more than once in the case of these people. If it were true? Had the great deliverance really happened? Those martyrs had said they saw the crucified Son of man and the heavens opened! If only he could have positive proof of it—he with his bleeding heart sore! His soul cried aloud to God.

According to the Acts it was mid-day when Saul approached Damascus. The land lay outstretched, dazzling in a scorching heat which hovered over the plain. At this mysterious hour of a southern day there lay over all Nature a soft stillness which appealed strongly to the soul. There, all at once, all this quivering, dazzling brilliance was outshone by a blinding light from heaven! A more than human countenance beams upon his entranced eye — everything around him is bathed in the supernatural radiance. Christ the Risen One is at his side! Terror, pain, and sorrow succeed one another in his soul, and a jubilant joy that such a vision is vouchsafed him. Suddenly he feels the great thing, the wonderful thing, coming to him: Christ has taken up His abode in his heart—a new and infinite sense of strength floods all his being. The man who a moment ago was under sentence of death—he lives—he lives for ever! "I live, yet not I, but Christ lives in me."[1] "If a man is in Christ, he is a new creature. Old things are passed away, all things are become new."[2] The good in him had conquered. With a strong hand his God had snatched him from the way of persecution. His strong and truth-loving soul could not lose itself in lies and fanaticism.

However we may imagine the details of the occurrence to ourselves we shall always recognise in the struggle of Paul's soul, in the mould of his character, his encounters with the Christians, and his personal fanaticism, the moving causes which ultimately transformed him in a sudden change.

Miracle may disappear from religion—we need no sign for a pledge of our faith, like the Jews. For us the "sign of the prophet Jonas" suffices, the appeal to the heart. Those who are unable to see the hand of God in the gift He makes us of such strong and truth-loving souls as this Pharisee, and in His dealings with body and soul in a man, let not such minds imagine they will rather discover the Divine in the Damascus miracle! Yet the life and the conflicts of such souls are, it must be admitted, signs, signs of the victory in the great fight fought by all God-seekers upon earth—and signs of hope, that tell us not to weary in the strife for God, not to let ourselves be overcome by whatever in us and around us wars against Him, but, like Paul, to wrestle and cry for the living God.

[1] Gal. ii. 20.   [2] 2 Cor. v. 17.

NIETZSCHE'S ACCUSATION AGAINST PAUL.

It may confidently be asserted that, among all the opponents of Christianity, from Celsus down to our own contemporaries, few have been at once bolder and deeper than Nietzsche. What especially distinguishes him from all the lesser minds who have directed their attacks against Christianity during the last generation is that he has not rung an unending series of variations on doubts as to the traditional dogmas of the Church, or on the criticism of the earliest form of Christianity in the light of the modern gospel of culture, or on the difficulty of belief in a personal God and in a world to come. It is, of course, true that all this is to be found in his writings. He would not be a child of his own time if it were otherwise. But he possessed something which was lacking in many of his contemporaries—a delicate psychological perception of the essence of religion and a knowledge of the believer's heart. Only, in his hatred against the gods of his youth, Christianity, Schopenhauer, Wagner, whom he confounded together—everything was distorted and transformed into monstrosities.

Nietzsche was well acquainted, too, with St Paul and his conversion. His criticism of the apostle is likewise free from all externality; it is a deep and penetrating moral and even religious criticism. If it were correct, we should needs have to acknowledge Christianity to be " the foulest blot in the history of humanity."

A good deal can be learned from Nietzsche, for there is no weak spot in his enemy's armour which escapes his eagle eye. But his criticism is essentially dangerous and confusing. He delivers historical judgments which have no foundation in fact, with a positive certainty as though they had long been incontrovertibly established. It is especially four pages in the *Morgenröte* (pp. 64–68) which contain the most vehement accusations against Paul.

After a somewhat lengthy introduction, Nietzsche portrays the Pharisee: " Paul had become the fanatical champion and defender of God and His law. He was ever on the watch, ever prepared to do battle against all who questioned the authority or transgressed the ordinances of the law: he would show them no mercy; no severity was too great for them. And now he made a discovery. He found that he himself, passionate, sensual, melancholy, and malicious as he was, could not fulfil the law; nay, stranger still, that his domineering spirit was continually urging him to transgress it, and that it was useless to kick against this prick. . . . He had a great deal on his conscience. He alludes to enmity, murder, sorcery, idolatry, impurity, drunkenness, and the love of carousing; and however much he tried to satisfy his conscience, and still more his lust for power, by the most fanatical veneration and defence of the law, there came moments when he said to himself: ' It is all in vain. This torture of the law that is unfulfilled cannot be escaped.' The law was the cross to which he felt himself crucified: how he hated it! what a grudge he bore against it! how eagerly he sought about for a means, no longer of himself fulfilling it, but of destroying it!"

In this representation of the struggle in Saul's

breast two complete misinterpretations of his words are used in order to make out his conversion to be an act of moral inferiority. Saul, too, according to Nietzsche, seeks refuge from the exacting claims of duty in a feeling of religious exaltation, a description which, it must be confessed, applies to many "conversions." With this end in view, Nietzsche describes Saul as a man full of the worst vices. Such a man he certainly never was, as little as was Luther, in spite of all his self-accusation. In St Paul's letters we frequently come across enumerations of different sins, the so-called catalogues of vices. But it is surely a complete misunderstanding of his words to apply all these to himself. The contrary can be proved. Such catalogues of vices were a favourite form of ethical instruction at that time, both in the Gentile and in the Jewish world. We find them repeated, almost word for word, in various writings of the time. Moreover, St Paul has himself told us that he was a strict Pharisee. Is it likely, then, that he should ever have come to practise sorcery or idolatry? Nor can we accuse him of sensual excesses without at the same time convicting him of untruthfulness, for we have again his own statement to fall back upon: "God," he says, " gave him a special gift in this direction which enabled him to remain unmarried while others were obliged to marry in order not to 'burn' and to give way to temptation."[1] Saul hated and killed, it is true, but can these acts of the persecutor of the Christians be simply labelled as "murder," by the side of sorcery and impurity? But above all, the state of feeling which gave birth to

[1] 1 Cor. vii. 7.

Paul's conversion is completely misrepresented. It was not hatred against the law that he felt, nor was it the attempt to evade the requirements of the law, but it was a reverence for the law and the honest confession that he was a sinful man and therefore lost. Such was the sentence of death which he pronounced upon himself. The law is holy, righteous, and good. Hence Nietzsche's representation of the conversion is likewise altogether distorted: " At length he found salvation. A thought flashed through his mind, accompanied by a vision, as was inevitable in the case of an epileptic subject such as Paul. On a solitary road there appeared to him, the fanatical champion of that law of which he was heartily weary, Christ, with the glory of God about His head, and he heard the words: 'Why persecutest thou me?' What really happened was this: The confusion in Paul's thoughts was cleared up. 'It is irrational,' he said to himself, 'to persecute Christ, of all men. Why, here is the way of escape, here is the completest form of vengeance; here and here alone I have Him who can make the law of none effect.' Paul suffered keenly from tortured pride. All at once his sufferings vanished, his moral despair rolled away like the mist, for the moral law itself was destroyed, *i.e.* fulfilled on yonder cross. Hitherto, that disgraceful death had seemed to him to be one of the chief arguments against the Messiahship of which the advocates of the new teaching made mention; but what if it were necessary in order to annul the law?"

So, then, it was tortured pride and a feeling of vengeance against this law, his torment, that turned a Saul into a Paul. He accepts Christ in order with Him to kill the law. What Paul really felt was the exact contrary of this, and surely everything depends on what he felt. When the law condemned him, God did not put him to death, but, through His Son and His spirit of childlike faith, the heavenly Father took him up, guilt-laden child as he was, in His arms. Thereby he was, it is true, freed from the law and the power of the law; not, as Nietzsche would have it, that he was liberated from the claims of the *moral* law —that is a popular, mostly Roman Catholic misunderstanding of Rom. vi.—but in the sense that the claims of the moral law now presented themselves to him as the claims of his own inmost being and ruled his outward life as the natural "fruit" of that being, only in a much purer and mightier form.

Morality and the striving after righteousness cannot be completely identified with the "law." It is the outer form of the law which distresses the unconverted sinner, the external authority with its menace of the terrible punishment of God, and the incomprehensibility of the will of God with its thousand and one worthless, petty decrees. Now the wave of religious enthusiasm brings with it a new understanding of the will of God. What God wants is an undivided allegiance—the new inner man—and in the furnace of this enthusiasm there is tempered a new will with an indomitable power of working righteousness and accomplishing the "fruits of the Spirit." The deliverance, then, which converted people experience is not that of manumitted slaves, but that of heroes who feel within themselves living sources of a new, an undreamt of, power.

Here, however, two ethical opinions part company and the chasm between them is hardly to be bridged over. For Nietzsche, every "conversion" was a monstrosity, an act of madness. In another place in the *Morgenröte* (p. 84) he says: "As to the physiological meaning of such a sudden, irrational, and irresistible transformation, such a change from the deepest misery to the deepest contentment, whether it be a veiled form of epilepsy or not, that specialists may decide, who have abundant opportunity for observing such 'miracles' (for instance, cases of homicidal or suicidal mania). The comparatively more agreeable effect in the case of the Christian makes no essential difference."

It is strange that a man who himself experienced two conversions—the first, a very sudden one to Schopenhauer's views, and the second, in several stages, as he gradually abandoned them—seems to have had no understanding for the conversion of a human heart. Perhaps this ignorance is assumed. This wild attack on conversion as an act of madness is, as is so often the case in Nietzsche, nothing but the expression of the hatred which he feels for that pietistic form of Christianity in which he was brought up and with which he renewed acquaintance in Pascal, whom he always held to be the typical Christian. The monstrous assertion of revivalism that morality is confined to the "converted," that all the virtues of the heathen are but "brilliant vices," the arrogance with which this form of theology regards as indifferent all that is otherwise counted as morality and is not related to this "miracle," making it, as Nietzsche rightly observes (p. 83), an object of fear by looking upon it as "self-pleasing and pride"—this outrageous "Christian" one-sidedness Nietzsche outbids in his hatred, by his accusation of mania and epilepsy.

Nietzsche, of course, knows that those attacks of "an angel of the adversary"[1] of which St Paul speaks, have been explained as epileptic fits—not without good reason, as we shall see later—and he turns this circumstance to account in forming his accusation. But, although the severe nervous affliction from which St Paul suffered—it was probably not epilepsy, but hysteria—may possibly have something to do with the form of his conversion, though it may have occasioned the vision in which it took place, yet the conversion itself was neither an epileptic nor a hysterical attack, but a long and serious struggle with his conscience and the hardly-gained conviction that every step further on the old path led still further away from God.

And here, finally, we come to the greatest injustice which Nietzsche does to Paul; he dissects him in his psychological analysis without once mentioning his faith in God, as though he were some modern atheist struggling against ethical imperfection. But the adversary with whom Paul is wrestling is far more powerful: it is the sense of guilt towards God and the fear of destruction with which the law threatens him in passing its sentence of death. From this he is saved, not by his own works, but by the working of God in his conscience, which assures him of God's forgiveness. He knows that it is true, because henceforth his heart is filled to overflowing with joy and moral strength.

[1] 2 Cor. xii. 7 *seq.*

After all, early Christianity, and Paul with it, has been a profounder observer of the moral nature of man than Nietzsche, and on this observation all else depends. Simple men are often better exponents of that which lies in the human heart than the cleverest of philosophers.

When Nietzsche says (p. 83) the New Testament sets up a canon of morality, but only of an impossible morality, " In presence of such a rule those who still strive after a moral life should come to feel themselves ever further and further distant from their goal, they should despair of virtue, and should finally throw themselves in the arms of the God of mercy," he is quite right, with one exception—the word " should." The New Testament is not an address delivered at a revival meeting, but a series of testimonies to an inner life of righteousness. But if we take the sentence as the statement of a fact and not of an ideal duty, then we come to a deep truth which Nietzsche has overlooked and which Luther and the Pietists have emphasised one-sidedly, but which is none the less true. As a man increases in moral strength of character, so his conscience becomes more sensitive; he realises more keenly the distance that separates him from the ideal, and hence the weight of the feeling of guiltiness oppresses him ever more heavily. Growth in goodness does not, therefore, necessarily imply increased happiness; on the contrary, it may mean greater unhappiness. And his unhappiness increasing in proportion to the elevation of his ethical standard, a man's end is either Buddha or suicide if he knows no God; while if he knows God, it is despair or that conversion which, having sobbed away its tears on the Father's breast, thence derives ever new strength to fight the battle of life, sure of the final victory. Nietzsche does not take this into account, and therefore he fails to show justice to the "twice-born" type of Christians who experience the joy of their lives in that moment when, in spite of all increase of unhappiness through the clearer voice of conscience, they can throw themselves in the everlasting arms and find comfort in a Father's love.

There is yet another, a more excellent way: it is to go forward with heart glad and thankful for progress in all that is good, and to look upon increased conviction of sin as a part of such progress. This path true and humble men of heart can alone tread, and neither Philistine, self-satisfied respectability, nor Nietzsche's "superman" can walk thereon, but only such as gratefully acknowledge that the wiser and the better they become, they receive all from their heavenly Father.

There is a Christianity which lies beyond that of the revival meeting.

THE PROPHET.

CHAPTER VIII.

THE NEW MAN. THE NEW GOD.

ON that day, on the road to Damascus, Saul died, having passed sentence on himself. Henceforth, a dead man wanders over the surface of the earth, without rest, without thought of self. With the labour of his hands he earns just enough to satisfy the modest needs of his hard life, but he is proud of the fact that he is no longer indebted to anyone for anything. He knows no home; he is a stranger to the affection with which the dear ties of a family would have surrounded him. He is a dead man. He has left behind him all that binds other men to the charm of life.

And yet he lives. For, if he lives no more, yet another lives in him, even the Christ of heaven, who made entry into his heart in that great hour, and now inhabits in his body as though it were His own. It is a marvel to him, and yet a fact. Since that day, a being from another world lives in his heart.[1] It is not enough for him to say he is living his present earthly life by faith in the Son of God, who loved him and gave Himself for him: no, it is Christ Him-

[1] Gal. ii. 20.

self that lives in him. A personal life from heaven, from that other world, has made a new creature of him, in which the old Saul cannot recognise himself. "Old things have passed away; behold, they have become new."[1] Like the other apostles, he has not only been a witness of the resurrection, he has not only seen the Lord. No; he has experienced that which they had experienced—a strange, new, heavenly life has sunk into his heart. That which they call the Holy Ghost he has experienced with the heavenly Christ: therefore the outlines of these two heavenly beings grow indistinct for him; now he calls his new inner life Christ, and now the Spirit; at one time the Spirit of Christ, and at another the Spirit of God.

He has described to us what he and all Christians at that time experienced in the hour of their conversion as follows:—

"You are no longer in the flesh but in the *spirit*, if the *spirit of God* lives within you. But unless a man has the *spirit of Christ* he does not belong to Christ. If, however, *Christ is within you*, then the body indeed is dead as a consequence of sin, but the spirit is full of life as a consequence of righteousness. And if the *spirit of Him who raised Jesus from the dead* lives within you, He who raised Christ Jesus from the dead will give life even to your mortal bodies for the sake of *His spirit* living within you."[2]

This certainty that the good man's reward, which is both great and wonderful, is no longer an uncertain hope for the future, but that it can already be found in human hearts, giving proofs of its living power in a courage that faces death without flinching, in a

[1] 2 Cor. v. 17.   [2] Rom. viii. 9 *seq.*

love which overflows all barriers, and in sighs that cannot be uttered, forms the great turning-point from Judaism to Christianity—Christianity in the specific sense of faith in the risen Christ, who lives in the believer in a supernatural manner. Christian mysticism has been born. The Jesus of history is lost in the heavenly Christ. The heavens are parted asunder and their costliest treasure has descended down to us, not merely once for all on the smiling shores of Galilee, but to-day and everywhere in each believer's heart. We are already in the heavenly place. The body needs but to fall from us like a loose veil, like the chrysalis from a butterfly, and lo! the new man of the heart stands there in bright glory, a picture of the risen Lord, into which we are changed from one splendour to another,[1] since the glory of God has appeared to us in the face of Christ.[2] The devils may strive with God's chosen saint, even the angel of Satan who buffets him may abide in his body: God's strength reaches its perfection in sickness, it is mightier than all the assaults of the adversary.[3] Placed as he is in the midst of this struggle with the demons whose worship he destroys, whose "vessels" he takes from them by his miracles, he fears them not—neither angels, principalities nor powers. He treads them under foot, for the Christ that lives in him is mighty to conquer them. Since the hour of his call he has been further vouchsafed the "signs of an apostle," the power to crush them. St Paul, too, has worked miracles: he has healed the sick,[4] though the demon whom he bore about with him

---

[1] 2 Cor. iii. 18.   [2] 2 Cor. iv. 6.   [3] 2 Cor. xii. 9.-
[4] Rom. xv. 19; 2 Cor. xii. 12; 1 Cor. ii. 3.

THE NEW MAN

in his own body—that is, his sickness—would not leave him.

Such is the new form which the religious life assumes in St Paul. There is something bold, defiant, and jubilant in it. He has not spent his life in burying that dead man who died on the road to Damascus, or in celebrating his memory with copious floods of tears. He boldly turned his back upon him once for all in order that the new life that had come to dwell in him might have room for growth and ultimate victory. There is nothing effeminate about St Paul, no morbid self-reproaches, no idle lamentation over the world, but a brave struggle with it, forgetting the things that are behind,[1] an onset like Luther's on death and the devil, with the certainty of victory. This is not the faith which wearily sings,

> "Take Thou my hand and guide me,
> I cannot walk alone."

It is the defiant challenge—

> "Yea, let the prince of ill
> Take whatsoe'er he will;
> Yet is his profit small,
> He cannot take our all."

Not that St Paul is unacquainted with the softer strains in the religious life. He has taught us the beautiful petition for the peace of God which passeth all understanding;[2] he knows the sighs that cannot be uttered[3] of the devout soul that comes into the presence of its God with a longing for its Master too great for words; but all this is but like the golden

---
[1] Phil. iii. 13.   [2] Phil. iv. 7.   [3] Rom. viii. 26.

gleams of sunshine which flit across a stern, majestic landscape.

This new and heavenly life has kindled a boundless activity in the apostle's breast: the energy of his life was increased beyond all calculation. A compulsion is upon him[1] to carry the good news from one country to another. His life has become that of the athlete in the stadium. It is his duty to make his body his slave, to render it capable of the severest exertions, to buffet it when it claims its rights, not to give way, not to look back.[2] "Straining every nerve towards that which lies in front . . . . I press on to the winning post to gain the prize of that heavenward call which God gave me through Christ Jesus."[3] Christian perfection consists in taking such a view of life.[4] Religion is a power, a strong, and therefore a glad life. "I am not ashamed of the gospel, for it is the *power* by which God brings salvation to every one who believes in it."[5] It is not correctness of doctrine or opinion, but a bold belief, a fearless will, and the jubilant certainty of victory:—that constitutes true religion.

It would be a complete mistake, however, to suppose that St Paul's religion was altogether confined to the sphere of feeling and volition. This rabbi, with his keen, well-trained intellect, whose previous religious life had consisted for the most part in the knowledge of the revealed will of God, was bound to develop no less decisively in the domain of thought after his great experience on the road to Damascus. Paul

---

[1] 1 Cor. ix. 16.　　　[2] 1 Cor. ix. 24–27.
[3] Phil. iii. 14.　　　[4] Phil. iii. 15.
[5] Rom. i. 16; *cp.* 1 Thess. ii. 13.

THE NEW MAN

built up a new knowledge both of God and the world, a new view of the history of humanity, a mighty structure of thought, not to say a system of theology. This he elaborated within the framework of that ancient conception of the world which he shared with all his contemporaries, and which we have already examined. This he defended with all the weapons of his rabbinical training, and maintained with might and main to be the true view of God, the world, and man. We shall have to examine this view of his more minutely later on. At present, it is sufficient for our purpose to point out that Paul, like every other fully developed man, placed the intellect in the service of his faith. He would never have endured that contradiction between head and heart which many, even of those who claim to be his followers, consider to be the normal condition of the Christian life. This faith was not only true, it was reasonable.[1] We may perhaps go so far as to say that, owing to his experience on the road to Damascus and the strong intellectual bias in his character, Paul was the first to intellectualise and thereby narrow the original gospel. Not that his faith is one in a supernaturally revealed dogma ; Paul knew as little of dogma as did Jesus or the early Christians as a whole. Nevertheless, "faith" is no longer for him simply the heartfelt trust in God's mercy, but something besides, the fervent acceptation of a fact—the Resurrection. It appears almost always as the object of the verb "to believe," or else Paul speaks of faith in Him who raised Jesus from the dead.[2] Hereby some of that "belief in facts"

[1] 1 Cor. ii. 6.
[2] Gal. iii. 6; Rom. iv. 17, x. 8 *seq.*; 1 Thess. iv. 14; Rom. iv. 24.

has crept into Christianity which so easily destroys the true, the inmost conception of faith. The outward occurrence and the inner psychological process were identical for St Paul. His failure to distinguish the two has for ever burdened Christianity with the danger of this twofold conception of faith. To this day we are suffering from this uncertainty. A further difficulty arose as follows: Conscious as he was of deriving every thought and feeling from the plenitude of the divine being that lived in him, he stamped every advance that he made in knowledge with the character of a divine revelation. "For the Spirit searcheth all things, even the profoundest secrets of God."[1] The consequences on Christianity as a whole were less important then when Crispus and Sosthenes and every simple Christian claimed the like character for his thoughts.

In the course of the second century, however, the Church again became the religion of a sacred book, and denying the inspiration of all the faithful, attached the divine character to the thoughts of Paul and the other "apostles" exclusively, and was thus compelled once more to intellectualise and narrow the Pauline ideas, of which process only a very small beginning is, after all, to be found in St Paul's own writings.

But while taking into account a certain rigidity occasioned by his intellectualism, which has become a danger more through the natural course of development than through any fault of his, we must not forget the great debt of gratitude under which he has laid us by the decision with which he formulated

[1] 1 Cor. ii. 10.

the new experience in a series of sharply-defined articles of the creed. By this decision, with which he conceived and expressed his thoughts in formulas, St Paul became the saviour of Christianity. Not only did he die to the law just as it was on the point of making its way into Christianity again amongst the disciples of Jesus, in order to live henceforth as a new man, but he killed the law by his hard sayings, and thrust it mercilessly out of religion. St Paul was the first to realise that the law as such, in its formal character, was the cause of sin and misery in the end, in spite of all that it contained that was holy, righteous, and good, and that it must therefore be annulled. That was his great discovery. He was the man of one idea, and to make it prevail he employed all the keenness of his intellect and all his rabbinical training. His theology is nothing but the proof of this one thesis, and for this very reason it is the defence of his holiest, his most cherished possession.

When humanity has arrived at such a crisis in its history, when the forces of the new order of things are already massing themselves together, or when sometimes, as in the present case, they stand clearly visible to all, if it were not that they are concealed from some by the old ruins that have tumbled down and covered them, then such iconoclasts, such devourers of formulas, as Carlyle says, must come and find the sharp, incisive word which will open men's hearts and eyes, tearing down everything that is moribund, as a storm in spring sweeps away the dead branches in the forest. Mankind made a great discovery in that age. They realised the truth that the religion of Nature and of the law was ended. Something new was to take its place: the religion of the good heart, the religion of the children of God, the religion of the might of the Spirit, in the old sense of the word Spirit—that is, the overflowing power of a soul that has found its God in spite of sins and of guilt, and which feels itself uplifted by Him out of and beyond itself into a sphere of purity and goodness, of peace and blessedness and ultimate victory, that rests on something far greater than our own strength.

Paul and Jesus are alike heralds of this truth with which mankind are to rise to another stage in their ascent. The difference between them is this: Paul formularised the idea, and confined it within the strict limits of a dogmatical and scriptural proof, equipped for this task with a keen intellect, and urged thereto by bitter vexation for a blinded life. Thus formularised, the idea was more immediately effective than in the pure beauty and inwardness in which Jesus rather lived than taught it.

The New God.

The new man implied a new God. Saul's experience on the road to Damascus had revealed the God of his fathers in a new light.

He had always known that Jehovah was a holy and a mighty God, who with a mighty arm and with an outstretched hand directs the fortunes of the nation before whose greatness the heathen are as drops in a bucket. He had also believed that this Almighty God guided the righteous, and had their good deeds ever before His eyes no less than their sins, even their secret faults.

But now, in the light of his conversion, all this is exalted into a new and still more powerful picture of the God who, with a strong hand, guides the fate of man, who separates and calls a man from his mother's womb,[1] who shows mercy on whom He will and hardens whom He will.[2] True, Paul was not the first to express thoughts such as these; many pious Jews and devout heathen had already had similar experiences of God, and no doubt this experience had found expression in books which Paul had read—the wisdom of Solomon, *e.g.*—but such a faith in God is not to be learnt out of books but in the hard school of life. It is true, too, that there always have been individuals who have been carried away by stronger characters and just repeat their belief in the passive guidance of men by God. So Melanchthon was Luther's echo, but Paul has himself experienced his God as the Power who has guided his life at every step; who led him down the road of error down to the deepest abyss, in order to uplift him all at once, and to set his feet on the bright high place of a new life full of energy and love. Nor did Paul gain this belief of his in predestination by abstruse philosophical reflection: it is neither determinism nor any system at all, but it is religion. It rests neither on the problem of the freedom of the will, nor on the recognition of the law of universal causation, but on the question, "How can I be saved?" and on the feeling of a wonderful, divine guidance, higher than all laws of cause and effect. And when he found himself no longer able to give the old answer

[1] Gal. i. 15.   [2] Rom. ix. 18.

to the question as to salvation, viz., "by works, by mine own righteousness," then the other was revealed to him and brought him light and joy: through Him that "calleth me."[1] God is all and man is nothing, and yet the object of God's constant care.

And how does one attain to the knowledge that one belongs to the number of those "of whom God took note from the first, and also marked out from the first to be transformed into likeness to His Son, so that he might be the eldest among many brethren"?[2] whom He then "called" in accordance with His purpose in a great hour of their lives and "justified," *i.e.* accepted, as righteous, and "brought to glory"? How does one learn it? One learns it in that great hour of one's life when faith comes through hearing the message;[3] one learns it daily by that love for God which ever since fills the heart with a warmth that never grows cold. "We know that God makes all things work in harmony for the good of those who love Him. I mean, of those who have received the call in accordance with His purpose."[4]

But while this faith in God fills the single man or woman who possesses it with happiness—for by the love they bear to God and the delight they take in Him they feel that they are of the called—yet it is a gloomy and a hard creed when it has to be applied to the surging mass of humanity round about us. Two objections have therefore been raised against it which no one—not even Paul—has been able to refute to this day. The first objection met

[1] Rom. ix. 12. [2] Rom. viii. 28 *seq.*
[3] Rom. x. 17. [4] Rom. viii. 28.

THE NEW GOD 105

the apostle when he thought of his own people, how they had thrust away the proffered salvation, and had even trodden it under foot (Rom. ix. 11). His heart, overflowing with love, is like to break when he thinks of it.[1] But he accepts the fact. It is no one's fault that it so came about; it is fate—*i.e.* it is God's free choice, as in the case of Esau and Jacob. Rebecca was told, before they were born and before they had done anything either right or wrong, that the elder would be a servant to the younger, as it is written, "I loved Jacob but I hated Esau." What is the inference then? Can God be guilty of injustice?[2]

That is the question. And though Paul at once answers, "certainly not," yet he can give no conclusive reasons for his answer.[3] For the proof from Scripture which now follows, merely repeats Paul's own assertion, and is no solution of the problem itself, though it establishes the apostle's view in accordance with the conceptions of the time. And so, too, Paul merely concludes this scriptural proof with the words, "Therefore God either takes pity on people or hardens their hearts just as He chooses."[4] He brings forward a second reason in the following words: "Who art thou, O man, that art arguing with God? Does a thing which a man has moulded say to him who moulded it, 'Why didst thou make me like this?' Has not a potter in dealing with clay a perfect right to make out of the same lump one vessel for show and another for the commonest use?"[5]

[1] Rom. ix. 1 *seq.*   [2] Rom. ix. 11–13.   [3] Rom. ix. 14 *seq.*
[4] Rom. ix. 18.   [5] Rom. ix. 20 *seq.*

All this, however, is of no use. The problem continues to present itself bristling on all sides with difficulties. If God is at once almighty and capricious, if without rhyme or reason He shows compassion on one man and hardens another's heart, is not injustice His chief characteristic?

St Paul puts the second question, which arises in the sphere of ethics, in the same manner without giving an answer: "How, then, can God still blame any man[1] if He Himself shows mercy on him or hardens him? Where is man's responsibility, where his free will?" To this question Paul has given no answer here. In Rom. vi. he puts the same question from another point of view, and emphasises in the strongest possible manner the necessity of responsibility and the moral life in bringing forward two objections to his doctrine of justification: (1) Shall we continue in sin that grace may abound?[2] and (2) Let us sin, we are no longer under the law but under grace.[3] Paul meets both these perversions of his predestinarian theory with an emphatic negative: "Sin must not reign in your mortal bodies."[4] And yet, after all, he has recourse once more to the imperative, for he could do nothing else: "Once for all give up yourselves to God as those who, though once dead, now have life, and give up to Him your members as instruments of righteousness." "Give up your members as slaves," no longer to impurity, but "to righteousness which leads to holiness."[5]

Paul felt the contradiction involved between his

[1] Rom. ix. 19.   [2] Rom. vi. 1 *seq.*   [3] Rom. vi. 15.
[4] Rom. vi. 12.   [5] Rom. vi. 13, 19.

faith and his moral sense, and though it vanished in the unity of his own life, from God for God, he was never able to discover a theoretical solution.

Probably the real difficulty of the problem was concealed from him by the thought that all men being sinners they had all deserved death, and that it was God's love alone which saved some, so that predestination to evil is not taken into account. For Paul continues after the last verse quoted from Rom. ix.: "But what if God, although He intends to reveal His displeasure and make His power known, bore most patiently with the objects of His displeasure, fit only for destruction, so as to make known the wealth of His glory in dealing with the objects of His mercy, whom He prepared beforehand to share His glory?"[1] The very delay in the execution of this sentence of death on the wicked is an act of God's love. Even thus, however, the difficulty is but put away out of sight and not solved. For to be merciful without due reason towards some involves an equally groundless mercilessness towards others. For one thing is certain—in this case we must go further; we cannot accept a position which is at once non-merciful and yet righteous.

After all, it is not this philosophical conception which formed the final unity in Paul's heart, but an altogether different feeling which might be described in connection with a third possible objection. If we conceive of God as showing mercy to some and hardening the hearts of others, what room is there for love to all men, for that love which, in St

[1] Rom. ix. 22 *seq.*

108   THE PROPHET

Paul's own convincing words, "believeth all things and hopeth all things"?[1] The predestinarian cannot love all men or he would just die of grief; and he would be better than his God who felt no such pain or love.

The difficulty is not really felt as long as we merely think of extreme instances such as Esau and Pharaoh,[2] the deterrent examples of a sacred book; but as soon as our thoughts turn to the men and women in whose eyes we look, whose hands we clasp, our fellow-workers and fellow-soldiers, then we realise the enormity of this doctrine of predestination. Nor could the apostle's heart suffer him to go any further when he had got so far. Chapters x. and xi. of the Epistle to the Romans are sufficient evidence of this. Paul conceives of his people as lost, and yet: "Brothers, their salvation is my heart's desire and my prayer to God.[3] Nor are they altogether lost and accursed, for I can testify that they are eager for God's honour, but ignorantly." And so he cannot believe that God has rejected His people.[4] At present, it is true, it is but a remnant that has been converted, the remnant of which the prophets of old already prophesied; the rest are hardened.[5] This hardening, however, is but a means to a great end: it is to furnish space and time for the mission to the Gentiles.[6] The heathen are to be grafted on to the old stem in place of the branches that have been cut away because they had become useless.[7] And at length the apostle's heart wins a complete victory:

[1] 1 Cor. xiii. 7.   [2] Rom. ix. 13–17.   [3] Rom. x. 1.
[4] Rom. xi. 1.   [5] Rom. xi. 4–10.   [6] Rom. xi. 11 *seq.*
[7] Rom. xi. 11–24.

when the heathen have entered into the kingdom of God, then all the people of Israel will be converted and will enter in.[1] "For God has included in the prison of disobedience all alike, that to all alike He may show mercy." Paul wrote down these sentences as a "mystery"—he trembles with joy as he endeavours to find utterance in solemn words for this, the climax of his message; he is conscious that it is a divine revelation, the light has burst upon him after many a hard time of trial which this problem has occasioned him.

He came to conceive that his mission to the Gentiles was realised in the best and highest manner possible when he looked upon it in the light of this revelation as a means of rousing his fellow-countrymen to jealousy,[2] and thus making them in their turn stretch out their hand for that which the heathen were so gladly accepting.

The light of this "revealed mystery" fills him with rapture. The stern experience of his life and the love of his heart united in this bold, but too bold, hope, and his song of praise ascended jubilant:—

> O the depth of the riches of the wisdom and knowledge of God!
>
> How unsearchable are His judgments,
> And His ways past finding out!
>
> For who hath known the mind of the Lord;
> Who hath been His counsellor?
>
> Who hath first given to Him,
> So that He may claim some return?
>
> For of Him and to Him and through Him are all things:
> To Him be glory for ever and ever. Amen.[3]

---

[1] Rom. xi. 32.   [2] Rom. xi. 14.   [3] Rom. xi. 33–36.

The philosopher for whom this world contains no riddles that he has not solved, may smile at such a hope and such helplessness in solving the great riddle presented by the juxtaposition of the human and divine wills and the coincidence of the feelings of freedom and dependence; does not a long history of eighteen centuries brilliantly refute the apostle's hope, his expectation that all mankind would be saved in his generation? Are there many signs even to-day that the fulness of the heathen, and thereby the people of Israel, are about to enter into the kingdom of heaven? One thing, however, he too will learn. For whichever solution of the great riddle of human destiny he may decide—whether he be a predestinarian or not, a determinist or an advocate of the freedom of the will, he will be continually meeting with facts which can only be harmonised with a one-sided theory by doing violence to truth.

It is certain beyond all manner of doubt that Paul conceived of his God as the irresistible power in whose hand his own life and that of all other men was as clay in the hands of the potter, and yet he ventured to appeal to all men to be converted, and he was instant in admonishing his converts to lead a righteous life. The whole of his life as missionary is one great contradiction, and the contradiction was only solved in the certainty that the God whose strong arm he had experienced was a Father of compassion and a God of all consolation,[1] that the God and Father of our Lord Jesus Christ[2] is likewise our Father, ready to bestow upon all that ask, as the apostle does at the beginning of every one of his

[1] 2 Cor. i. 3.   [2] Rom. xv. 6; 2 Cor. xi. 31.

THE NEW GOD 111

letters, both grace and peace; a God to whom he can cry Abba, Father,[1] who has shown His love in suffering His son to die for sinners[2]—the God of love and of peace.[3] But the message of God's love never becomes weak or unreal in St Paul's mouth. For behind his words there stands the experience of that all-powerful God who leads men with His mighty hand whichever way He will, and will summon them before His judgment seat, where all, even the inmost secrets of the heart, shall be revealed. And there is one thing needful for him that has heard the Father's call: he must walk worthy of this God who has called him to His kingdom and to His glory.[4]

[1] Rom. viii. 15; Gal. iv. 6. [2] Rom. viii. 32; v. 8.
[3] 2 Cor. xiii. 11. [4] 1 Thess. ii. 12.

THE PROPHET.

CHAPTER IX.

MAN'S COMMUNION. THE NEW FELLOWSHIP.

THERE are two ways in which from the earliest time God has come down to man: revelation and sacrament; and there are two ways in which man has ascended to God: prayer and sacrifice.

Whether revelation and prayer came first—God's revelation in the heart and the word of the heart to God, or the mysterious union with the holiness of the Godhead and the offering of man to God, that is, sacrament and sacrifice, who shall decide? Only he perhaps could find an answer who could tell us whether mankind thought and spoke before they acted, or whether they represented by gesture and by action that which stirred mightily within them, before speech flowed from the abundance of their heart.

One thing, however, is certain—the way from God to man, be it revelation or sacrament, is the earlier. It is not man who first sought God, but God who first sought man. God made known to man His life of all power and might, and granted him to share in this life as his costliest possession, as the highest realisation of his life. Religion is primarily a receiving, secondarily a giving.

Such were the feelings of primitive man when there was revealed to him in the ever-green tree, in the never-failing fountain, in the sheer ascent of the cliff, in the quivering lightning and the rolling thunder, in the rustling of the wood and in the soul of man himself, a power of life which went beyond his own power, that he might receive from it blessing and life, and render to it thanksgiving and the requests of his heart and the first-fruits of all that he possessed. Such were the feelings of the cultured believer of our own day when he defined religion in our colourless scientific language as a feeling of absolute dependence upon God. This is the feeling that makes the whole world kin from our remotest ancestors downwards. It is only the superficiality, the hurry and the bustle of our modern life, that have dulled our hearing and rendered the ears of many insensible to those tones in which it echoes in us all.

For Paul, too, the fact that not he had come to God, but God had come to him, and spoken to him in his heart without ceasing, took precedence over everything else. Since Christ, the Spirit of God, has taken up His abode in him, he has ears for this inner voice; he listens to all that is declared to him, revelation of the future, interpretation of the past, direction for the needs of the day. On the road to Damascus Paul became not only an apostle, but, above all, a prophet—a prophet in the right meaning of the word current in his time, not an oracle-monger.

No more grievous mistake has been committed by our religious instruction, which continues in the old ruts, than that of changing the prophets into these oracle-mongers, and that to such an extent that one can scarcely understand how there can have been any prophets at all after Jesus. For the prophets, we were taught, had to prophesy the coming of Christ, and the last of these men whose work it was to deliver oracles was John the Baptist. This, however, was not the essence of the prophetic office to those who themselves knew prophets, still less to the prophets themselves. To the early Christians, the prophet was a man of inspired speech which flowed from the fulness of the Spirit and the great new experiences, he was one who built up the faith of his hearers and furthered their moral growth, giving them comfort and encouragement of every kind,[1] because his words came from a heart filled with God, and therefore found their way straight to the heart. This does not, of course, hinder the prophet from foretelling the great events which the faith of that day pictured to itself as about to take place, those mighty catastrophes of the last days to which Paul refers when he says to the Thessalonians, "We are certain to encounter trouble,"[2] and amongst which Agabus described more especially a famine, which prediction was fulfilled, it was generally believed, in a time of dearth that followed not long after.[3] But he, too, is a prophet who reads history in the light of his new life as Paul does (Rom. ix. 11), or who finds his way to the heart of the heathen weighed down by the sense of guilt and filled with longing when they come to the Christian assembly—he can do it, for he has suffered as they are now suffering, and the key of sympathy is in his hands. "If all use the prophetic gift, and an unbeliever or one without

[1] Cor. xiv. 3.   [2] Thess. iii. 4.   [3] Acts xi. 27 *seq.*

the gift enters, he is convinced by all, he is judged by all, the secrets of his heart are revealed. Then, throwing himself on his face, he will worship God and confess, God is indeed in you."[1] So powerfully do the words of the prophet affect the heart, so inexplicable is the way in which he reads the most secret thoughts and feelings, that even the heathen must needs ascribe to the God that abides in the Christian his superhuman knowledge and the mighty form of his speech. Thus the fire smouldered which the prophet Paul had kindled in the hearts of his converts, and thus it burnt in his own, an inextinguishable flame, ever since that day on the way to Damascus. In visions and in revelations, in words which the " Spirit of God " whispered to him, in pictures which He showed to him, in new phases of knowledge which appeared suddenly, as though from unfathomable mysterious depths, so God revealed Himself to him.

The deepest longings of this heart athirst for God were satisfied. Paul's religion was no longer based upon a sacred book. His God no longer spoke to him from the faded leaves of old riddling writings, or from the explanations of subtilising pedants. St Paul only looked for Him there when he wished to prove a point to others. But it was from the flame of fire that burnt within his own heart that his God spoke to him. He spoke to him in the silent watches of the night, and in the work of the day, and Paul heard His voice.

Such is religion: these are the marks of a living religion. And in spite of all that official Lutheranism

[1] Cor. xiv. 24 *seq.*

and Anglicanism have said and done during the last three hundred years to "quench the Spirit" amongst Quakers, Methodists, Pietists, and the like, in spite of all their efforts to kill the prophets of to-day and to garnish the tombs of the prophets of old, religion still lives in our midst. Happily, religion is mightier than old creeds, and the life with God has never quite been killed by the dogma of inspiration. We have here something essentially human at war against the aberrations of our national churches, and it will conquer. Even supposing scientific criticism should effect no change, we must remember that it was in Pietism in Germany, and in similar tendencies in England, that the religious life first broke through the old hide-bound narrowness, and if the Pietism and Evangelicalism of to-day have suffered themselves to be led away captive, in the person of most of their representatives, by their old enemy orthodoxy, then a more living and a more liberal piety must take up their work and continue it. For a man's religious life dates from the day when he realises that God speaks to him as well as to others—speaks to him individually, and he hears the voice distinctly, and it is irresistible.

So God spoke in times of old to the fathers, and so too He spake again to Paul. This personal element in the apostle's religion is something at once everlasting and yet quite new. But Paul is a child of his own time too, he belongs to antiquity. And so he knows yet another way in which God comes down to man: viz., in sacraments. There is but one true explanation of sacraments, the Catholic and the Lutheran; all others, especially all modern theological explanations, are but compromises and modifications of this pre-Christian idea, the contradiction of which with our religion we have felt since the Reformation in an ever-increasing degree. Sacraments are the external means by which, according to the faith of primitive man, God imparts Himself, and that so that He suffers man to share in His Almighty superhuman life and in His holiness. In the sacrament man eats and drinks God Himself; or he makes a covenant of blood with Him, when he smears His altar or stone or stake and then himself with the blood of the sacrificed beast, or eats the flesh with the blood. In thus accomplishing the sacramental rites he becomes a "participator," he is initiated into the mysterious life of the Godhead.[1]

Out of the dim dawn of prehistoric times remnants of this ancient belief, long abandoned by philosophers, and survivals of the old ritual, had lasted till the age of the empire. They had even started into new life during the centuries immediately preceding the Christian era. They had been amalgamated with the hope of immortality and united with the worship of the gods of light, of the sun, and of spring. By initiation into these mysteries through going to witness the dramatic performances at Eleusis and drinking the magic draught, in other places perhaps by submitting to the baptism of blood of the "great mother," or of Mithras, through the cup and the bread, which he gave to those that believed in him, the converts participated in the divine life— "died" with the deity in winter and during the night, and rose with the deity to a new life in the

[1] 1 Cor. x. 21.

blessed springtide and in the new day of eternity. Such were the feelings of the worshippers in the mysteries, such their experiences, such the benefits which they derived from participation in the sacraments. Just about the time of Jesus' life on earth, this form of religion had begun to conquer the world, unsatisfied as it was with a merely material life, and filled with longing for immortality and for some tangible proof of an everlasting life of future blessedness. Jesus Himself did not baptize, even if He suffered Himself to be baptized—the meaning of the baptism of John we are no longer able to understand — He instituted no sacrament, even if on that last night He did compare the broken bread and the red outpoured wine with His tortured body and His shed blood. It was a picture, a parable— no sacrament. But in that age the Last Supper was bound almost at once to become a sacrament, and the baptism of Jesus to furnish a warrant for a sacramental consecration of all the disciples. It was an inevitable tendency, common to mankind. But He who knew that nothing that entereth into a man's mouth from without could defile a man[1]— neither flesh of swine nor strong drink—He could not believe either that any holy food could make a man pure or give him the gift of everlasting life. We do not know who first transformed the Gospel by incorporating the two sacraments. But no more pregnant decision was ever taken by Christianity. When we come to Paul's life we already find the accomplished fact. The words of administration have already been changed so as to harmonise with the

[1] Mark vii. 15.

MAN'S COMMUNION 119

change of view. The bread is no longer the picture of the broken body, nor is the wine the blood shed for many,[1] but the bread is "my body which is for you," and the cup is "the new covenant, in my blood."[2] The emphasis is laid on the food, and on participating in the food. Baptism and the Lord's Supper are already mentioned side by side as two similar ceremonies,[3] and the only reason for doing this was the analogy presented by the mysteries. Bread and wine are already conceived of as substances in which, and with which and in the shape of which one partakes of the body and blood of Christ in a sensual and at the same time supersensual manner, through which we therefore enter into a real connection with the heavenly Being.

The fundamental idea of the sacrament has perhaps nowhere been expressed more clearly than by St Paul in 1 Cor. x. 15-21. Those who eat the sacrifices from the altar at Jerusalem are "sharers" with the altar, have communion, enter into fellowship with it, *i.e.* with the life and holiness of Jehovah. Those who eat the sacrifices offered to idols enter in like manner into fellowship with demons. And then Paul turns in the third place to the Lord's Supper: there in the same material manner one partakes of the body of Christ, has a share in Christ, enters into fellowship with Him. Even at this early date Paul speaks of baptism just as the worshippers of the mysteries who die and live with their God. "Know ye not that all we who were baptized into Jesus Christ were baptized into his death? So then we have been buried with him by baptism

[1] Mark xiv. 22. [2] 1 Cor. xi. 23 *seq.* [3] 1 Cor. x. 1-6.

into death, that like as Christ was raised up from the dead by the glory of the Father, even so we also should walk in newness of life."[1] When Paul here says "should walk" he is giving an ethical turn to a point of view which occurs very frequently in his writings.[2] The effect of the sacrament itself is such that by fellowship in the death of Christ we attain to fellowship in the life. Hence that vicarious baptism for the dead, *i.e.* for those who died before conversion, which we know to have been practised at Corinth in the apostle's time. Even thus early, therefore, a magical efficacy for the next world was ascribed to the sacrament. The fact that Paul argues from this custom as from something perfectly justifiable and efficacious,[3] shows us how profoundly the sacramental idea had penetrated into Christianity.

In St Paul's writings we have the two forms of religion—the subjective and the objective, the sacramental and the purely spiritual—standing side by side without any attempt at co-ordination. At one time it is faith that produces the Spirit, at another baptism, now union with Christ is through faith, and now again it is through the Lord's Supper. These two series of conceptions have not as yet been united under any one system. They cannot be harmonised. For two entirely different religions have here met together. The pre-Christian religion has made its way again to the very heart of godliness. Here the first breach was made in the walls of the new faith. Instincts which had been handed down through thousands of generations united with the new longing and wove the fantastical veil of the symbolical

---

[1] Rom. vi. 3 *seq.* [2] *E.g.* Rom. vi. 8. [3] 1 Cor. xv. 29.

about the young religion of inward and spiritual grace; and the only shape in which it was as yet possible for mankind to conceive of symbols was the magical, in sacraments.

Paul himself did not feel the problem at all which arose through the collision of the natural religion of redemption contained in the mysteries with an ethical faith like the Christian. It is true that when his converts threatened to lapse into immorality through a too unquestioning faith in the natural form of religion, he warned them very earnestly and blamed them very severely: sacraments do not save a man from the judgment of wrath which God has appointed to the sinner. The Israelites in the wilderness had baptism, says Paul, for they were covered by the wonderful heavenly cloud, and they had Holy Communion, for they had the wonderful food from heaven, the manna, and they drank the heavenly water from the rock that was Christ; so they had the same sacraments as the Christians. And yet they were destroyed by the Angel of Death, because they became idolaters and committed acts of immorality and other sins. "Wherefore he that thinketh he standeth," *i.e.* whoever thinks that through the sacrament he, *ipso facto*, possesses eternal life with God, "let him take heed lest he fall."[1] Now it is not the ethical religion of redemption that St Paul opposes to the sacramental form of religion in this argument, which we may take as a crucial instance, but it is the religion of ethical retribution. He did not say: "As God's children ye cannot sin: if you sin you do but show that you are not yet God's children; you must grow;"[2] but he

---
[1] 1 Cor. x. 1–11.   [2] 1 Cor. iii. 1–5.

thought that he could only attain his object by using these old ideas of retribution. And thereby he took the first decisive step towards Catholicism. For Catholicism may be defined as the co-ordination of the ethical religion of the law with the sacraments. The grace of God, supernatural in its origin but mediated naturally, connected with definite external objects; and then a legal form of ethics—the amalgamation of these two forms the faith of the Catholic Church.

While the primitive conception of the sacrament survived from the earliest dawn of man's religious history down to St Paul's own day, with scarcely any change—one may even say with a renewed vitality and an increased extension—sacrifices, in the original sense of food offered for the needs of the deity, had died out long ago. The continued efforts of the prophets had borne fruit at last. The people had abandoned their naïve confidence in their offerings to God. They had learnt the lesson which the Greeks as well as their philosophers had likewise learnt: that God was too great that He should delight in the sweet odour of burning pieces of fat, or that they should be necessary to support His life. Again and again the prophets had preached that mercy was better than sacrifice, that God loved not a brilliant ritual, but righteous thoughts and righteous deeds; and so by degrees sacrifices came to be conceived of less and less as a real gift to God: they had come to be part of the law, they were propitiatory, *i.e.* they had become sacraments. God had commanded the sacrifices to be offered, the sacrifices at Jerusalem, the priests, and all the pomp of the temple: and they were offered as a part of His will and His commandments. But there was besides a belief in the propitiatory and consecrating effect of the blood and of the covenant by blood, of the rites of sprinkling. Hence it is that "blood" stands so frequently in the New Testament for "sacrifice."

For St Paul sacrifices had been abrogated, as a matter of principle, together with the law as a whole. They are just as little necessary to man's salvation as any other part of the law. The only sacrifice which Christians are bound to offer is that of their bodies, which they are to present as a living, holy sacrifice, acceptable to God; that is the only reasonable worship which exists.[1] Never did St Paul criticise sacrifices more severely than in these words: It is not reasonable to offer up animals, "a male without blemish." God's greatest pleasure is the body of a man unspotted by sin.

But we have already seen that St Paul was not able to maintain his footing on these spiritual heights: the partaking of sacrifices as a sacrament was a reality for him. Nay, more. In the stress of argument, when compelled to defend the death of Jesus as an atonement against his Jewish adversaries, he too, like the first disciples, had recourse to the idea of a sacrifice. Christ is for him the great sacrifice of all Christians, His blood has brought reconciliation,[2] He has been offered up as our Paschal lamb.[3]

Here polytheism, for a second time, made a breach in the walls of the religion of spirituality, of the inner spiritual motive. Sacrifices were at first only external symbols, but gradually they came to be realities. And

[1] Rom. xii. 1. [2] Rom. iii. 25; v. 9; viii. 3. [3] 1 Cor. v. 7.

124   THE PROPHET

as the idea of the sacrifice of the mass came to be developed, with the ever-repeated offering—a bloodless offering, it is true—polytheism celebrated its decisive victory. Men wanted to have their sacrifices again as their fathers had had theirs. They wished to unburden their souls; they were not willing to offer up the only reasonable sacrifice, that of their own bodies, and so they looked about for some compensation.

It is very remarkable that we cannot as yet affirm with certainty whether Paul himself sacrificed in the temple at Jerusalem after he became a Christian. There can scarcely be any doubt in the case of the disciples of Jesus. According to the Acts[1] Paul did too, and there is no particular reason for refusing to accept this statement. We cannot, however, be absolutely certain, as sacrifices already played too small a part in Judaism. They are never mentioned in the course of St Paul's arguments with the Judaisers as one of the points on which they insist. Nor indeed were they of any great importance for the Jews outside of Jerusalem. It was only a little later in the history of Christianity that the sacrificial system was seriously attacked. The Epistle to the Hebrews, and that of Barnabas, are the earliest writings which formally declare sacrifices to be abrogated and engage in a regular polemic against them.

Whatever St Paul's practice may have been as regards sacrifices, the way in which he sought for communion with God and for His gifts was not sacrifice but prayer. A Christian's life consists for him in joy and prayer.

"Rejoice always, pray without ceasing, give thanks

[1] Acts xxi. 21–27.

for everything: this is God's will for you as made known in Christ Jesus."[1] "Rejoice in the Lord always; I will say it again, rejoice. Let your gentleness be known to all men. The Lord is at hand: do not be anxious for anything, but make what you want known to God with prayers, supplication, and thanksgiving. So will the peace of God, which surpasses every human conception, stand guard over your hearts and thoughts in Christ Jesus."[2]

Here we have the keynote of the Christian life as Paul conceived it. Jesus Himself could not have described the life of the children of God more beautifully. Like rays of bright sunshine, such words break forth from the dark, heavy masses of Pauline polemics.

And as he described the Christian life to others, so he gave an example of it in his own life. He begins no letter without turning the customary salutation into a request for grace and peace from God and our Lord Christ; he concludes no letter without praying in some form or other: "The grace of our Lord be with you. Amen." And this first request is followed everywhere by a longer introductory prayer—save in the Epistle to the Galatians, where it would have been impossible for the apostle to pray or to give thanks sincerely, so greatly disturbed was he at the fickleness of his converts. But to make up for this harsh beginning he added a hearty "My brothers" to the concluding petition in this letter and in this alone.

St Paul's peculiar phraseology is imitated by so many, that it is very difficult for us to realise at the

[1] 1 Thess. v. 16 *seq.*; Phil. i. 3.   [2] Phil. iv. 4–7.

present day that we have something here that was once entirely fresh and new. His language has been fossilised in liturgies, or worn away by such frequent use, that we no longer feel the force and the originality with which these words once came pouring forth from the lips of one whose heart was filled with the living God. For though you can tell that St Paul was born and bred among a people that had been in the habit of using psalms and liturgies for many hundred years, yet there is something quite his own in these prayers of his. So characteristic were they supposed to be, even in the early days of Christianity, of Paul and no one else, that almost all who afterwards wrote letters in his name imitated this peculiarity. Of course even the longer thanksgivings at the beginnings of the letters do not give a full and perfect picture of the way in which Paul prayed; too much attention is paid to the style for that, and then after the first few words addressed to God they pass very quietly into an exhortation to the congregations. Paul, in fact, is not the man to wear his heart upon his sleeve; he shrinks, even in the most confidential letters, from appearing to pray a written prayer before his congregations in the real sense of the word.

Few more striking instances can be found of the way in which he managed to rejoice always, and to foster this happy disposition by thanksgiving for all things, even misfortune, than his prayer at the beginning of the second Epistle to the Corinthians.

"Blessed be the God and Father of our Lord Jesus Christ, the Father of mercies and God of all comfort; who comforteth us in all our trouble, that we may be able to comfort those who are in any trouble, by the comfort wherewith we ourselves are comforted by God. For as we have our full share of the sufferings of Christ, so through Christ we have also our full share of comfort. Whether we suffer, it is for your comfort and salvation ; whether we be comforted, it is for your comfort; which will make itself felt in you when you endure the same sufferings that we ourselves are enduring. And we have good hopes for you, for we know that as you are sharing our sufferings, so you will share our comfort."

Prayer is for the apostle the most beautiful feature in the Christian life. The best, the most real result of the Palestine famine fund, are the words of heartfelt gratitude that the recipients will offer up to God.[1] The apostle is absolutely certain that his intercessory prayer will be granted. Often he expresses his conviction in the shape of a statement that something will assuredly take place : " And God himself will strengthen you to the end, so that no one will be able to accuse you in the day of our Lord Jesus Christ."[2] So in the introductory prayer, in the letter to the Philippians, we have not a petition but a positive statement, following immediately upon the thanksgiving : " I thank my God whenever I think of you ; for whenever I pray, I pray for you, and my prayers are full of joy ; for you have co-operated with me to the furtherance of the Gospel from the first day until now. For of this I am quite sure, that he who has begun the good work in you will complete it in readiness for the day of Jesus Christ."

As he always prays for his congregations, so in turn he requests them to pray for him: the Romans are

[1] 2 Cor. ix. 11.   [2] 1 Cor. i. 8.

to wrestle with him in prayer, that he may be delivered out of the hands of the Jews, and may come to them in answer to their prayers.¹ And in joyful confidence he told the Philippians who had supported him—they were the only congregation of whom he accepted such support—that the only way he could requite them was through prayer. But then Paul trusted his God as implicitly as the child trusts his father. " My God, so great is his wealth, will give you richly all that you need." ²

Even Paul's prayers were not always granted, but they were always heard by his God. Thrice he prayed to God to take away the severe affliction, the trial of his life, but neither health nor alleviation of his suffering was granted him, only the answer: " Strength is made perfect in weakness. My grace must be enough for you." ³ As the apostle thus prays, the same voice " answers " him as that which spoke in Jesus: " Not my will, but thine, be done ; " it is that most perfect form of faith which trusts in God and doubts not, even though sufferings and necessities abound.

Once again Paul's prayers are like the prayers of Jesus in that his petitions are first and foremost for the coming of the Kingdom of God, taking this kingdom in the apostle's sense of peace and joy in the Holy Ghost.⁴ The petition for daily bread occupies but a small space in the prayers of Paul. What a contrast between them and many of our liturgies, where this petition seems almost to have absorbed every other — for the Church and its servants, for

[1] Rom. xv. 30 seq.   [2] Phil. iv. 19.
[3] 2 Cor. xii. 8.   [4] Rom. xiv. 17.

whom so great a portion of these liturgies is reserved, and who occupy therein the most important place, belong likewise to this fourth petition and not to the second, are daily bread and not visible Kingdom of God. The only occasions on which Paul in his letters prays for the supply of bodily wants are when he wishes to help others. Thus he prays for a prosperous journey,[1] he thanks God for deliverance from danger,[2] and for prevention of a step in his missionary procedure easily liable to misunderstanding.[3] His chiefest care—that which he has most at heart—is the growth and development of his congregations, and he has given expression to this anxiety of his in the most heartfelt and tenderest of prayers and blessings. " God will bear me witness that I yearn over you all with the tenderness of Christ Jesus, and what I pray for is this, that your love may grow yet stronger and stronger with increasing knowledge and with moral perception, so that you may learn to test what is good and bad, so that you may become pure and blameless in readiness for the day of Christ, filled with the harvest of righteousness which comes through Jesus Christ, to the glory and praise of God."[4] And his thanksgivings, too, strike the same key. " We thank God always for you all while we mention you in our prayers, for we never fail to remember your work of faith and labour, of love and patience, of hope in our Lord Jesus Christ in the sight of our God and Father."[5]

Many similar passages might be quoted. Let these few suffice. Thus Paul prayed. Nowhere does his brave, strenuous, kind and loving personality

---
[1] 1 Thess. iii. 9 *seq*. [2] 2 Cor. i. 10. [3] 1 Cor. i. 14.
[4] Phil. i. 9. [5] 1 Thess. i. 2.

stand forth revealed more clearly than in his prayers. Our prayers are our judges not less than our hopes; for prayer is the will of hope. Unfortunately, the very fact which proves Paul's prevailing power in prayer has come to be the reason that we so often fail to recognise it: viz., the fact that to this present day the Church lives on his prayers, and many to this day simply repeat them. That is why so many of his phrases no longer have the genuine ring for us that they once had. But he that can get rid of this impression will find rich stores of much that is pure, good, strong, and genuinely human in all the apostle's prayers.

Thus St Paul prayed "with the understanding." He knew besides, however, those transcendent moments of prayers when the cry "Father" burst from his soul and escaped from his lips;[1] and again those quiet hours, the source of so much strength, in which the "spirit" prayed in his heart in his stead to God with sighs that could not be uttered.[2] For him, too, those were the supreme seasons in his life, when, filled with the certainty that he had found the Father, and carried away and uplifted by thoughts of God, his heart engaged in that speechless communion with God, and he experienced that great longing in which prayer itself is swallowed up in the one feeling—

"Nearer, my God, to Thee,
Nearer to Thee."

THE NEW FELLOWSHIP.

Every religion strives to realise a fellowship. Whenever man has found "life and full content,"

[1] Gal. iv. 6; Rom. viii. 15.   [2] Rom. viii. 26.

THE NEW FELLOWSHIP

the full heart overflows in speech. He preaches because he has believed, just as he believes because he has heard the preacher.

Thus men are encircled by the chain of a common experience, a stronger tie than that of class or state, of race or nationality, even than that of the love of wife and children. More especially is this true of enthusiastic religions which produce ardent and zealous devotees. So, too, Paul's faith seeks for fellowship and communion,—it impels him to go forth into the mission-field.

Now there lies a great danger in this direction, and that for enthusiastic religions more than for others— the danger of mysticism, the danger of sinking into selfish enjoyment of the deity, of encasing oneself in cold reserve towards others, of looking down from a very lofty level upon the common herd, "the multitude that knoweth not the law." Nor is this aristocratic exclusiveness of the religious coterie the mark of Pharisaistic and dogmatic forms of religion only, the result of theological corruption; it is often to be met with in the more fervid creations of the revivalist and sectarian.

But all such illiberality is entirely alien to St Paul. His inmost being is heartfelt love. Whatever great experiences God may have vouchsafed him, speakings with tongues and visions, revelations and ecstasies: " Were I to speak with the tongues of men and of angels, yet have not love, I am become sounding brass or a clanging cymbal; and though I have prophecy, and understand all secrets and all knowledge, and though I have all faith so that I could remove mountains, but have not love, I am nothing."

His religious experience is not that of the mystic who is wrapt up in himself. Love, his heart's irresistible impulse, bids him lay bare his inmost soul to others, in order to win them, and let them share in that which shall make their hearts just as glad and as strong, as happy and as blessed, as his own has become.

Besides, Paul's personal religion is of an essentially social type. Individual as was his original experience, he was incorporated in Christ, the Christ who dwells in the whole body of Christians; he was plunged into that great ocean of the Holy Ghost which surges and rages in all others just as it does in him. Thereby he has become part of a great organism, every member of which is of equal value and significance for the whole, which can only live if all bestir themselves in helpful activity: "For if one member suffers, all members suffer."[1] That is what makes the apostle's mysticism so pure. It is equally removed from pious egoism and from pious self-exaltation. His only way of experiencing religion is to enter into a great fellowship with others, and to recognise that in all of his fellows the same power is at work, and that everyone of them realises this power in that particular way which makes his life to be of especial value to the whole. It is no polite but insincere form of speech, it is the simple truth when he says to the Romans:[2] "I am longing to see you, I would gladly impart to you some spiritual gift, and give you fresh strength. In other words: I would live in your midst, and be comforted together with you by the faith which we share in common."

[1] 1 Cor. xii. 12; Rom. xii. 4, etc. [2] Rom. i. 11.

That is Paul's conception of the Church: an organism of people who have been brought together by the same experiences, and who are retained in this union by ministering love. Or rather, it is not his conception of the "Church," but it is the *fellowship* in which his new life has placed him, it is the "congregation of God." In later ages this simple form of fellowship was no longer supposed to be sufficient, it fared as the similar fellowship of the disciples of Jesus. As men's living experience grew weaker, creeds and articles were devised; when love no longer held them together, its place was taken by canon law. And whenever the attempt has been made, throughout the history of Christendom, to do without creeds and external regulations, the result has always been a reaction which one should have the courage to term a "fall," even though a "fall" is no historical category, and however much one recognises the necessity of this fall. Will there never be a change? Will the law never suffer itself to be completely rooted out from the religion of the Divine Fatherhood, and will those that bear rule amongst us ever seek to exercise authority and decline to serve?

THE PROPHET.

CHAPTER X.

THE NEW MORALITY. ORIGIN OF CHRISTIANITY
AND NIETZSCHE'S CRITICISMS.

IN describing the new fellowship, we have already passed from the domain of the religious life to that of morality. Here too Paul's experience on the road to Damascus marks a new epoch, even though Paul did but rediscover what Jesus had already experienced before him and preached in another form. Through Paul the moral life of mankind has been enriched by the realisation of two great facts. First, there is the truth that morality, in the full sense of the word and in its highest development, can only blossom in the fiery heat of religious enthusiasm. As a Pharisee Paul could not perform the works of the law, although all that it bade him do was righteous, holy, and good. He could not do the good that he would, he fell from one sin into another. Moral compulsion was not enough. But when he had passed sentence upon himself, when he had died, to begin the new life, a power had been developed in this mighty transformation of his life which destroyed all the roots of selfishness in him, which impelled him to live henceforth only for God

THE NEW MORALITY

and others. Instead of the works which he had not been able to do, there grew up in his heart, a blessing to himself and others, the "fruits of the Holy Ghost," love, joy, peace, long-suffering, gentleness, generosity, trustfulness, kindliness, and self-control.[1] We have a completely new kind of morality which harmonises with Christianity. Man is no longer governed by "thou shalt," but by "I will"; like the flower from the bud, like the fruit from the blossom, so morality grows gradually in the transformed man. An irresistible feeling of happiness issues forth from the new religious life, and, filling the heart to overflowing, completely destroys that hankering for little pleasures which incite to sin. It is not two souls that live within the Christian's breast, but a single new man. Duty and desire have been fused together in the heat of religious enthusiasm. This is what Jesus and Paul intended, this is what Luther rediscovered. Nor is a man like the Silesian hymn-writer, known as Angelus Silesius, far from the kingdom of heaven when he says, in the affected language of the seventeenth century:

> "Ask you why a Christian should righteous be and free?
> Ask rather why no little lamb can e'er a tiger be."

Or when he gives this thought a somewhat different expression and manifests a really profound conception of that which constitutes genuine goodness in the words:

> "The rose-tree blooms because it blooms,
> Nor knows the reason why."

It "blooms because it blooms": that is Christian

[1] Gal. v. 22.

morality which has overcome all legality. Morality has become a second nature: that is the great secret which the master spirits have read. Not all the dross had yet been smelted out of Paul's character, but his whole being was so permeated by the new elements in his life, that when he encountered a difficult problem he could rely on a revelation of his subconscious self; and that his conscious moral being expressed itself in such words as we find in 1 Cor. xiii. or Rom. xii., passages which would be the priceless possession of all mankind even if they were recorded in no sacred book.

The apostle's realisation of the second great truth destroys legal morality in its outer form. As morality develops in the course of history, it finds expression in single commandments. It was only by very slow degrees that these commandments came to be recognised as the single component parts which together formed one ideal. Thus Jesus showed in His explanation of the "commandments," "Thou shalt do no murder," "Thou shalt not commit adultery," etc. how, behind and above these commandments, there existed for Him an ideal, that of inward purity, in which all these commandments were deepened and unified.[1] It was not to be a new law, but a collection of examples of a "higher righteousness"[2] proceeding forth from this inward purity. Neither did Paul set up a new law of Christian ethics. What he wanted was that Christians should be free to consider each ethical question as it presented itself. He has, of course, left us a multitude of single moral precepts, but these are, so to speak, only headings to whole

[1] Matt. v.   [2] Matt. v. 21.

chapters of decisions which each man must take for himself.

Thus, as we have seen above, he described the fruits of faith; thus again he analysed love,[1] passing it through his ripe Christian experience and breaking it up into its elements.

Love suffereth long, and is kind, love envieth not,
   Love vaunteth not itself, is not puffed up,
Doth not behave itself unseemly, seeketh not her own,
   Is not easily provoked, nor does she reckon up her wrongs,
Rejoiceth not in iniquity, nay, rather rejoiceth with the truth.
She covereth all things, believeth all things, hopeth all things,
   suffereth all things.

And in Rom. xii. we find a whole series of the noblest ethical precepts :—

"Let love be without insincerity. Abhor that which is evil, cling to that which is good. Let your brotherly love be affectionate; where respect is to be shown, put others before yourselves; be thorough in your diligence and fervent in spirit. Serve the Lord. Rejoice in hope, be patient in tribulation, persevere in prayer. Relieve the wants of your fellow Christians. Show hospitality gladly. Bless those who persecute you; bless, and curse not. Rejoice with those who are rejoicing, and weep with those who weep. Let each look upon his neighbour as his equal, cherish no thoughts of social pride, but associate with the humble. Do not grow conceited. Never pay back injury with injury. Think always of that which is honourable in the sight of all men. If it be possible, at any rate as far as depends on yourselves, live at peace with all men. Beloved, avenge not yourselves; but leave room for the judgment of wrath (of God).

[1] Cor. xiii. 4 *seq.*

For it is written: Vengeance is mine, I will repay, saith the Lord. No, if thine enemy hunger, feed him; if he thirst, give him something to drink. If you do that you will heap coals of fire upon his head. Do not be overcome by evil, but overcome evil with goodness."

Here we certainly have a great number of single commandments, but they and many others are all grouped together under this appeal:—

"I beseech you then, brethren, by the mercy of God, to present your bodies as a living and holy sacrifice acceptable to God, which is your reasonable worship. And do not conform your life to the fashion of this world, but transform your lives by the renewing of your moral nature, so that you may learn to understand what the will of God is, all that is good and acceptable and perfect."

Paul's aim, therefore, is not a new law, but a new moral sense, a new conscience, one harmonious whole. Commandments are only special instances. Hence too we must be allowed to judge the apostle himself by his own standard, by the new moral nature which he brought over to Europe, and to sift out the traces of Judaism which still cling to him, such as the ascribing of vengeance to God, and the "coals of fire," taken from the proverbs of Solomon. For we too, children of a later day, must give heed to his admonition: "Brethren, whatsoever things are true, whatsoever things are honourable, whatsoever things are righteous, whatsoever things are pure, whatsoever things are lovable, whatsoever things are attractive, if there is anything in virtue and praise, think of these things."[1] And by this standard the next sentence must be judged: "All that you learnt and received from me, all that you heard and saw me do, do that."

One of the boldest hopes ever cherished by Christianity has been the possibility of raising mankind to such a height that each individual should be a moral law unto himself; hitherto no nobler Utopia ever took shape in the brain of man. The experience of fourteen centuries seemed to provide a brilliant demonstration of the futility of this ideal, but then came the Reformation. Protestantism set it up again, whilst Roman Catholicism finally abandoned it by adopting, especially among the Jesuits, a casuistical system of ethics, and so it descended again to the old level of a legal religion. In that church either the priest, or a manual, teaches you every single commandment.

Will the reformed churches be strong enough to transform this great hope of Christianity into real life, will they ever really attain to this new stage in ethical development? Will they succeed in changing the masses into personalities, each man with a conscience of his own, an independent moral being? What endless work, how vast a system of national education, this one hope necessitates! What countless social institutions will have to second and continue the work of the school if this hope is ever to be realised!

Well, if our hope be but transformed into work, we need not despair.

[1] Phil. iv. 8.

The Origin of Christianity and Nietzsche's Criticism of Paul's Personal Religion.

Very soon after Jesus' death the ethical religion of redemption, which came with Him into the world, experienced the most decisive formal transformation through which it ever passed. The religion of the Divine Fatherhood was changed into the faith in the divine nature of the man Jesus. The visions in which the disciples saw their living Master seemed to prove that He was a heavenly being and no mere man, or at least that He was now exalted into heaven. Hence the disciples made faith in Him, as the Messiah exalted to God's right hand, and in the conception of His death as a divinely ordered propitiation for all sins, a necessary condition. The religion of Christ, Christianity in the narrower sense of the word, begins with this experience of the resurrection and with this dogma of the death of the Messiah.

But Paul was the first to develop these ideas and to secure their ultimate victory by his system of Christian mysticism. Wherever at this present day the old forms of our faith are united with a living, personal religion—as is the case amongst many true and genuine Pietists and Methodists—there they draw their vitality from this mystical view of Christ. These men are "much cheered with thoughts of Christ, the living bread." There are, it is true, a good many other religious conservatives of a different stamp, who talk about the "living Christ," but the words have no genuine ring, they only appear to be used as an ecclesiastical weapon with which to slay inconvenient opponents—but that does not alter the undoubted fact that Christian mysticism is to this day full of life and ardent enthusiasm.

That is why Nietzsche's attack upon Paul's mystical view of Christ is so peculiarly vehement. He rends him tooth and nail, as though he were dealing with a living adversary.

"The endless consequences of this idea, of his solution of the mystery, quite dazzle him. All at once he becomes the happiest of men—the fate of the Jews, nay, of all mankind, seems to him to depend upon this idea, to be linked to the second when he was suddenly illuminated; he has discovered the thought of all thoughts, the key of keys, the light of lights: henceforth he, Paul, is the centre of all history. For henceforth he proclaims the annulling of the Law!
. . . He has become one with Christ, *i.e.* he has, like Him, become the destroyer of the Law; he has died with Him, *i.e.* he too has died unto the Law!
. . . Now the Law is dead, now the flesh, in which it lives, is dead—or at least continually dying, so to speak, decaying. Yet a little time in the midst of this decay! Such is the Christian's lot before he rises with Christ, having become one with Him, and shares with Christ in the divine glory, becoming like Christ, 'Son of God.'" Here Paul's intoxication reaches its climax, and he throws off all reserve. As he realises that he has become one with Christ, every sense of shame, every sense of subordination, vanishes, every barrier disappears; the domineering spirit of one who brooked no control revealed itself in this anticipated revelling in *divine* glory. Such is the first Christian, the discoverer of Christianity! Hitherto there had only been a few Jewish sectaries.

In another place (p. 182), he compares him to Madame de Guyon, and in so doing repeats his charges against him: "There stands Madame de Guyon, one of the little group of French Quietists. All that the apostle Paul's eloquence and enthusiasm had ever dreamt of the Christian's all but divine nature, of that union of sweetest charm and most dread majesty, of completest repose and intensest rapture, are there realised,—while the Jewish forwardness, so characteristic of Paul's relations to his God, is eliminated, thanks to a genuine, womanly, refined old-French naïveness both in word and manner."

Here again one cannot reproach Nietzsche, as one can so many modern opponents of Christianity, with ignorance of the object of his criticism. He is right, too, in noting that in her experience of God, Madame de Guyon strikes a tenderer, a more refined and womanly note than St Paul. But then, her experience is so much less constant, so much more variable, exposed to all manner of catastrophes and attacks of frailty. St Paul's religious life scarcely ever gives one the impression of anything that is morbid. Madame de Guyon lives almost entirely in an abnormal condition, at any rate it is the foundation of her ordinary life; and Kerner's remarks on the "Visionary of Prevorst" apply to the whole period of Madame de Guyon's religious life: "She makes the impression of one that is already dead, of a soul that hovers between this world and the next, so extreme is her nervous excitability." In spite of the attacks of the "messenger of Satan," and in spite of his visions, Paul's life, on the other hand, distinctly makes the impression of a healthy man at the height of his powers, who is not to be diverted from his course by dangers by land or by water, by hardship and privation, by scourging and cruel punishments. Nothing like Madame de Guyon's long descriptions of her varying moods is to be found in Paul's writings. There is something decisive, clear, and sharp, something firm and manly, perfectly sane and sober, serious and defiant in Paul's character and in the character of his religion, in spite of all his raptures. Moreover, these abnormal states are by no means of frequent occurrence. They are not the source of his life, as is the case with the Quietists, nor does he conceive himself to be separated from God in the quiet hours of his existence; they are no regrettable interruption in a life devoted entirely to an ecstatic state of contemplation. It is true that he spoke much in the ecstatic state, "he spoke with tongues more than they all,"[1] but he has to go back as far as fourteen years in order to find another instance when he was thus hurried into a higher sphere from his ordinary everyday life, when he was caught up into paradise and the third heaven.[2] Paul's piety is akin to that of Kerner's ecstatic visionary; but it is something more than ecstasy, it is a quiet, courageous, constant, and happy life in the Spirit or in Christ.

But this is just what Nietzsche criticises as a shameless forwardness towards God—(see the latter of the two passages above quoted from his writings). The expression is peculiarly ill-chosen—Paul very rarely speaks of a life in God. What he exhibits is not a genuine Jewish forwardness, but a genuine Jewish reverence for God—a reverence which far

[1] 1 Cor. xiv. 18.   [2] 2 Cor. xii. 2 *seq.*

exceeds any feeling that other peoples conceived for their gods. In God the Jews worshipped a Will, highly exalted, far above anything human in might and in power, the will that could save and could damn to hell fire. Never could Seneca's idea of seeing the gods "on a level with himself" have occurred to any Jew. Nothing is further from Paul's thoughts. On the contrary, his God is exalted to so terrible a height that He rather inspires awe and terror, as we have already seen.

But perhaps we are too literal. It might be urged on behalf of Nietzsche that it is all the same whether Paul speaks of God or of His spirit, or of Christ,—the forwardness, the presumption is the same. This is by no means the case however; for the belief that the Spirit of God seizes hold of a man, and that a new and mighty life from on high comes over him, was deep-rooted in the religious history of Israel. Such was the explanation of certain definite experiences, *e.g.* those ecstatic states, which are facts and not fancies, which "occur" to a man like thoughts and recognitions, like feelings, sensations, and dreams. But Nietzsche takes no account of this explanation, and so he is constantly guilty of injustice towards Paul. He is deficient, after all, in the genuine historical sense. He lacks the patience to so steep himself in a bygone age as to look out upon the world with the eyes of a past generation. The motive force in Paul's soul in that decisive hour of his life was his longing for purity and goodness, for a full, complete, and true life, for the certainty that God would forgive him his sins and would save him from certain destruction. In that hour when his evil conscience showed him the innocent, persecuted Nazarene living in the glory of heaven, this longing was transformed into the glad certainty that God had deemed him worthy of salvation, and that simply because such an experience was vouchsafed him.

Looked at from a psychological point of view, it was his soul of goodness which, in the shape of a bad conscience, won the victory over his previous conception of God and the way of salvation. He, too, perceived that if God were *just*, He would and must destroy Himself. The law cannot be the last word of His will. It is neither forwardness nor a domineering spirit that is the cause of Paul's belief that a new, a heavenly life, has begun in him, but a fact—the fact that *a new inner life really has begun in him*. He no longer seeks to take his stand upon his own deserts, he no longer strives to secure the recognition of his righteousness in God's sight by means of his own works and merits. No, he has received all: just as he was beginning to despair, the certainty came over him that God took compassion upon him, that He sent forth the spirit of His son into his heart, so that he could now say, "Abba, Father," and need no more be afraid of the righteous God.

So we simply have to reverse Nietzsche's assertion. It is humility that the apostle feels in that he ascribes not to himself but to One higher the new life that has begun in his heart. It is not the sham humility, so often called Christian, which talks so much about being humble, but it is the true humility which enables him to take up a proud and bold position towards the world about him. It is true that man seeks for "dominion" in religion, that is to say, the certainty that he has aims and objects beyond this world, that his life is destined for eternity, and that the whole world cannot compensate him for the loss of his soul.[1] True religion imparts this certainty to him, for it fills his soul with a power which lifts the man up above himself and his previous life and assures him that all his aims and all his activity are now part of God's eternal will, and that as God's fellow-worker he inherits eternal life. So he becomes lord over all kings. But while thus exalting man and his position, religion ascribes everything to a Being higher and more than man. The greater the man, the greater the readiness to recognise the new life as God's gift, as a life in God; and so with the sense of his high calling comes that profound humility without which human greatness is like a flower without scent. And by giving man a share in God's work, religion makes him once more a servant in the ministry of love to his neighbour.

Nietzsche himself is a striking instance how an experience similar to that of Paul's, if it be unaccompanied by faith in God, leads to the heights of self-glorious pride from which the fall to the flat sands of vanity inevitably succeeds. He too, proud and self-confident man that he was, experienced a conversion, and from it he received a new life; he too was filled thereby with the conviction that he ought to go forth and prophesy to his people, and, like every prophet, he thought that "henceforth all history turned round himself as centre," himself and his "overman": but in his case the effect is terrible and repulsive, for he has thought all this without any

[1] Mark viii. 36.

belief in God. What else can we call it but boundless self-sufficiency that he could only speak of himself when he spoke of the great things that he was conscious of experiencing and showing to others: his assumption of the rôle of Zarathustra does not alter the case. Again and again one is forced to the conclusion that he never went down upon his knees before the mystery in his own soul, that he could never lift up his eyes with gratitude to One who had given him the most precious of all that he possessed. From a purely human point of view, the religious man has this great advantage over the irreligious,—pride and self-confidence are no snares of vanity for him, but are changed into humility. Of course it is only genuine religion that can do that—the spurious can always be detected by its mistaking the want of pride and self-confidence for humility, or by its affectation of humility covering a really vain nature.

We have one last accusation to notice: the intoxication in Paul's soul. It is strange that Nietzsche, of all men, should be the one to level it against the apostle. Usually it comes from the Philistines and other wise people who understand the intoxication of the body, while that of the soul appears to them something uncanny and akin to madness. Nietzsche cannot have meant it as a reproach when he too joins in the cry, "Paul, thou art beside thyself." He was himself too much of a poet for that, he himself knew this intoxication of the soul, and knew that the highest upon earth can only be attained by those souls that have experienced it. It was only the form in which Paul experienced it, and the religious soil in which it took its rise, that were strange and unfamiliar to

Nietzsche. There are others, however, besides Nietzsche, who say, when the apostle is thus depicted to them, that he was a mad fanatic; and there are religious people, quiet and unemotional folk, who turn round and rend anyone who ventures thus to present the real Paul. To such we must answer that not those men are full of the deity who find their utterance in well-turned phrases, but those whose hearts are filled with "groanings that cannot be uttered," whose message bubbles forth from the soul in stammering sounds and joyful cries; and that it is not the words of human eloquence that move the souls of men, but the proof of an indwelling spirit and of power. Enthusiasm is kindled by enthusiasm alone, and not by wisdom; faith only by faith, and not by logic. And that alone is the right faith which believes in hope against hope.[1] But such faith springs up only in souls that are "full of new wine."[2]

It is not enough, however, merely to negative Nietzsche's accusations. They deserve very careful consideration. There are two things which our educated religious laity, and still more our clergy and theologians of conservative tendencies, should learn from Nietzsche. First, that they are quite as un-historical and quite as unjust towards their contemporaries as Nietzsche is towards Paul, when they call every man a heretic who cannot accept Paul's mysticism or repeat their shibboleth of "the living Christ," because his modern outlook on the universe forbids him to do so. The particular form which Paul's conversion assumed was surely caused quite as much by the strange psychology which was then

[1] Rom. iv. 18. [2] Acts ii. 13.

universally accepted, as by the picture of Christ taken over from Judaism. It was a psychology which always represented a man as possessed as soon as he felt within himself powers that he could not ascribe to himself, possessed either by the devil or by God, by an angel of Satan or by Christ, sometimes by both at once, as Paul believed in his own case.[1] But we can keep Jesus stedfastly before our eyes and treasure Him in our hearts, we can realise how He, how His living form within us, works in and on us, without accepting the somewhat gross psychology of a bygone age, any more than we accept its belief in spirits in its entirety. Even he who is perfectly well aware that what he sees with his mind's eye is but a picture of the imagination formed by historical tradition and his own creative energy, may still experience its life-giving power in his own case.

Secondly, our friends ought to recognise that their insistence on this mysticism, created as it is by means of an antiquated psychology, constitutes a danger to Christianity itself. They make of it and of the dogma of the Atonement the narrow gate which leads to the Kingdom of Heaven, and, forgetting that it should be Jesus' high ethical demands [2] which constitute this gate, they close the door of the Kingdom in the face of many.

But still more important than this is the question whether " Christianity " has not altered the contents of the religion of Jesus in many essentials, whether Paul's personal religion does not represent an entirely new departure. Such is not the case. In Paul as in Jesus one realises that the living core and centre of

[1] 2 Cor. xii. 9.   [2] Matt. vii. 14.

the whole religion is joy in the Divine Sonship. It is neither the law nor single external works which save a man, but the entire surrender of the whole man to God, and a new life which results from this surrender. Whether this conversion of the whole inner nature be called repentance and forgiveness of sins, or a life in Christ, in the Spirit, does not alter the fact itself. If we except a few remnants of the old system, which we have already noticed and will have to notice again, it was both in Jesus' as in Paul's case an ethical religion of redemption which issued from the ethical religion of Judaism—in the former through an inner spiritualising process, in the latter by a sudden convulsion. When they reach the highest ground of all, Paul and Jesus are at one, however much their formulas may differ, however much they may themselves differ in their inner character. There a Being who, in spite of all struggles and changes of mood, is transfigured through and through by communion with God and the goodness of God, and here a man wrestling and struggling mightily, who has to fight a hard fight against the flesh, and against devils in himself, whose nature is shaken by passion till late in life, a passion which destroys all harmonious repose.

THE APOSTLE

CHAPTER XI.

THE CALL OF THE MASTER. THE SOIL OF THE MISSION FIELD. THE MISSION FIELD.

THE new man born on that day of Damascus has stood before our spiritual eye. We have seen the prophet of a new religion, and have listened to the conflicting dispute as it went on within his heart. Whatever may have developed in after years of the peculiar piety alive in Paul, the initial point of departure for it all was that Damascus day. However rudimentary and imperfect the beginnings may have been, they yet carried within them the earnest of the full-grown saint.

But that great hour had shown the Pharisee too a new public aim; the "vocation" to be "an apostle of Jesus Christ," His Messenger, sent with the glad tidings to the Gentiles.

Apostle of Jesus Christ. This is the only title Paul values, which he always proudly claims again when others attempt to dispute it, with which he presents himself before his own and before stranger[1] churches, when he wants to be impressive, to command, or to rebuke.[2] Only when he is particularly

[1] Rom. i. 1. [2] 1 Cor. i. 1; 2 Cor. i. 1.

friendly and cordial, when he is corresponding with beloved churches as their fatherly friend, he lays aside his proud title and addresses himself as a brother to his brethren.[1] But whenever his apostleship is hotly attacked or called in question, wherever in the churches there are signs of their deserting the apostle, he writes bluntly and sternly : "Paul an apostle not from men, neither through a man, but through Jesus Christ and God the Father, who raised Him from the dead, and all the brethren which are with me, unto the churches of Galatia." His pride and joy, his life's force and supreme offering, was, to be a messenger of Jesus Christ.

No man, but God, appointed him to this work, for it was the Damascus experience which showed him his new path. God chose him from his mother's womb and revealed His son in him, that he might preach Him among the Gentiles; he saw the Lord, and so became an apostle.[2]

Why does Damascus mean a new vocation to Paul?

We have seen already how the apostle's very piety constrains him to communion and fellowship: the prophet must needs become an apostle. The assurance of redemption from sin and guilt, from pain and death, sets up an exuberance of the heart out of which the mouth must speak. And love for others, who are in the way of perdition, whom the prophet sees reeling to the abyss, impels him no less to seek and to save. And with Paul there was this further, that throughout the long restless time before conversion, he had been forced to condemn himself, to

---

[1] 1 Thess. i. 1 ; Phil. i. 1.   [2] Gal. i. 16 ; 1 Cor. ix. 1, xv. 7.

speak his own sentence of death. Now he had found new life, it could only be one complete consecration to Him who had given it: *God through Jesus Christ* is his battle-cry. He had persecuted the Lord in the past, he had slaughtered His servants: now he could show only by the devotion of his whole life that he was in very truth converted. He adjudged himself, so to speak, a second time to death; not now indeed the death from which there is no escape, but the participation in the sufferings of Christ, that were to bring for him and others salvation, life, and resurrection with Christ.[1] All this was surging together in the apostle's heart. And thus he conceived his new calling not as "I will," but as "I must": "For if I preach the gospel, I have nothing to glory of, for necessity is laid upon me; for woe is unto me if I preach not the gospel."[2]

It is easily comprehensible that the prophet became the apostle, yet it is difficult to understand just why he became the apostle of the Gentiles. Was it not more natural he should preach to his fellow-countrymen, to whom he was bound by birth and education, with whom he must have had more inward affinity than with the Greeks? Could he not do far more to help them than he could do for the foreigner? Did he not himself say he could wish himself anathema, and for ever severed from his Master, if thereby he might save them?[3]

Perhaps the two passages, Gal. v. 11 and 2 Cor. v. 16, will furnish us with a clue for the explanation of our question, if we consider them in psychological connection with the apostle's own statement, that he

[1] 2 Cor. iv. 10 *seq.*   [2] 1 Cor. ix. 16.   [3] Rom. ix. 3.

received his new vocation in that Damascus revelation. In these passages we can trace the idea that Paul had once known and preached circumcision and Christ after the flesh—that is, he had, when he was still Saul, recognised and proclaimed an earthly Jewish Messiah, and that he had already been a teacher, possibly also a missionary. In this case it may have been a pre-existent calling, or at the least perhaps an incipient though hidden desire which awoke within him in full force in that supreme moment. Thus he may have recognised that now, when the law no longer barred the way of the Gentiles, the great hour for their entering into the Kingdom of God had come, and that to him, with his new enlightenment as to the law, it was specially given to be their guide. On the other hand, he knew how matters stood in the hearts of his people, that here the "offence of the Cross" was still too great, and that his people would perhaps only then enter in when they should see the Gentile multitudes become Christians. All this must have been present to his mind, not in such logical clearness, yet half-consciously, and this it may have been which urged him in the new direction. The argument is further supported by the fact that Paul laboured for fourteen years as missionary in his own immediate neighbourhood of Cilicia and the adjoining Syrian district. The religious aspirations of those Gentiles, whom he had known from his youth, who must have long filled his heart with yearning affection, now appealed to him more than ever, here was the ground which first seemed to him suitable for his new mission.

THE CALL OF THE MASTER 155

Many passages, of Jewish and Roman writers alike, testify that the attention of the Jews, who were scattered over the whole empire, was bent upon winning the Gentiles for Jehovah; and that the mission to the Gentiles was zealously carried on. Jesus Himself, in a few graphic words, has characterised the zeal of the Pharisaic missionaries, "compassing sea and land to make one proselyte."[1] And Paul has thus described for us the lofty self-consciousness with which the Jew performed his mission: "Thou bearest the name of a Jew and restest upon the law, and gloriest in God, and knowest His will, and canst distinguish good from evil, being instructed out of the law, and art confident that thou thyself art a guide of the blind, a light to them that are in darkness, an instructor of those who are wanting in sense, a teacher of the childish, having in the law the model of knowledge and of the truth."[2]

How often the youthful Saul must have sighed: "A day in thy courts is better than a thousand elsewhere; I will rather lie on the threshold of the house of my God, than dwell in the tents of the wicked!"[3]

He knew not what blessing was to spring for him and for all nations from the fact that he had dwelt in "the tents of the wicked," that he had known and could share their yearning and their experience, understood the language of their lips and of their hearts, and that he had looked on all that with a burning zeal for the cause of Jehovah and with a heart full of love. True, all this could only become fact after the new religion had, with all its

[1] Mat. xxiii. 15.   [2] Rom. ii. 21.   [3] Ps. lxxxiv. 11.

stupendous might, taken hold of his heart, freed it from all fear and carefulness, and given him a force which irresistibly carried away with it the hearts of men.

THE SOIL OF THE MISSION FIELD.

There is a mighty power in a man who stakes his life unreservedly for a cause. Paul, at the time of his death, had achieved extraordinary things. When his conversion took place, Christianity was really only a small Jewish sect, who believed the Messiah had come, held milder views about the law, gave special prominence to its moral meaning, and interpreted it prophetically. Their most precious possessions were the words of their Master, yet they did not fathom the whole significance of these. For even after numerous churches had arisen quite outside the law, independent of it, the congregation of the disciples attempted to establish the new religion on the old lines by the introduction of a legislation in matters of eating and drinking,[1] which, though mild in form, was, after all, really framed according to Judaism. At the time of Paul's death, there existed independent Gentile Christian Churches as far as Rome, churches with a growing consciousness that they were in possession of a new religion and that they were themselves a new race, a third kind of people, something more than Jew or Gentile. Not that Paul's own work can be traced in every part of the empire: on the contrary, even some such important churches as that of Rome were founded neither by Peter nor by Paul; unknown missionaries, travelling artisans,

[1] Acts xxi. 25.

THE SOIL OF THE MISSION FIELD

merchants and physicians, did this work of world-historic importance: but it was Paul who, with strong hand, broke through the magic circle of the oldest mission of the disciples: above all, it was Paul who pressed on straight along into the enemy's centre—into Europe—and definitely started on the way to Rome, although indeed he only arrived there as a prisoner after being overtaken by others. Others were fired by his great example. Some were his pupils and successors, some his adversaries and rival missioners, who now set out all over the great empire to proclaim Christ. What has been so often observed in the history of the world, repeats itself here: a man of genius seldom stands alone; as a rule he will arouse a whole host of other men; and even when he is not able to lift them to his own level, he yet lifts them above themselves and spurs them on to achievements such as without him they would have found positively unattainable.

Yet even all this would not be sufficient to explain the enormous success of the new religion. Great men, too, may stand alone and disappear, solitary,—flaming harbingers in the lurid morning sky, when the new day is still far off. With Paul it was not so; the times were ripe for his message. From our schooldays we are still only too prone to regard Paul's missionary journeys as something quite unique in their kind, having hardly any connection with the great history of imperial Rome. They are treated in a special Scripture lesson and studied from the meagre standpoint of a traveller's journal: Cyprus to Perga, Perga to Antioch, Antioch to Iconium, and so on. To the schoolboy they thus appear to gather their importance from a few beautiful speeches which the apostle made by the way. But this is turning things upside down.

The early Christian mission is a mere wave in the great stream of Oriental religions which at that time was pouring itself over the Roman Empire. And it was sustained by social requirements and social currents of manifold nature, with which it had affinities, or to which it accommodated itself; and also by widespread common needs for which it brought help.

The temporal power of the empire in itself was of material assistance to the mission. Paul has indeed still much to report of dangers which beset his way, yet on the whole he travelled as a citizen of a great and well-ordered empire, with a fair amount of security and speed. And he was able to carry on his profession for many long years before the hostility of his countrymen ultimately delivered him over to the Roman authority.

But more important still was the inner structure of the empire for the development of the mission. Rome had completed what Alexander the Great and, in part, the great Asiatic empires, had begun. Rome united in itself the nations from India to the Pillars of Hercules, and, although they continued to carry on their individual life, they were all alike tinged with the same great culture. Their religion was for the most part Oriental, their thought Greek, their administration and army Latin, but the common character of all—mingled of these various elements and a thousand popular peculiarities into the bargain—was on the whole homogeneous. It is only gradually that

THE SOIL OF THE MISSION FIELD 159

we are beginning to understand what Hellenistic culture was and what it meant for Europe. Amalgamated with the Church, it has become for us the great medium of classic art, science, and religion; in a curious conglomerate it has rescued for us the building stones of a great future, and now with the Church it is rapidly passing away, after having been mistress of Western civilisation for nearly two thousand years. From Babylon and Egypt, from Syria and Asia, Thrace and Greece, Rome and Punic Africa, from everywhere flowed the springs and streams into that vast sea on whose shores we are living still to-day. We may pronounce never so hard a judgment on the " chaos of peoples," its immense significance and its educative value for the civilisation of the West cannot be seriously called in question.

The common medium of intercourse, which was understood practically everywhere—excepting the extremes of West and East—was Greek, and this neutralised, at least outwardly, the differences in the great empire. With his knowledge of Greek, Paul was able to address his hearers wherever he went without an interpreter, and, while this may not imply as much as one is ready to imagine, it certainly was a very real help and afforded him an advantage over Peter who, according to a reliable tradition, was obliged to use an interpreter in his preaching. True, it was possible to get on very well indeed in Further Asia with Aramaic (Syrian), which Peter spoke—it was a very widely spread medium of communication in those regions. Paul probably spoke this language too, which the Jews had for many generations back adopted in place of their ancient Hebrew tongue.

Thus, in the matter of speech too, he could be a Jew to the Jews, and a Greek to the Greeks.

As regards the organisation of new churches, the mission was powerfully assisted by the fact that the ancient forms of political and public life generally, however busily appearances might still be maintained, were in reality fallen into decay. Apparently the empire was a constitutionally governed state; in reality it was an absolute military monarchy. Consequently, public life and the desire for political activity took refuge in associations, which sprang up in amazing profusion, being now persecuted and now tolerated by government. They were for the most part combinations of the common people and the middle classes, and afforded opportunity to shopkeepers and labourers for satisfying the instinct of the natural heart towards mutual help, associated work, and associated aims, and for free utterance in the circle of like-minded fellow-members. Here they could rule and command on a small scale, when it was no longer possible on a great one. Burial unions, life insurance societies, were probably the commonest forms of these associations. To outsiders, the infant church fell into the ranks of these associations, and thus its quiet growth was, for the time being, assured.

Perhaps it may even have also adopted one or other of the official titles, such as bishop (ἐπίσκοπος = overseer, president), possibly the very office itself, from such sources. These associations never indeed stood for much in the internal development of the new religion, but they did secure a protection from without; and the tendency to co-operation which

THE SOIL OF THE MISSION FIELD 161

they fostered, certainly rendered the organisation of the primitive church easier. It drew its first disciples from the same circles in which the unions flourished: Paul himself sprang from them, and, spite of his theological culture, really belonged to them. In modern parlance, the apostle was an itinerant factory hand, a weaver of the rough goats'-hair cloth that was manufactured in Cilicia and employed for all kinds of purposes, more especially in tent-making. The early church as a social agent worked among these classes, not only by means of its active benevolence and by procuring employment for the brethren, which it did on a very large scale, but also especially because of the fact that in this brotherly fellowship the rich shared the Lord's Supper with the poor, the rich man was not ashamed to sit at the same table with the slave, the sometime robber and thief was not treated with condescending indulgence in Christian refuges, but welcomed with thousandfold joy as lost and found, really esteemed as a brother, not only graciously called one. Such enthusiasm, that appears excessive to us, and that nowadays is only to be found in the Salvation Army, did more for the social reformation of mankind than all the fine theories in which those times were no less prolific than our own. This phase of primitive Christianity is unfortunately still much misunderstood; but it was of the highest significance in the pioneer work of this earliest age. The types of the prodigal son, of the woman that was a sinner, and of the adulteress, of the tax-gatherer, and of the beggar Lazarus, were then more than beautiful words, they were very deed and life.

Finally, Christianity was furthered in a still deeper way by the religious need, the eager longing which met it half way. It is true that it was just this religious yearning of the age that, on the other hand, more than anything else, transformed primitive Christianity. Philosophy had destroyed the ancient gods of the national faiths, though that was at first only the case in the cultured classes. But the people, too, heard and knew about this "wisdom," this philosophy, and bandied the watchword "culture" not less passionately than to-day. "The 'Greeks'" says Paul, "seek after 'wisdom' as the Jews ask for signs."[1] And the apostle is himself fully conscious that he has a wisdom to preach.[2] Christian monotheism spread to the Occident not alone as religion, but above all as culture.

But far stronger than this yearning of the lower classes for culture was the longing after revelation, which permeated all grades of society. To satisfy this longing, all the gods of all the world and all the wisdom of the priests had been called into service. These religions and revelations were esteemed the more highly the older they were and the farther they had travelled out of the East. An age in which doubt sifts all plain and patent truths, is always ready to rush into a wild desire for supernatural revelation, and is all the more inclined to give easy credence where the absurd and the eccentric are presented.

Beneath this passion for the strange and the exotic, however—a passion which greedily devoured all that hailed from the East—there was a real and deep though hidden yearning for purity, goodness, and eternal life.

[1] 1 Cor. i. 22.   [2] 1 Cor. ii. 6 *seq.*

THE SOIL OF THE MISSION FIELD 163

In order to find purity and blessedness, men were willing to be initiated into all possible mysteries: they had recourse to baptisms of blood and libations, dramas and liturgies, by way of alleviating this thirst of the soul. Despairing of their own powers, men penetrated into the mysterious life of divinities, hoping thereby to find deliverance and glory. If they were to believe in a god, then it must be a saviour-god, a redeemer; he must impose upon his followers high demands and mysterious rites. There existed indeed some licentious cults under imperial Rome, but, speaking generally, the religions that were at that time the object of men's search, nearly always demanded from their adepts, the " perfect," asceticism, abstinence from meat and wine, marriage and family.

Such was the ground primitive Christianity first trod. It came indeed " when the time was fulfilled,"[1] fulfilled even in a far deeper sense than Paul himself knew. And a great door was opened for it, not only in Ephesus, as the apostle tells us,[2] but everywhere over the whole empire. The soil was ready, the sower had only to come to scatter his seed. And Paul was a skilful sower. He had penetrated deeply into the hybrid religions of his day, with their initiatory rites and sacraments; we have already considered their influence on his own moral religion of redemption. That such experience was valuable for his mission is just as clear as that it threatened to become detrimental to the nature of his piety. He was enabled to represent Christianity in the form which his age needed: to the Jews as righteousness, to the Greeks as wisdom, to all alike

[1] Gal. iv. 4.   [2] 1 Cor. xvi. 9.

redemption and revelation—the supreme blessings for which mankind yearned then as now.[1]

THE MISSION FIELD.

Our habitual idea of Paul's mission is entirely determined by the influence of the account given in the Acts. Yet this account itself can establish no claim to accuracy. Only in some isolated features does it correspond to the statements in the apostle's epistles, and it plainly betrays the fact that its reliability as a historical document is invalidated in many points of detail by the defective state of the original sources from which it is derived; it is vitiated in essential traits of detail by want of authority, as in its whole plan, by the intention of the writer to have Paul appear in Jerusalem as often as possible. The impression one gathers from the story in the Acts is that of three great circular tours undertaken by the apostle, originating at Jerusalem, actually starting from Antioch, all three closing with the apostle's return to the twelve and to the home church in Antioch. A solemn scene inaugurates the great Foreign Mission: five prophets and teachers of the church at Antioch pray and fast, whereupon the Holy Ghost by the mouth of one of them commands: "Separate me Barnabas and Saul for the work whereunto I have called them." Then they fast and pray, and lay their hands on them, and send them away.[2] So Barnabas and Saul now travel *via* Cyprus to Pamphylia and Pisidia, and from there they come back by nearly the same route, leaving out Cyprus. Now takes place the solemn assembly of the apostles

[1] 1 Cor. i. 30.   [2] Acts xiii. 1–3.

in Jerusalem. Some time after returning from there, Paul begins his second journey, which takes him first of all among the communities in Syria and Cilicia, then over the mission field in Pisidia, afterwards on to new ground: through Asia Minor to Europe, where he preaches, particularly in Philippi, Thessalonica, Berœa, Athens, and Corinth. After a sojourn of nearly two years in Corinth he returns by sea to Syria, having on his way broken ground at Ephesus, whither the Gospel had travelled before him.[1] Arrived in Cæsarea, "he goes up and salutes the Church," presumably in Jerusalem,[2] and then goes down to Antioch. The third journey finally takes him from here through Galatia and Phrygia to Ephesus, where he remained over two years; from here he visits Macedonia and Achaia, with its capital Corinth, returns by the same route, and sails along the coast of Asia Minor to Jerusalem, where he is taken prisoner.

Of his missionary activity up to his meeting with the twelve in Jerusalem, Paul has himself given us some hints in his Epistle to the Galatians,[3] from which we gather a different impression. According to Gal. i. and ii., he was only once in Jerusalem during this whole period—three years after his conversion: the fourteen or seventeen years[4] subsequent to this event he passed in Syria and Cilicia. Possibly he laboured also in Galatia, beyond the limits of his home neighbourhood—Gal. ii. 5 may be understood to mean this. At all events, the success of his enterprise was so great as to draw attention in

---

[1] Acts xviii. 19 *seq.*   [2] Acts xviii. 22.
[3] Gal. i. 17-21.   [4] *Cp.* Gal. ii. 1; i. 18.

Jerusalem to his mission. The Jerusalem concordat, which he now managed to bring about, secured peace for a time, but in Antioch he had left Peter in open strife, after having found from experience that it was impossible to maintain the compromise arrived at in Jerusalem.

From this moment he leaves his eastern mission field in order to press forward straight to Europe. Whether the dispute with Peter was the real occasion of the sudden extension of the mission field in the west, or whether slowly ripening resolutions needed this impulsion from without in order to transform themselves into action, cannot now be determined. It is a matter of fact, that the apostle's missionary methods were also changed henceforth. For if Paul had been evangelising so many years in his own home neighbourhood, he must have already laboured in the smaller, even in the very smallest places—while from this point, on the contrary, he takes the great commercial roads and carries on his propagandism in the large towns. By this means Christianity in the west became a town religion in a special sense; in Syria it had always been different. The book of the Acts, in chaps. xiii. and xiv., has preserved for us a picture taken from the period of the first eastern mission. It is indeed a question how far this may or may not really correspond to history. For the very beginning, which we have considered above, will not easily fit in with Gal. i. 1: either we have to very greatly modify the sense of the words, "apostle not from men, neither through a man," or we must minimise the importance of the scene at Antioch considerably. And Paul's great speech in chap. xiii. is, in spite of certain particulars, on the whole too much of a kind with the other speeches in the Acts, and in the only passage in which Paul's doctrine of justification appears,[1] so unlike Paul's style, that in it too we can only recognise the pen of the disciple, not that of the master. But provided we first deduct something on account of the popular exaggeration of the miraculous, we may safely take such scenes as the one with the sorcerer Elymas in Cyprus, or the one in Lystra, where Paul and Barnabas, after the healing of the lame man, are taken for gods and then presently dragged out of the city half-stoned to death, as specimens of the manner in which this missionary activity was carried on.

It is a matter of controversy whether the places on this journey—Iconium, Lystra, Derbe—belong to the Galatian churches to whom Paul addressed his letter, or if they are to be sought further north, where in fact some remnants of scattered Galatian, *i.e.* Celtic, Gallic races, were living, having got so far in their wandering, predatory expeditions. No certain grounds for decision on either side of the question have as yet been brought forward; what speaks most of all for the north is the appellation "Galatian" Celts, applied to those who were to receive the epistle. It is a play of fancy not without charm that has at various times tried to place some Germans among these Gallic races who came in part from the left Rhine bank, thus attempting to make Paul the first apostle of the Germans too.

According to his letters, we must assume that Paul only once returned to Jerusalem from his great

[1] Acts xiii. 38.

westerly missionary tour, undertaken after his explanation with Peter, and that it was in order to deliver the great money gift which he had unceasingly been collecting for the impoverished brother church, thus faithful to the promise he had once given the apostles.[1] He intended after this to go by Rome to Spain.[2] He saw Rome indeed, but only as prisoner.

The apostle's epistles report of his second great missionary enterprise, but we have also in the Acts the travelling notes of one of his companions, telling us about its beginning and its conclusion. It is a pity these notes were only partially utilised. The beginning (to be found in the nine first verses of chap. xvi.) is particularly interesting, clearly betraying, as it does, the thoughts and feelings that filled the apostle on this new path. There is a rich field for a mission work everywhere in Roman Asia, but when the missionaries coming from Phrygia and Galatia are about to proceed into Asia, *i.e.* the region of Ephesus, "the Holy Ghost forbids them to speak the Word." Then they turn northwards, travelling through Mysia. Once again they attempt a halt in the interior in Bithynia, but the "Spirit of Jesus" suffers them not. Now they are led right through Mysia to Troas. Here they stand on the seashore: over yonder Europe is outstretched before their eyes. The first Europeans they see are the Macedonians, with their outlandish dress, on the beach and in the streets of the town. That same night Paul had a dream: a man of Macedonia appears to him and says to him: "Come

[1] Gal. ii. 10.   [2] Rom. xv. 23 *seq.*

over and help us." Now he knows why the Spirit has led him hither: "And when he had seen the vision, straightway we sought to go forth into Macedonia, concluding that God had called us to preach the Gospel unto them."[1]

With irresistible power the apostle is drawn to Europe, for now the great idea has laid hold of him to proclaim the Gospel to the "whole world," even unto the ends of the earth as far as Spain. Now he presses forward with his mission more vehemently than ever: he travels all over the Balkan Peninsula, making the great commercial city of Corinth, where people from the whole empire thronged together, the headquarters of his labours. He ran through the whole chain of the coast cities from Philippi, where he made the start,[2] by Thessalonica[3] and Athens[4] to Achaia, and up along the west coast as far as to Illyricum.[5] He also intended to push on to Rome by this overland route, but he was always "hindered"[6] from doing so. These words, in the Epistle to the Romans, were written by Paul after he had in the meantime found a new field of activity in Ephesus, where he remained for long. We do not now know what attracted him thither, he only tells us himself that a great and effectual door is opened to him there.[7] True, he also found many adversaries: and once he was even in mortal danger, from which it was probably the devoted affection of Prisca and Aquila that saved him.[8] From Ephesus the apostle went at

---

[1] Acts xvi. 10.   [2] Phil. iv. 15.
[3] Phil. iv. 16; 1 Thess. ii. 2.   [4] 1 Thess. iii. 1.
[5] Rom. v. 19.   [6] Rom. i. 13.   [7] 1 Cor. xvi. 8.
[8] 2 Cor. i. 8–11; Rom. xvi. 3 seq.

least once more for a short time to Corinth and Macedonia before he left for Jerusalem.

The question of the dates of the missionary journeys of the apostle can be determined with just as little positive certainty as many other of the details. I cannot here even allude to the critical researches necessitated by this unreliability, which attends the relative and the absolute chronology alike. Only let us here remind ourselves of the two quite positive statements—that Paul's missionary labours belong to the years 30 to 64-68 at the latest, and that his missionary activity as we know it, covered about twenty-five to twenty-eight years. Since he must have been already a man above thirty years of age at the time of his conversion (we judge by his prominence in the persecution), he was able to devote the full power of his best years to his great vocation. So that he had the same good fortune as Luther, whose vast activity lasted almost exactly as long.

The last verses of Acts[1] just hint that, after the two years of his Roman imprisonment, Paul was no longer able to remain in his own house in Rome, to move about at will, nor to proclaim the Gospel. The apostle's speech to the elders of Miletus is so evidently intended by the writer of the Acts to mean a last will and testament, the reference to the coming gnostics and to his own death[2] is so unmistakably prophetic, that we may fairly assume the author's own knowledge of Paul's condemnation and execution after the "two whole years" mentioned by himself. There is an ancient opinion in contradiction to these hints which says Paul got his freedom

[1] Acts xxviii. 30.   [2] Acts xx. 24 *seq.*

again, and that he not only evangelised in Spain, but also visited his churches in the east. This last idea is of course only an invention for the purpose of dating the epistles to Timothy and Titus, because they cannot be located in the apostle's life as we know it. On the other hand, the Spanish journey is not to be lightly declared impossible. It rests on an ancient tradition, and is probably referred to in the first letter of St Clement, written about A.D. 100, where we also get the oldest mention of Paul's death: "Let us set before our eyes the good apostles: Peter, who for the sake of unjust hatred bore not one nor two but manifold afflictions, and so became a witness unto blood, and went to the place of glory which was his due. Through hatred and through strife Paul had to win the palm of patience: after he had seven times borne chains, had had to fly for his life, had been stoned in the east and in the west, he won the glorious prize of his faith: after he had taught the whole world and had been as far as the frontiers of the west, he left the world and went to the holy place—he, the perfect pattern of patience. After these men, who were so holy in the way of life, came a great multitude of imitators, the elect, who, through hatred suffered manifold horrors and torments, and thereby have become for us the fairest examples."

In these last words the Roman clearly refers to the victims of Nero's persecution, and calls them all "noble examples of our own day." It is, however, not quite certain from the text of the passage whether Peter and Paul suffered death together, and if they really were victims of this persecution.

At all events we have positive accounts of Paul's

two great mission fields only: the eastern on the ground occupied chiefly by the Syrian population, and the western, that on Greek territory. In the former Paul laboured fourteen to seventeen years, in the latter eleven. We have detailed knowledge only of the western field from the apostle's letters. What therefore we have to tell about Paul's missionary activity refers above all to the mission in Europe.

THE APOSTLE.

CHAPTER XII.

THE LIFE OF THE MISSIONARY. THE MISSION
PREACHING.

THE dead are mightier than the living: primitive man believed this, in fear and dread of the spirits that leave their graves at night to hurt or to help him. That the dead are mightier than the living, is an experience that forces itself upon us too, again and again, in quite another sense. Not those who loved life have done the greatest things in the world, but those who despised it and had done with it. He best overcomes life and lives most vigorously who has died to live. We can observe this in religious and irreligious people, in Paul as in Rousseau. The dead are mightier than the living.

From the hour when Saul died on that road to Damascus, and the body, that had once been a man, now became only a member of Christ, his life was nothing but one complete offering for the mission, which lay on him as compulsion,[1] on behalf of Greeks and barbarians, wise and foolish, whose debtor he had become.[2] We are indebted to a pupil's faithful affection, such as St Clement cherished in his heart,

[1] 1 Cor. ix. 16.   [2] Rom. i. 14.

for a brief account of this life full of suffering and of patience; we have discussed it in the foregoing paragraph. We are indebted for another picture to the mean attacks of Paul's adversaries, who forced him to tell his threatened Corinthian church on one occasion how wrong it was of them to begin to doubt him on account of these his enemies. He was able to say to them proudly and plainly: "I have had more than my share of toil, more than my share of imprisonments. I have been flogged times without number. Often I have been at death's door. Five times I received one short of forty lashes at the hands of the Jews. Three times I was beaten with rods. Once I was stoned. Three times I was shipwrecked. I have wrestled with the waves a whole twenty-four hours. My journeys have been many; I have been through dangers from rivers, dangers from robbers, dangers from my own people, dangers from the heathen, dangers in towns, dangers in the wilderness, dangers on the sea, dangers among false brothers. I have been through toil and hardship. I have often had sleepless nights. I have endured hunger and thirst, I have often passed days without food; I have been cold and poorly clad."[1]

And to the same church, when a portion of its members attempted to lower the apostles to the level of party leaders, and then, as it seemed to Paul's lofty moral conception, to turn them into types of their own vanity and human passion, he remonstrates: "I think God hath set forth us, the apostles, as the 'last of all'; as men doomed to death; for we are made a spectacle unto the universe,

[1] 2 Cor. xi. 23–27.

THE LIFE OF THE MISSIONARY 175

to angels and to men. We for Christ's sake are
'fools' (the apostle is here referring to the scornful criticisms on his preaching which were made by the followers of Apollos), but ye are wise in Christ; we are weak, but ye are strong; ye have glory, but we have dishonour. Even unto this present hour we both hunger and thirst, and are naked and are buffeted, we are homeless, and we work hard, toiling with our own hands. Being reviled, we bless; being persecuted, we endure; being defamed, we console. We are made as the filth of the world, the offscouring of all things even until now."[1]

We know next to nothing in detail about the occurrences to which Paul here alludes, as the book of the Acts has only furnished us with a few meagre items about the imprisonments and scourgings of Paul. It is just by these gaps in the story the author proves how little accurate information was at his disposal whenever he neglected to utilise the old source of the travel-journal which tells us, for instance, with such lively touches of the apostle's later shipwreck on the way of captivity to Rome.[2] Another piece of news he gives about the apostle's escape over the city wall in Damascus,[3] is confirmed by Paul,[4] even to the detail that the flight was effected in a basket which was let down through an opening in the wall; only about the pursuers there is a divergency in the two accounts, Paul mentioning the governor and the guards of King Aretas, while the Acts, in accordance with the object it has in view, gives "the Jews." True, this difference does not necessarily mean any essential

[1] Cor. iv. 9–13.   [2] Acts xxvii.
[3] Acts ix. 24 *seq.*   [4] 2 Cor. xi. 32.

contradiction, if the King acted at the instigation of the Jews. The second detail which Paul mentions is the peril of death, when Prisca and Aquila "laid down their own necks for his life"[1]—perhaps, as we said before, the same danger referred to in the words:[2] "We were weighed down exceedingly, altogether beyond our strength, so much so that we actually despaired of life. Indeed we had within ourselves decided we must die [and God sent this trouble], that we might not trust in ourselves, but in God· who raises the dead."

Besides danger was anxiety; not anxiety for his own life, to be sure. The questions: What shall we eat? what shall we drink? wherewithal shall we be clothed? played no part in Paul's economy. Yet day by day a host of cares pressed upon him: "Beside those things that come as a matter of course, there is that which presseth upon me daily [with inquiries and appeals], I have my burden of anxiety about all the churches. Who is weak without my being weak [with him]? Who is offended without my burning with indignation?"[3]

He was besieged on all sides. So much, everything indeed, was incomplete in the young churches. The new converts knew so little, with their new world in their hearts, how to see their way in the old world without. Doubt and scruples, faint-heartedness and effervescent enthusiasm, strife and bickering, old and new sin, influences of all kinds from without, shook the tender new life again and again to its very roots. A host of cares for the man's loving heart, and a continual question for his conscience; for he

[1] Rom. xvi. 3 *seq.*   [2] 2 Cor. i. 8.   [3] 2 Cor. xi. 28 *seq.*

THE LIFE OF THE MISSIONARY 177

knew he would have to render an account at the Day of the Lord for every soul the Father had given him.[1]

The life of constant sacrifice led by the apostle becomes moreover a life of continual self-conquest in asceticism. For Paul was an ascetic for the sake of his calling. He had to separate himself from his people and his country, however much he still loved them. All things, once so dear to him, he had to count as less than nothing, as dung.[2] His people requited his apostasy from Judaism with grim, life-long hate. Even by those Jews who had gone over to Christianity, he was here and there bitterly maligned as a destroyer of the law, and even for centuries his memory was dragged into the dust. His life long Paul must have suffered greatly from this. We do not know if his own parents were dead when he became a Christian; but it is perhaps not less painful to lose one's dead parents inwardly, than it hurts to have to separate oneself from them when alive. Neither do we know on what footing he was with his sister; that her son saved his life[3] is not sufficient to prove that he and his mother were in spiritual communion with the apostle. For Paul the love and care of a wife never made the missionary's life easier, as they did for Peter and the Master's brothers, who travelled about with their wives.[4] And, although it was a matter of course that an apostle should be supported by the hospitality of his congregations, just as much a matter of course as that the soldier lives on his pay, the vine-dresser from his

---

[1] 1 Cor. iii. 13 *seq.*   [2] *Cp.* Rom. ix. 3; Phil. iii. 7 *seq.*
[3] Acts xxiii. 16 *seq.*   [4] 1 Cor. ix. 5.

vine, the herdsman from the milk of his herd; and although "the Lord himself did ordain that they who proclaim the gospel should live of the gospel" —yet Paul never availed himself of this permission.[1] He never accepted gifts from anyone, except the church at Philippi, to whom he was attached by a peculiarly close bond of affection. He supported himself by his difficult and poorly paid handicraft, because he wanted to escape the reproach of bartering the good news for money;[2] and also because, as he says himself, he too wished to have something to glory in before God, something for which he trusted to have a reward from God.[3] Here again there is a dash of something Roman Catholic in the apostle's piety; he appears to regard his renunciation in matters of money and hospitality as a good work worthy of special acknowledgment, just as Roman Catholic theology does with its so-called evangelical counsels. But yet there is a great difference between the two. Everything, whatever Paul has and does, is given him by God,—is an imperative inward I have, I must. Now he would still like to have something with which to do God honour; he wants to be able to come before God's judgment throne and say: See, I too, I as a man, have done something. It is perhaps not correct Lutheran, not even correct Pauline doctrine; but from a human point of view it is as natural as the joy of the child that gives his father a birthday present out of his father's own money,—as the joy of a man who looks upon his accomplished work with pride. We may smile at it, or we may mourn over the unconverted state of the hearts that are still so

[1] 1 Cor. ix. 15–18.   [2] 1 Cor. ix. 18.   [3] 1 Cor. ix. 16 *seq.*

proud: whoever loves sound human hearts will share their joy. Such a mood becomes unhealthy only when it addresses itself scornfully to others: Paul is free from this.

Thus he regarded his asceticism, after the manner of Jesus, as the inevitable condition for the right fulfilment of his vocation. Marriage alone he estimated as of only secondary importance, in accordance with the decadent opinions of his time, and because he could only appreciate it from the sensual side.[1] But in everything else he has the sane and sober point of view of the Gospel, and once he gave expression to it in words so beautiful and so suitable as hardly anyone after him:[2] "I rejoice in the Lord greatly that now once more your care of me hath flourished again [he means the supplies they have sent him]: ye were indeed not wanting in thought, but ye lacked opportunity. Not that I speak in respect of want, for I have learned to be content with what I have. I can live in want, I can live in abundance; in everything and in all things have I learned the secret: both to be filled and to be hungry, both to abound and to be in want. I can do all things in him that strengtheneth me." Thus, apart from his words on marriage, he stands inwardly above asceticism, as did Jesus: to him it is no service of God and no peculiar purity, it is the special duty and suffering attendant on his vocation. "Every man that striveth in the games lives in strictest temperance. And yet they do it to receive a corruptible crown, but we, an incorruptible. I for my part will not run with an uncertain aim. I

[1] 1 Cor. vii. 1 *seq.*   [2] Phil. iv. 10 *seq.*

will not fight like a man hitting at the air. No, I treat my body roughly, and make it my slave, lest by any means while I preach to others I myself should be rejected."[1]

Such was the apostle's life: an unceasing sacrifice for others, a difficult, hard labour, a sharing of poverty and peril, a restless wandering without home and loved relations, not an hour without trouble and care, girt around with dangers and with the prospect of a dreadful death from the stone-throwing of an enraged mob. Yet not one instant did the apostle shrink back from such a life: it was God's will, he had to go through with it.

And yet it was a life full of supreme joy too, joy such as a dull, commonplace existence, in its lazy security, cannot know—and full of that vigorous affection that springs from human hearts that are at one in the highest and innermost things. Primitive Christianity in general was no sullen slave service, and no melancholy lachrymose salvation out of this vale of tears. Paul especially lived a life full of cheerful valiance; for beyond all mortal danger and all suffering he sees the loving eye of God watching him, of the God who "raiseth from the dead," and who is ready to help men over suffering and peril. Joy is a word that plays an important part with him. All his epistles, even those written in the darkest moments, such as Philippians and second Corinthians, are full of exclamations of joy and challenges to joyfulness.[2] We might write as motto to his life what he

[1] 1 Cor. ix. 25-27.
[2] 2 Cor. i. 24, vi. 10, viii. 2, xiii. 10; Phil. i. 18-25, ii. 17, iii. 1, iv. 4; *cp.* 1 Thess. i. 6, v. 16.

THE LIFE OF THE MISSIONARY 181

once said himself:[1] "And even if I am offered upon the sacrifice and service of your faith, I joy and rejoice with you all. And in the same manner do ye also joy and rejoice with me."

The ground for such joy is not only the love and friendship which met him in those with whom the bond of the new life brought him into a closer communion than that of any natural love-bond—an affection and friendship that, after all, illuminates all the care with which his disciples burden him, for it is nothing but pure, trembling, pleading attachment, nothing but trustful love. The ground for such joy in suffering lies higher still. Never was he more conscious of the nearness of God, never did he feel the hidden Christ more living and more mighty, than when for him there were "fightings without and fears within."[2] When he feels old powers of darkness leagued against him, feels Satan is trying to hinder him from doing his work—then his assurance shines all the more brightly within him that his work is God's work, and hope becomes all the stronger: "hope grows out of tribulation and hope putteth not to shame, for the love of God has been shed abroad in his heart by the Holy Ghost.[3] The power of the new life that has arisen in his heart becomes only greater in every temptation, in distress and danger: "Though hard pressed on every side, we are never hemmed in; though perplexed, never driven to despair; pursued, yet not forsaken; smitten down, yet not destroyed; always bearing about in the body the dying of Jesus, that the life also of Jesus may be manifested in our

[1] Phil. ii. 17 *seq.* [2] 2 Cor. vii. 5. [3] Rom. v. 3–5.

body. For we which live are continually being given over to death for the sake of Jesus, that the life also of Jesus may be manifested in our mortal nature."[1] Thus the apostle is present to our souls, as he has drawn himself in a solemn hour of his life, defending his honour in perfect loyalty against outrageous charges: "Giving none an occasion of stumbling in anything, that our ministration may not be made a mock of. On the contrary, we commend ourselves in all things as the ministers of God: in much patience, in afflictions, in difficulties, in strifes, in imprisonments, in tumults, in toils, in watchings, in fastings; by purity, by knowledge, by long suffering, by kindliness; in the Holy Ghost, in love unfeigned, in the word of truth, in the power of God; through the weapons of righteousness for attack and defence, through glory and dishonour, through evil report and good report; as the 'impostors,' yet we are true men; as the 'people nobody knows,' yet we are well known, (to God); as 'at death's door,' and behold, we are still alive; as the 'chastened' (referring to his malady, which he himself considered demoniacal), yet we are not killed; as being overwhelmed with sorrow, and yet we are always happy; as poor, yet making many rich; as having nothing, yet we possess all things!"[2]

So lived the first great missionary of Christianity.

THE MISSION PREACHING.

From Paul's epistles we can still plainly see what was the contents of his message and in what manner he may have preached. But we should be greatly mistaken if we were to suppose the contents of his

[1] 2 Cor. iv. 8–11.   [2] 2 Cor. vi. 3–10.

epistles coincided exactly with the contents of his preaching. Just the contrary is the case. For in the epistles the apostle writes precisely about such things as he explained either not at all, or certainly not particularly, to his congregation. If therefore we want to learn what he preached, we must compare his own express statements on the matter.

He himself describes the contents of his preaching in a few plain words when in a passage he says to the Thessalonians: "Ye turned unto God from idols to serve the living and true God, and to wait for his Son from heaven, whom he raised from the dead, even Jesus, which delivereth us from the wrath (judgment) which is coming."[1] Here one point is plainly put into the foreground which has but little attention in the epistle—the struggle against the idols in favour of the one living and true God. So the preaching began: Leave your gods; they are dead idols, stone and wood! They are but "so-called" gods and lords.[2] And even though it is not to be denied that these gods give evidence of their power, in many wonderful effects, in healings and in dreams, yet after all these images are in themselves "nothing,"[3] for they are dumb and dead. Wicked demons produce these miraculous effects, demons that delight in the smoke of sacrifices, and for whom therefore the sacrifices are intended[4]—but they show their evil, demoniacal nature by precipitating their worshippers into folly and sin. The wise Greeks, who talk so very much about wisdom and culture, appear to be blind to the fact that they, instead of

[1] 1 Thess. i. 9 *seq*. [2] 1 Cor. viii. 5.
[3] 1 Cor. x. 19. [4] 1 Cor. x. 20.

adoring the great God and His glory, which they too should and could have seen in the visible world, worship only images of corruptible beings, of men, birds, and four-footed beasts, and even of reptiles.[1] Such senseless blindness in such cultured minds can only be attributed to the agency of evil demons, it is only explained by the abyss of moral darkness into which these same devilish spirits first lured the Greeks. And with that Paul's preaching against the gods turns into a sermon to his hearers' consciences.

God has given you over to the evil passions of your hearts, that make you so miserable, which you yourselves feel to be shameful and degrading to your own bodies, vile lusts that destroy alike body and soul. And not your men only act in this way; your women too have lost all dignity and sense of shame, and your youths and boys are sunk in depravity. And in the train of vice that lowers the soul and leaves it shameless, come all the coarse and baser sins: malice, greed, envy, murder, strife, lying and deceit; you become tale-tellers, backbiters, haters of God, insolent, arrogant, boasters, intriguers, disobedient to parents, senseless, unsteady, without natural affection, unmerciful. Such are your lives![2]

And yet, just as God did not leave Himself without witness in His work of creation in visible nature, just as you seek Him there, and just as you yourselves sometimes perceive a breath of His spirit, so He has given you His voice in your hearts for warning and reproof.[3] Or do you not yourselves know that your lusts make you vile? Do you not recognise —by the very thoughts that in your own hearts accuse

---

[1] Rom. i. 20-23. [2] Rom. i. 24-30. [3] Rom. ii. 14-16.

you—God's decree: That they which practise such things are worthy of death? Nevertheless, you not only do them, but also approve others who do the same.[1] Verily, the god of this age has blinded your eyes and blackened your minds.[2] It is he and his demons that lead you in mad intoxication astray to those dumb idols![3]

Therefore, turn yourselves away from them, and turn to the one, the living God. Life, eternal life, is what you are seeking. Only the living God can give that, He who in very truth is God, who proves His divinity and also His life in His works, and in your consciences, who has proved His life and His divine power above all by raising up His Son from the dead!

And with that Paul has got to the heart of his preaching. Everything else draws its force and substance, its life and glow, from this point. That there had come forth a man out of Nazareth, mighty in deed and in word, that the Jews had killed him, that they made him die the ignominious death of a criminal, that this man was the Son of God, that His death had taken place on account of sin, that God had manifested Him as His Son beyond and after death by raising Him from the dead in the sight of all men, and that this resurrection was known by experience to the disciples, and last of all to him too, him, the aforetime persecutor, who now stood here before them devoting his whole life to this Son of God—this was Paul's supreme message.[4] He gave himself up to it completely, his heart and his lips

---

[1] Rom. i. 32.
[2] 2 Cor. iv. 4.
[3] 1 Cor. xii. 2 *seq.*
[4] 1 Cor. xv. 1–11.

were opened, and his own life's struggle and need, its transformation and its victory, thrilled his hearers to their very hearts. When he was enabled to proclaim thus, how God had taken hold of them all, the apostles, one by one—how their Master had shown Himself to them, living and mighty—then the glow of enthusiasm burst into flame even from cold souls that had long been dead. And with amazement, those who had just before stood the fire of his accusations, saw the happiness that shone in the preacher's eyes. Paul did not tell them much about Jesus: he only talked about His death and His power. He says himself that he had set forth Jesus to the Galatians "before their eyes" as the Crucified.[1] And in his first mission in Corinth he preached only the Crucified,[2] for he had determined "not to know anything among them but Jesus Christ, and Him crucified."[3] Here he could show the seriousness of sin, the love and power of God in all their moving magnitude—quite apart from the fact that the cross had been the great "stumbling block" in his own old life and had become the very pivot of the new. Paul talked little or nothing about the actual life of Jesus. The moral laws—in common with the Church he had already taken for such the sayings of Jesus—probably were first brought prominently forward in the course of later teaching. And to this later teaching belonged too the detailed proofs from the prophecies of the Old Testament, although the very earliest preaching certainly included references to the ancient revelation of God.

---

[1] Gal. iii. 1. [2] 1 Cor. i. 23 *seq*.
[3] 1 Cor. ii. 2; *cp*. 2 Cor. i. 19.

But the preaching, after dwelling on Jesus, came back again to the subject of God: God had indeed proved His own existence, but He will afterwards prove it still more fully, when His wrath breaks forth against all transgressors. Terror and tribulation will come upon them with the flame from heaven which destroys all iniquity. Only those will be saved who by faith belong to Jesus[1] and flee from evil. For the unrighteous shall not inherit the Kingdom of Heaven: neither the impure, nor idolators, nor thieves, nor covetous, nor drunkards, nor revilers, nor extortioners.[2] Like Jesus, Paul too grounds his call to repentance on the announcement of the latter days: Become new creatures! for the Kingdom of Heaven is at hand. Only now the message runs: Believe and be baptized, for the Son of God will come, to judge and to save. How graphically Paul may have drawn his pictures of the judgment or of future felicity we do not know; but we may be sure that he too, like Jesus, showed great reserve in this matter; for not only the Christians of Thessalonica —where he only laboured a short time—but the Corinthians too, come to him with questions about the last days, and indeed with such elementary questions, we are obliged to wonder how it was Paul had not yet said anything to them about these things.[3]

Paul's mission had a threefold aim: a religious aim, a moral aim, and an ecclesiastical, although this last word may only be pronounced reservedly.

The first aim was religious. After the old belief in gods had been shaken, and the thirst awakened for

[1] 1 Thess. i. 9 *seq*.   [2] 1 Cor. vi. 9.
[3] 1 Thess. iv. 13; 1 Cor. xv.

the living and true God, after sin which had been suffering was shown to be sin as guilt towards this God, His greatness, and His love, salvation was offered to the penitent in Jesus, the propitiation for all guilt, the living, everlasting Lord. The missionary presented this salvation not alone as the inward act of becoming a believer, of which indeed he could only bear testimony, the virtue of which was vouchsafed to them by his own irradiating happiness; no, he offered this salvation also, as the time needed it, in two mysterious sacramental acts to be apprehended by the natural senses: in the baptism out yonder by the solitary banks of the river, and in that singular meal, to be watched by none but those who shared it, about which there presently circulated the strangest stories ever invented by the bloodthirsty fancy of human curiosity.

Secondly, the mission preaching required the solemn vow of a new moral life. We have already listened to the most elementary interdictions. But there certainly always came the positive side as well: the fruits of the Spirit as Paul has detailed them [1] in love, joy, peace, long-suffering, kindness, goodness, faith, meekness, and temperance. This picture of a new life, drawn in a few vigorous strokes, surely moved hearts no less than the picture of the Judgment which Paul had before disclosed. In all his epistles Paul accompanied his theoretical discussions with such practical moral applications, clearly following a custom which he had probably developed while preaching.

Finally, the third aim, the ecclesiastical, is likewise

---

[1] Gal. v. 22.

realised through baptism and the promise to lead a new life: the admission into the new fellowship. All the baptized received the same spirit, all may eat of the same body of the Christ, and all become His associates, welcomed in the mysterious communion with a Being from the beyond, and so bound in stronger bonds to one another than the bonds of blood and personal choice can bind.[1] While thus becoming the "elect" of God and "saints," taken up into the life of the Godhead, lifted above this unholy world—for this, and not moral goodness, is meant by the term "saints"— they have become brethren to one another, they belong to one another in life and in death. True, they are to remain in that standing and condition in which they were called;[2] yet they do belong to a new fellowship which dictates to them the rules they are to live by, which teaches them, outwardly too, to live with and for one another in quite a new way, not at all as they had hitherto lived together.

All this was contained in the one great requirement of conversion and baptism.

After all that Paul outlines for us of his mission preaching, it appears to be certain that it did not contain just what we call "Paulinism," that is to say, the peculiar Pauline doctrine of justification and redemption. His preaching is concerned with far more general, more simple thoughts, thoughts such as Jesus' disciples probably also placed in the foreground of their preaching. It even ran to some considerable extent on the lines of the Jewish mission preaching, alike in its attack on the heathen gods and

---

[1] 1 Cor. x. 17, xii. 27 ; Rom. xii. 5.
[2] 1 Thess. iv. 11 ; 1 Cor. xii. 24.

in its moral appeal and its prophesying of the latter days.

If we survey the whole chain of ideas of Paul's mission preaching, it appears amazingly simple, and just on that account perfectly typical. Has not all Christian mission preaching, indeed all revival preaching to this day, followed in the same steps? Certainly this sort of preaching has up to now met with immense success, it is the manner of preaching of Methodism in the broadest sense. Simple great threatenings and demands, all issuing in immediate action, there baptism, here confession, and in both cases admission into the new fellowship as well as the vow of the new life. We must not, however, shut our eyes to the fact that this form of revival preaching has its effect to-day only on certain souls, and only there where the influence of Christianity, *i.e.* traditional Christian teaching, is still strongly at work in the imagination. Educated people, who have abandoned the traditional faith, no longer respond to the spell of such a chain of ideas at the present day. We require different grounds for morality, and above all a deeper foundation for a belief in God. Hence, too, the proportionately greater difficulty we experience in implanting the fundamental thought of our religion—that sin is not merely suffering, but guilt—in the heads and hearts of our hearers.

But even at that time, when Paul started his mission preaching, the influence of what was at the back of it counted for far more than did the thoughts themselves; and this was the yearning of the people and the apostle's personality. He himself was well aware of this. He expressed it too: not the words of wisdom, and not the aptest application of proofs, and not correct rhetoric, was what won him men's hearts, but the demonstration of the Spirit and of power.[1] The joy of the redeemed soul that beamed in his countenance, and which from his God-filled heart poured itself into others—this was what made them sound and strong in body and in soul.

[1] 1 Cor. ii. 4.

THE APOSTLE.

CHAPTER XIII.

THE PREACHER. THE ORGANISATION OF THE MISSION.

IF we were to make a picture for ourselves from the criticisms of his antagonists of how Paul preached, and what immediate effect his preaching had on his hearers, and, if we were to take his own remarks about it literally, we should get quite a wrong impression. Again and again Paul declares that he too considers eloquence a "second-rate virtue," he emphasises that he himself was no trained orator [1]— Luther translates still more vigorously, yet he misses the turn that he was rude in speech—and his adversaries tell him scoffingly his letters are weighty and strong, but his bodily presence is weak and his speech contemptible.[2] Evidently Paul was not a man likely to captivate his audience by a striking and triumphant appearance; nor was he one of those wondrously attractive Orientals such as the Jewish race even now produces from time to time, but a man who seemed at first sight insignificant and ugly. In the second century, one of his admirers described him in this respect still more particularly, but this

[1] 2 Cor. xi. 6.   [2] 2 Cor. x. 10.

description may possibly have no foundation in remembrance, but rather in the dogma that God uses the base, the ill-favoured, the despised of the "world" as tools for His purposes. The fact is, however, in itself sufficiently vouched for by Paul's own epistles. And further, Paul never enjoyed the advantages of a complete Greek education. His Greek is not the worst, but neither is it the best in the New Testament, in which indeed only one piece of writing—the Epistle to the Hebrews—may be said in some measure to satisfy the demands of æsthetic style; and so those people who set store by rhetoric in the sense of that age, found no satisfaction in him. He lacked correctness and elegance of speech. And very likely our present-day churchgoers would not have been "edified" by him. For they are too much spoiled by the liturgical pomp of our ceremonial pulpit style, and far too much accustomed merely to inquire if the parson preaches "beautifully," for most of them to be responsive to the plain word springing directly from the soul.

Yet three things make it quite certain that Paul really was a great and heart-stirring speaker: namely, the success of his mission as a whole; further, the positive accounts of his demeanour in Galatia and Corinth; and finally, parts of his epistles in which we still have direct evidence of a powerful preacher. According to these witnesses, he too certainly preached *not as the Scribes*, but as one who has power over men's hearts, over good and evil spirits. The glow of a rude yet persuasive eloquence still burns for us in these letters. There is nothing here of the polished cleverness of the Greek sophist, no affectation of the rough and tumble wit of the demagogue of the day. No, this flows from a soul steeped in the kind of eloquence that permeates the Old Testament, one that has fed itself on the vigorous imagery and poetry of prophet and psalmist. The Old Testament pattern comes out clearly, even in forms of frequent antithesis and parallelism. This kind of speech did indeed correspond to the apostle's inmost being. Just as his whole life was one constant struggle, so is his speech too a continual play of contrasts, a contest with contradictions and objections. He places the person of his opponent before him and speaks with him face to face. In the beginning of the Epistle to the Romans, as he is showing how the Gentiles are lost in ignorance and iniquity, all at once he sees the Jew standing at his elbow, nodding a smiling approval out of the comfortable sense of his own superiority. He turns sharply round on him and attacks him: "What I say concerns everyone; everyone, him too, and that particularly, who fancies he may allow himself to be a judge of others. It concerns you and me! First the Jews and then the Greeks! Are you any better? You have indeed the law; but do you obey it? You preach against stealing, and yet you steal yourself! You forbid adultery, and yet commit it! You loathe the idols, and yet rob their temples! You are indeed proud of your law, and yet you dishonour God by breaking it!"[1]

Such was Paul's way of speaking: thus he grappled with his opponent: individual against individual, man to man: with this he overcame, he prevailed. This complete surrender of his personality,

[1] Rom. ii. 1–23.

this mode of attack, makes it all an entirely personal affair for the hearer. And this comes out clearly too even in the form of his sentences. The whole style of speech is by leaps and bounds, and often it is astonishing; it takes much for granted and leaves still more to be read between the lines. It is precipitate, it rushes to its mark, and thus is obliged to fill in much by way of supplement or parenthesis, it moves in query and retort: What shall we say then? God forbid! and so on. All these things are symptoms of the warm temperament that characterises our apostle, who is not wise and serene at all. They are so characteristic of him, that the mere fact that the Epistles to the Ephesians, to Timothy, and to Titus have nothing whatever of this style about them, but are throughout pitched in the key of ceremonial ecclesiasticism and legality, proves that they cannot be from the same man who wrote the letters to the Corinthians and Galatians. It was, on the other hand, a blunder of taste to declare the letter to the Galatians spurious by reason of the fits and starts in style, for the epistle is one of the most genuine products of this turbulent, fiery soul, and was thrown off at a time when the waves of anxiety and of anger were rolling over it.

The pieces of oratory which here and there shine out in the apostle's letters, one and all testify to this his fervency of soul and to the elevation of his prophetic speech. The principal section of one such great delivery, the speech in defence, 2 Cor. xi. 8–31, has already been quoted (p. 174) almost entirely. Another passage,[1] which plainly reveals the

[1] Rom. viii. 28–39.

overpowering impressiveness of the preacher who wrote it, is reproduced here, with an appropriate distribution of the verses according to the sense; let the reader read it out aloud to himself. For, properly speaking, all the apostle's letters are to be read aloud, for the plain reason that he dictated them all, and so was speaking in the tone of his pulpit delivery:

> We know, that to them that love God, all things work together for the best, for they are the called according to His will.
> For whom He chose, them He also foreordained, to be conformed to the image of His Son, so that He might be the first-born among many brethren;
>> but whom He foreordained, them He also called,
>> and whom He called, them He also justified;
>> whom He justified, them He also glorified.
>
> What then shall we say to these things?
>> If God is for us, who can there be against us!
>> He indeed spared not His own Son,
>> but delivered Him up for us all;
>> how then shall He not with Him freely give us all things!
>
> Who will bring a charge against God's elect?
>> It is God that acquits them!
>
> Who is he that shall condemn them?
>> Christ Jesus is here, He that died,
>>> nay, rather, that rose again,
>> That stands at the right hand of God:
>> He also makes intercession for us!
>
> Who shall separate us from Christ's love?
>> Tribulation or anguish or persecution or famine or nakedness or peril or sword?—as it is written:
>>> For thy sake we are being killed all the day long,
>>> We are regarded as sheep to be slaughtered.
>
>> Nay, in all these things we are more than conquerors through Him that loved us.
>
> For I am certain:
>> neither death nor life,
>> neither angels nor principalities,
>> neither present nor future (spirits) nor any powers,
>> neither height nor depth, nor any other creature, is able to sever us from the love of God in Christ Jesus our Lord.

When we read this hymn, with its passion and its swing, we understand how it prompted our greatest hymn-writer Gerhard to one of his finest lyrics ("If God is for me"), and furnished him with his theme line by line.

What was denied to Paul outwardly in beauty and impressiveness, and in cultivation of the intellect, was compensated by the force and intensity of his inner life. In fear and trembling and in weakness, perhaps in sickness, he stood before the Corinthians when he preached to them for the first time.[1] He knew well all he lacked, and yet he came with the demonstration of the Spirit and of power. He carried his audience along with him. Even if he was not master of his subject, the subject mastered him. The hidden life that flashed within him, as he spoke of his great subject, transfigured his insignificant and ugly figure. The more afraid he was, the more palpable his anxiousness became, the more mightily were many of his audience overcome, when his eye began to glow with marvellous power, at once menacing and gentle. And as it was with Jesus, so also here, when Paul spoke: the emotion was so intense that miracles happened. This is what Paul means by the demonstration of "power": the sick were healed, anguish-stricken hearts humbled themselves and declared, thrilled and happy: God is in you indeed![2]

Similarly in Galatia. Paul was intending to go to Europe, when a sharp attack of his malady prostrated him: the messenger of Satan buffeted him once more. Was Satan to get the upper hand? No, God's power is made perfect in weakness.[3] He roused

[1] 1 Cor. ii. 3. [2] 1 Cor. xiv. 24. [3] 2 Cor. xii. 9.

himself, and won the victory over his body. He was obliged to remain where he was, but it should be seen that the messenger of Satan had here too become an instrument to the furtherance of God's work. Paul preached. And the triumphant might with which he overcame his infirmity and the "Devil," overcame men's hearts. As a rule men turned their backs on such invalids with shuddering horror; here one of them was welcomed "as an angel of God," and the people would have plucked out their eyes and given them to him, if they could have made him well again.[1] As an angel of God: here too again we have the amazement at the mighty force, the marvellous power that lifted the apostle above himself, at the Life that imparted to the body a strength that overcame everything.

Again, another scene presents itself to our mind when Paul reminds the Thessalonians of his first appearance in their midst:

"You know yourselves, brethren, that our visit to you was not without results; but after all the suffering and ill-treatment which we, as you know, experienced beforehand at Philippi, we yet came forward full of valiant trust in our God, to declare unto you the gospel of God in spite of great opposition."[2]

It was instinctively felt with this man and his preaching: he was no sounding brass, and no tinkling cymbal. He pledged his very life for his message, and this was the secret of the great impression his preaching made. He may indeed yield where brutal force robs him of his sphere of labour, but none can

[1] Gal. iv. 12-14.   [2] Thess. ii. 1 *seq.*

rob him of his labour. Whoever speaks thus out of the abundance of his heart, and whoever thus stands at the back of his words with his life, can cheerfully do without rhetoric and homiletics; his speech may perhaps not be beautiful, but it will be a demonstration of the Spirit and of power.

Paul has expressed this himself in the three-versed Hymn on Love,[1] full of matchless poetry, surely the most beautiful thing he ever wrote:

> If I speak with the tongues of men and of angels,
>   And have not love,
>   I am sounding brass and a clanging cymbal.
> And if I am able to preach wonderfully
>   And know all mysteries and all knowledge,
>   And if I have all faith
>   And can remove mountains,
>   And have not love,
>   I am nothing.
> And if I give away all I possess,
>   And if I deliver up my body
>   And let myself be burned,
>   And have not love,
>   It profiteth me nothing.
>
> Love is long-suffering and kind: love envieth not.
>   Love vaunteth not itself, is not puffed up.
>   Doth not behave itself unseemly. seeketh not its own,
>   Is not provoked, nor doth she reckon up her wrongs.
>   Rejoiceth not in unrighteousness, but rejoiceth with the truth.
> She covereth all things, believeth all things, hopeth all things, endureth all things.
>
> Love never ceaseth.
>   Prophetic gifts—they shall pass,
>   Tongues—sometime they will cease,
>   Knowledge—it shall be done away.
>   For our knowledge is incomplete,
>   Incomplete, our prophesying;
>   But as soon as perfection comes—
>   Then what is incomplete will be cast aside.

---

[1] 1 Cor. xiii.

> When I was a child
> > I talked like a child,
> > I felt as a child
> > I thought as a child.
> > When I became a man,
> > > Then the child's world was put away.
> > For now we see a riddle in a mirror,
> > > But then face to face !
> > Now my knowledge is incomplete,
> > > But then I shall know as fully as I am known.
> > Faith, hope, and love abide for evermore, these three,
> > > But the greatest of these is love.

THE ORGANISATION OF THE MISSION.

The Acts of the Apostles makes Paul carry out his mission work according to a fixed plan. He invariably goes first of all into the synagogue of the place to which he has come, and preaches a sermon to the Jews. Some let themselves be persuaded by him, but the majority turn away from him with indifference, or even turn against him in enmity. Thereupon Paul solemnly bears witness against them that they have rejected salvation, and goes to the Gentiles, who listen to him gladly and welcome his message.

Although the apostle (even after the concordat in Jerusalem that he and Barnabas were to go to the heathen, the twelve, on the contrary, to the Jews)[1] may perhaps sometimes here and there have proceeded in this manner, his epistles prove on the other hand that he considered himself the apostle of the Gentiles and that he had Gentile converts. It is certainly possible that he, as the travel document of his companion in Philippi[2] has it, went to the Jewish place of worship, in order there to meet such Gentiles as were generally attracted to monotheism and to the

---

[1] Gal. ii. 9.   [2] Acts xvi. 13.

moral teaching of the Jews by their own religious needs. These were the people with whom he was to break ground, especially such proselytes as had not become Jews completely and had not been circumcised, the so-called devout, who shrank from the Jewish ceremonial law and from admission into the nation, yet found Judaism interesting, and were its adherents on account of its ethical teaching and its monotheism, its antiquity and its prophecies.

Another time Paul very likely made use of the sort of quiet propaganda from lip to ear, such as has been developed by nineteenth-century socialism in its initial stages. In the circle of his fellow-craftsmen, or in other small circles with a religious interest, Paul may have started work; and however inconspicuous the results of such work may be, this is precisely the way to ensure the rapid spread of ideas, provided they meet the yearning of the inquirer half-way.

Again, it may have been in the lecture-room of a popular philosopher that Paul sometimes preached his new religion.[1] But most probably the large reception-room of a private house was oftenest the scene of Paul's preaching. That "devout man," Titius Justus, mentioned in the Acts;[2] Stephanas, who with his household placed himself at the "service" of the saints in Corinth;[3] Phœbe, the "servant" ($\delta\iota\acute{a}\kappa o\nu o\varsigma$) and patroness of the church at Cenchreæ[4]—are examples of people of means, who regarded the young churches of their native towns as placed, so to speak, under their protection, in whose houses the members assembled, who prepared all that was needful for the

[1] Acts xix. 1.   [2] Acts xviii. 7.
[3] 1 Cor. xvi. 15.   [4] Rom. xvi. 1.

regular service and for the Lord's Supper, uniting in their persons the parts of host and verger.

As a general rule, admission into the new community came remarkably soon. Whoever had listened once or twice to the mission preaching, had been deeply moved by it, and demanded baptism, was baptized and admitted a saint and saved soul to whom eternal life was assured, and who "would judge angels."[1] There is tremendous enthusiasm in this dependence on the fervent resolve and on baptism, an enthusiasm which derived indeed its vindication from the subsequent quiet and unwearying work with the converts. Everything great in the world is thus created. It is born in enthusiasm. It is nurtured and developed by a devotion to duty in details. Whenever one of the parts is lacking, no life will be awakened, or no life will be maintained.

It is not a nice epithet that we have formed to express the most beautiful aspect of a real pastor's activity: the word—cure of souls. It smacks of ailing and anxiousness: no true man, and no woman of delicate inner life, will ask for a "physician of souls." We should let the word drop, yet the thing rightly understood is the greatest service one man, and not only a pastor, can and ought to render another. This work of friendship with the newly won friends was what really became the apostle's chief life-work, and that he had a masterly grasp of it, his epistles are there to prove.

The highest quality that enabled him to do it was the absolute genuineness of his character. He buffeted

[1] 1 Cor. vi. 2.

THE ORGANISATION OF THE MISSION 203

his body and brought it into bondage, lest by any means, after preaching to others, he should be found a hypocrite himself.[1] He demanded only such sacrifices as he had himself offered. His own life of absolute surrender was the first such: it told. The life of enthusiasm that he led, and which he poured out in words to all who heard him, was embodied in daily intercourse in a life of loving service for others. His love was all the more winning, because people had seen, and saw again and again, how this man could flame into fury, how he could hate and threaten, when his cause, his God, and his Master were attacked or appeared to be so. A keen intellect kept this love from aimlessly evaporating, making it, on the contrary, possible to approach men on all sides in order to win them. However irksome it was to him, with his pronounced individuality, Paul knew how to accommodate himself to every sort of covering in which a man's upbringing, his personal or national individuality, hid him. He could always discover the human part of a man, and could turn this into an ally: "I became a Jew to the Jews, that I might win the Jews; to them that are under the law, I became as under the law, howbeit I myself am not under the law, to win them that are under the law; to them that are without law, as without law not being without law to God, but under law to Christ, that I might gain them that are without law; to the weak I became weak, that I might gain the weak; I am become all things to all men, that I may by all means save some."[2] Even in his lifetime his adversaries imagined they could forge a reproach

[1] 1 Cor. ix. 27.   [2] 1 Cor. ix. 20-22.

for the apostle out of this very thing, and indeed, taken literally, the statement certainly smacks somewhat of pliancy. But if we look more closely into the passage and into the context of the words, we shall soon find they are not the marks of an accommodating character, but rather of that downrightness and sharpness which the apostle everywhere manifests. Paul reckons this, his entering into the peculiarities of everyone, as a positive part of that asceticism which he has to practise as a "wrestler" for Christ. He regarded his amiability in the same light as his fasting and his celibacy; for the words just quoted stand between the two following sentences: " Although I was free from all, l brought myself under bondage to all. . . . I do all these things for the gospel's sake." [1]

We are indebted to the calumnies which his adversaries were never weary of circulating, for he was once moved to describe this quiet work of the missionary and educator more particularly as he carried it on in Thessalonica:

"Our appeal to you was not based on a delusion, nor was it made from unworthy motives nor in guile, but as God has chosen us, as worthy to be entrusted with the gospel, so we speak, not as pleasing men, but God, which proveth our hearts. Never at any time, as you know, did we use the language of flattery, or make false professions in order to hide selfish aims. God is my witness: nor seeking glory of men, neither from you nor from others; although as 'Christ's apostles' we might have stood on our dignity. But we were

[1] 1 Cor. ix. 19–23.

THE ORGANISATION OF THE MISSION 205

gentle in the midst of you, even as when a mother cherisheth her children. So did we feel drawn to you and strongly attracted, not only to impart unto you the gospel of God, but our very lives as well, because ye were become very dear to us. Ye remember well, brethren, our labour and travail. Day and night we worked, that we might not burden any of you, while we preached unto you the gospel of God. Ye are witnesses, and God also, how faithfully and righteously and unblamably we behaved ourselves toward you that believe, as ye know how we dealt with each one of you as a father admonishes his children, exhorting you and pleading with you, that ye should walk worthily of God who hath called you into his own kingdom of glory." [1]

It is here, in this detail work that Paul did, this work of training, where he was like a father to his children, that we have to look for the apostle's real mission. His epistles reflect this part of his work too in the best way; they were the best continuation of it for the churches, although of course they are kept within narrower limits than was the oral instruction itself. What he had to do was to counsel, to warn, and to console, constantly helping with word and deed, unwearyingly active, so as to vindicate by a corresponding life the high religious claims of these "saints," "elect," and "brethren" who were to judge men and angels, and so as not to have them become a byword among the people; he had with all his might to prevent these saints from living just as unholily as the heathen, to hinder these brethren from attacking and preying upon one another,[2] like

[1] 1 Thess. ii. 3–12.   [2] Gal. v. 15.

the covetous and deceivers, the revilers, extortioners, and robbers "of this world."[1] The hard fight against old habits of life and constant new temptations was rendered all the more arduous for the apostle because his converts' attention was fixed far more intensely on the first great moments of their new life, and they did not estimate the moral detail work of daily life as highly as he did.

For them the Holy Spirit, the new creation, the Christ within them, *was* that marvellous power that had fallen upon them, which they had first experienced in the apostle as he spoke to them in flaming, prophetic language; such they had felt when he spoke with tongues, when he, in the highest trance of the soul, left off speaking, when his lips spontaneously stammered in jubilation; it may be they had seen how a demoniac, after a last fierce attack which had broken out under the impression of his mighty emotion, had gone away healed, how a cripple had suddenly been able to walk. They had observed in themselves how the apostle's flaming words had opened up the depths of their souls and had forced them to their knees, how the same trance of enthusiasm fell upon them, how they themselves began to speak with tongues. And all this was blended for them in one with the supreme moment of baptism, when the waters of the river closed over them, and when they came up out of the water as new creatures, born again in one unique tremendous harmony of an unparalleled new fulness of life, which was given them by a miraculous power that came straight down from heaven and led them

[1] 1 Cor. v. 9-13.

THE ORGANISATION OF THE MISSION 207

of a certainty to an everlasting life, yea, which had already transported them thither. For it was thus: the fashion of this world was even now passing[1] away, like the wings of a stage this world was to vanish out of sight, and behind it all at once the truly real, the eternal world shining in glory would be revealed. This trance of the soul was for them the Holy Ghost, it ripened them with baptism, baptism confirmed and bestowed the Holy Ghost over again.

To show men in this state of mind the hard and thorny way of strict self-discipline, to show this as "the greater gift,"[2] to represent to them the Holy Ghost as just this plain, moral right-doing without branding the uplifting of the soul as empty rapture, not to preach like a wise patriarch to the young, but rather as a loving father and like-minded brother—such was the cure of souls the apostle had to carry on, that was the great task the "Home Mission" had to accomplish once the moment of conversion was out of sight. To tell men who, on account of their miracles and their ecstasies, took themselves for spiritually minded beings, that they were still "carnal," as long as they quarrelled and disputed,[3] everywhere to apply, as Ignatius has since said, cold bandages to feverish members, yet without quenching the spirit[4]—such was the great educational art of the missionary.

[1] 1 Cor. vii. 31.   [2] 1 Cor. xii. 31.   [3] 1 Cor. iii. 3.
[4] 1 Thess. v. 19, *Ignat. Polyc.* ii.

THE FOUNDER OF THE CHURCH.

CHAPTER XIV.

THE FOUNDER OF THE CHURCH.

ALL great human creations are the products of the unconscious element in man. Clever people who can read all secrets and are possessed of all knowledge may smile at this fact, but a fact it remains. It is as though man were no longer a personal being in certain moments of his existence, but came to be "beside himself," as the old Greeks said, as though he left his personality behind him and became a part of the universal whole, an instrument to do the work of humanity, unconsciously, or even against his own conscious will. It is as though there were in us, but outside of our own personality, a feeling and a will of the great whole, which drives us along and leads us a road we would not go but one which mankind has to travel. It appears strange to us, and yet it is not stranger than the birth of a child of man, which is always a work in which mankind as a whole participates, and not merely the father and mother, for in it something is created beyond that which two human beings can impart to a third. Man's unconscious life is greater than his conscious existence, and exceeds in importance his thinking and his willing.

THE BEGINNING OF ORGANISATION 209

When Paul went forth to rescue souls from a dying world for heaven, he had no thought of founding a church which was destined to become the richest, the most powerful organisation in the whole of history. When the poor Jewish rabbi and Cilician clothworker was dragged by Roman soldiers as a prisoner to the imperial city where "the beast sat upon the throne," it did not enter into his mind that he was destined to be the stay and support of this throne of the Cæsars when the hosts of northern barbarians would try and shake it to the ground, and that of this Rome, which he saw flaming with all its great sinful streets in the final conflagration of the world, he was fated to make the "eternal city."

THE BEGINNING OF ORGANISATION AND ITS NECESSITY

Paul is the founder of the Christian Church. He did not want to found it, but he was compelled to do so. And what he did he did unconsciously. What he understood by church or congregation (ἐκκλήσια) is something altogether different to what the term has ever connoted in later history. "Church" means for him all Christians, in so far as he looks upon them as members of that mysterious being that lives in them, that speaks from them, that works miracles through them, as members of the Spirit, of Christ. The church is no invisible community—you can put your hand on it in Paul, in Crispus, and in Gaius— but it is not the sum total of Paul, Crispus, and Gaius either, conceived of as forming a separate body in thought, but as constituting sacramentally a special sphere in this world, a magic ring, so to speak, on earth. Such, for Paul, was the congregation of the Lord.

The thought that this being—for a being it is—could or must be organised, never once occurred to him. What need was there for organisation? All human societies, guilds, burial clubs and the like, cannot of course do without an organisation if everything is to go on properly. In the present case, however, it was another who saw to it that everything was done in order: it was God's Spirit, for God is not a God of disorder, but of order;[1] it was Christ, for all are members of Christ; and can Christ be torn asunder?[2] A boundless enthusiasm is implied by this confidence in the new spirit that had entered into these little communities, consisting as they did of the illiterate, the weak, the socially insignificant.[3] And in spite of many dark hours through which it passed, this enthusiasm has not been put to shame.

There was, however, another reason for dispensing with any kind of organisation—and one more immediately effective than this confidence in God Himself. It was the expectation of the Parousia. When the morning broke red, people asked each other whether it was not a precursor of that mighty stream of fire which was to fall from heaven and destroy all the evil in the world. And when in the evening the golden beams shot like spears across the skies, "look," they said, "these are the angels' weapons. They have come forth to destroy, or perhaps it is the glittering of their sickles wherewith they are to gather in the harvest." To-day, to-morrow, at any time, the door of heaven might be opened and the last trumpet

[1] 1 Cor. xiv. 32.   [2] 1 Cor. xii. 27; i. 13.   [3] 1 Cor. i. 26.

THE BEGINNING OF ORGANISATION 211

sound which would call the dead from their graves. Was this the time for thinking of an organisation? So little did this idea enter into Paul's head, that he did not even give his little local communities any regulations of their own.

But there was another thinking and working for him, the "Holy Ghost." He gave the Christians gifts which none had known these men to possess before, gifts of speech and of ministry, not merely talking with tongues, prophecy and teaching, but also gifts of "helping" and of "guidance,"[1] of "giving," of "presiding," and of "distributing alms."[2] If "presiding" thus stands between "giving" and "distributing alms," it can scarcely be used in the later sense of "governing"; it is rather used in the sense of "protecting," and implies the relationship of a patron to his client. Like every true government upon earth, the Christian was not based originally upon any legal right, nor even a duty; it was founded upon natural superiority, generosity, and love, the affording of protection and the giving of help. Such was the creation of the Holy Ghost: He gave not only wonderful words and hearts overflowing with enthusiasm, but He also made hearts gentle and kind, and ready to give, to help, and to serve.

The first organisation was therefore the negation of every kind of organisation, according to the words of Jesus: "If any man desire to be first, the same shall be servant of all."[3] There was Stephanas at Corinth, "the first-fruits"[4] of Achaia to God; what more natural than that he should open his house to

[1] Cor. xii. 28. [2] Rom. xii. 8.
[3] Mark ix. 35. [4] 1 Cor. xvi. 15.

the little company of his fellow-believers and prepare the room for their meetings ? But there were others who wanted to help and join in working and do something too.[1] So a certain Phœbe did for the converts at Cenchreæ what Stephanas had done at Corinth. Paul calls her "a helper" (deacon), and says of her: "Aid her in whatever matter she may need your assistance, for she too has 'presided' over many, *i.e.* she has been a patron of many":[2] where we see again that "presiding" and "helping" were the same thing —the president was the man or woman ready to help everyone else in every possible way. Such was the organisation of the earliest churches. All the means usually employed in government were simply left on one side, and reliance was placed on two great instruments alone: the swords of the word and of ministering love—two weapons in which not only the world, but Christianity itself, refuses to place an absolute trust to this day.

And has not the later history of the Church amply justified this want of trust ? Was there not from the very first more in these "gifts" than might appear, more authority, more power ? Even in the first Epistle to the Thessalonians, at an earlier date, that is to say, than the time to which the passages we have just quoted refer, we find Paul saying: "We beseech you, brothers, to show regard for those who toil among you and preside over you in the Lord's service and admonish you, and that you hold them in the greatest esteem and affection for the sake of their work."[3] And later, in the Epistle to the Philippians,[4]

[1] 1 Cor. xvi. 16.
[2] Rom. xvi. 1 *seq.*
[3] 1 Thess. v. 12 *seq.*
[4] Phil. i. 1.

THE BEGINNING OF ORGANISATION 213

some of these people are already called "overseers" (ἐπίσκοπος = bishop), probably the only word which the early Christians borrowed from the heathen religious clubs and one which has again and again given proof of its tendency to an autocratic exercise of power. We may grant this, but the first state of things was after all quite different to that which prevailed later on. In the Pauline communities the "oversight" and the "admonishing" were still conceived of as services of love which one man rendered to his neighbour—notice the first *and* in the quotation from 1 Thessalonians v. But men are for ever clamouring to be led and governed, and it is easy enough to conceive how, having learnt to subject themselves in love and courtesy, they should once again learn to create their rulers.

As yet, however, enthusiasm and faith in the Holy Ghost remained unimpaired. Christianity has always trusted the masses. Not that it believed in the masses as such, but it ventured to recognise human beings in the masses, and to place its trust in the converted man full of enthusiasm. These little communities of converts were to govern themselves. Their enthusiasm was to govern them. Paul did not merely say this—he acted in accordance with his words. All the services done by individuals he demands of all alike, all the "rights" possessed by individuals he assigns to all alike: "Brothers, even if any one should be caught in a guilty act, you who are spiritually minded should in a gentle spirit put the man right, each looking to himself, lest he too should fall into temptation."[1] "We exhort you,

[1] Gal. vi. 1.

brothers, to admonish the disorderly, to comfort the faint-hearted, to lend a helping hand to the weak, and to be patient with all men."[1] Every individual in the community has the right of "presiding" and admonishing—it is his duty—a duty to be performed by the whole community as such. Its determinations are revelations of the Spirit, the apostle accepts a sentence carried by a mere majority of the Church.[2] The congregation as a whole exercises a censorship over the morality of its members, it appoints people to settle disputes between them,[3] it elects committees for other purposes, such as collections.[4] The meeting of all the members as yet exercised the executive as well as the deliberative functions, which arrangement was the simplest and the most natural for such small communities.

As the churches grew in size, a recollection of the earliest days remained in the shape of the congregations which met at this or that house; we find mention of such in 1 Cor. xvi. 19 and in Romans xvi. The family, with the servants, friends, and relatives, formed an independent group for religious purposes. In the days of persecution, when the congregation as a whole was scattered for long periods at a stretch, Christianity found a refuge in these "family churches," and so its life was preserved. In the second century, however, they were suppressed by the bishops and other ecclesiastical authorities, because they impaired the organisation of the Church as a whole, and because they proved to be the most powerful allies possessed by the heretics. Ignatius

[1] 1 Thess. v. 14.   [2] 2 Cor. ii. 6.
[3] 1 Cor. vi. 4.   [4] 2 Cor. viii. 18 *seq.*

THE BEGINNING OF ORGANISATION 215

and Hermas show us the campaign against them at its full height—the former in Syria, the latter at Rome.

The bond of union between the Pauline churches was love and their apostle. In him the unity of the ekklesia was, so to speak, symbolised. His letters, and his disciples, whom he despatched with answers and on errands,[1] were the instruments by which he exercised his "central power"; through them he upheld the tradition of his teaching: "I entreat you be my imitators. That is why I sent Timothy to you. He is my dear faithful child in the Lord. He shall remind you of my methods in Christ (= Christian methods), methods which I follow everywhere in every church."[2] He supports his messengers with his own authority: "When Timothy comes, see to it that he has no cause to feel timid while he is with you. For he is doing the Master's work no less than I am. No one therefore should slight him."[3]

In all probability there were other similar instances of the beginning of an organisation grouping itself round the personality of some important missionary. They were the precursors of later provincial and still wider organisations, even though the latter did not directly proceed from them, for the growing Episcopal power destroyed these traces of a patriarchal organisation wherever they had been preserved.

We have completed our survey of the beginnings of ecclesiastical organisation. From these beginnings the great executive power of a later age was developed. *But the church itself is far more than its government,*

[1] 2 Cor. ii. 13 *seq.*; vi. 13 *seq.*; viii. 16 *seq.*
[2] 1 Cor. iv. 16.   [3] 1 Cor. xvi. 10.

the church is a peculiar expression of religious faith, with a law of life of its own, a law which can indeed be developed by the governing powers, but cannot be exhausted in them. It was a historical necessity that the Gospel of Jesus should be turned into a church, and it was Paul who took the first steps, and who had to take them, to make of this necessity an actual fact. Even in him the enthusiastic faith in the Holy Ghost had to be turned into hard and simple work, because mighty destructive forces soon arose which threatened to destroy his works and to rend the body of Christ. I am not thinking of the human, the all too human elements, which could not be quite suppressed even in this earliest community of brothers—personal vanity, petty ambition, scandal, and slander—but of certain great dangers, no figments of the imagination, but founded on real fact; and above all of the following three:

1. The church at Jerusalem fell ever more and more into the hands of an extreme Jewish legal party which demanded of the Gentiles under all conditions that they should become Jews before becoming Christians. It imposed circumcision and the observance of the law on every convert, and endeavoured to sunder the bond between the apostle and his congregations by an active campaign of agitation, hoping thus to win them over to their own way of thinking.

2. In Paul's own congregations little groups gradually arose which developed ascetic tendencies. They thought it a sin to eat meat or to drink wine, and they fancied they could not continue to live side by side with their more liberal-minded brethren. Here

THE BEGINNING OF ORGANISATION 217

we have the first signs of those aspirations after a peculiar sanctity which appeared still more distinctly in the course of the gnostic controversy, and which led finally to the formation of an especial class of ascetics—the monks.

3. The third danger lay in the Holy Ghost Himself; hence efforts to "quench the Spirit" can already be clearly traced in the Pauline churches. In the earliest days of Christianity, just as later in the time of the Reformation, the watchword of freedom threatened to break up these little communities and to plunge them into a state of anarchy. The less restraint a man put upon himself, the more did he appear to certain sections, even of Paul's own congregations, to be driven by the " Spirit." No state could tolerate such licence, and thus the very existence of the churches was at stake.

Such were the three destructive powers against which Paul battled indefatigably. His God is a God of order and of love. And so, unintentionally, he laid the foundations of the Church. What he did want was to save his congregations from absorption in the whirlpool of a religious revolution, from imprisonment, from decay, and uncharitableness.

THE FOUNDER OF THE CHURCH.

CHAPTER XV.

THE STRUGGLE FOR FREEDOM FROM THE LAW AND FOR THE INDEPENDENCE OF CHRISTIANITY.

THE most dangerous crisis which Paul's congregations had to traverse was the period of open rupture with the strict Jewish-Christian party, fomented by the attitude of Jesus' disciples towards the apostle of the Gentiles. As far as we can see, they appear to have wavered, subsiding from time to time, however, into a position of hostility.

The thought of founding a church had been even more absent from Jesus' mind than it was from Paul's. Jesus looked away from the external to the inner life of man. In the future there loomed the great final catastrophe which shut out every other prospect. Even great practical questions, which must have already presented themselves in His time, were scarcely noticed by Jesus. Such were the two important questions of the validity of the law for Himself and His disciples, and of the mission to the Gentiles. Neither appears to have been thoroughly examined or considered in its connection with the other. Jesus was animated by the glad confidence that the law could be fulfilled; for, rightly understood, it was the expression of the two great demands of love to God and love to man. Every true disciple of Jesus would have a heart so full of love that it would be easy for him to fulfil the whole law and the prophets better, more thoroughly, than the Pharisees. But had not Jesus set aside single commandments, such as that concerning the Sabbath and portions of the ceremonial law, in the glad certainty that as child of God He need not be over-scrupulous? In answer to His opponents, Jesus took His stand upon that which appeared to Him to be God's will in the law as against this or that special commandment. But he did not reject the law as a whole in consequence of this position. Just like His fellow-countrymen, His general attitude was that of an observer of the law. What His opponents criticised was not a regular disregard of the law, but the occasional breach of certain commandments. Thus Jesus, according to His own opinion, had fulfilled the inner meaning of the law. In reality He had surpassed it. For Paul rightly emphasises the fact that the law as law presents an alternative between which there is no middle ground: all or nothing.[1]

The consequences of His position to the law remained completely concealed from Jesus even while He was uncompromisingly opposed to one of the fundamental thoughts on which it rested, viz., that of ceremonial holiness.[2] It was only Paul who made the discovery in the fierce struggle of his life.

The question as to the mission to the Gentiles remained in like manner practically untouched. In all our present gospels we have of course words

[1] Gal. iii. 10; Deut. xxvii. 26.   [2] Mark vii. 17 *seq.*

ascribed to Jesus, which order His disciples to go forth and evangelise the heathen world, but the way in which they are ascribed is very significant. Each evangelist puts them into the mouth of the risen Lord, but each in his own way and in a different place. In Mark we find the passage in the conclusion, which is certainly not genuine, though it may still date from the first half of the second century.[1] In Matthew Jesus gathers His disciples together on a hill in Galilee and bids them "Go forth and make disciples of all peoples, baptizing them in the name of the Father, of the Son, and of the Holy Ghost, and teaching them to observe all things whatsoever I have commanded you."[2] The threefold baptismal formula is sufficient to prove the passage to be of a late date. In the earliest time the only baptism was that in the name of Christ.[3] In Luke the risen Jesus assembles the disciples on the Sunday evening at Jerusalem, and sends them forth to all nations with the message of repentance unto remission of sins.[4] And the gospel closes with the parting of Jesus from the disciples, and the description of their harmonious life. The second volume of Luke's work, the Acts, begins with the same two pictures; and here too the disciples immediately receive the command to evangelise the world.[5] Finally, John ventured to transfer the great "hour" of the conversion of the Gentile world into the life of Jesus, and to justify the mission by those wonderfully solemn words addressed to the Greeks that came to Jesus: "The hour has come that the Son of man should be

[1] Mark xvi. 15. [2] Matt. xxviii. 19 *seq.*
[3] 1 Cor. i. 13. [4] Luke xxiv. 46 *seq.* [5] Acts. i. 8.

glorified. Verily, verily, I say unto you, Except a corn of wheat fall into the ground and die, it abideth alone: but if it die, it bringeth forth much fruit."[1]

In reality this passage too bears witness to the fact that it was only after Jesus' death that His disciples thought of any kind of missionary work. And at first they confined their mission to the Jews: until Paul came, they held aloof from missionary work among the Gentiles. Jesus Himself thought of this work as little as did His disciples: was not the time until the end so short that they would "not have gone over the cities of Israel till the Son of man be come"?[2] As a matter of principle, Jesus would of course have raised no objection to the reception of the heathen: the Gentile is no worse than His "Samaritan." He always beheld the man in all men, even in the Jew; and where a ray of warm human love fell upon Him from a heathen heart—as in the case of the Canaanite woman—or of suppliant faith— as in the centurion of Capernaum—then He too, perhaps, once believed and said that many would come from the east and from the west, and would lie down at the banquet in the Kingdom of Heaven with Abraham, Isaac, and Jacob.[3] He did not mean that they would have to be first circumcised or baptized. He did not think of them as Jews or Christians, but as loving, trusting children of men. But words such as these were only occasional utterances, which bore witness to a heart free from all prejudice and full of love. They were not intended as indications for a definite organised work.

[1] John xii. 24.   [2] Matt. x. 5 *seq.*
[3] Matt. viii. 11; Luke xiii. 29.

Such was the position of uncertainty therefore in which Jesus left His disciples when He parted from them, and they never succeeded in clearing up the ambiguity. Two men alone took up a perfectly clear position: one was James, the brother of the Lord, who had not been His disciple, but soon came to play a leading part in the early church; the other was Paul. The former wanted to go back to Judaism—the latter had recognised that Christianity was a new religion.

For fourteen, perhaps seventeen years, Paul had successfully preached his gospel free from all connection with the law, in Syria and Cilicia. Congregations had been formed, and far and wide there were men who believed in Jesus as the Christ, their Saviour and Lord, without being Jews and without observing the law. But the further his work extended, the more anxious did Paul become. His one concern was "lest by any means I should run or had run in vain."[1] For all at once there appeared all kind of strange folk in his congregations. They called themselves brethren, and they did believe in Jesus as the Christ. But they were never tired of expressing their astonishment at what they saw round about them. "What, did their dear brothers here really eat things strangled and the flesh of swine? Were they really not circumcised? And had Paul made these arrangements? A strange thing, this so-called freedom! Well then, they probably lived as they liked in other respects too, like the Gentiles? Free, without law, that meant lawless, did it not?" "Licence they mean when they cry

[1] Gal. ii. 2.

liberty." And then they began to say how everything was quite different in Jerusalem; but then the "pillars"[1] of the church of God lived there, a Peter and a John, Jesus' favourite disciples, and James too, the saint, the brother of the Lord, who was so blameless in the law that even priests and scribes marvelled at him.[2] In Jerusalem—yes, there men lived a strict and righteous life. Perhaps, after all, they would know what was right there, better than here. And pray who *was* this Paul? Was not Judaism the true religion, did not Paul himself continually refer to the Old Testament? To be a pious Jew and to believe that Jesus is the Messiah—that is true Christianity. So spake the people who came down from Jerusalem, " the mother of us all."

And thus approached Paul's severest hour of temptation, and a struggle harder almost than that which he had had to fight on the road to Damascus. For here too the travail in the apostle's soul ended in a revelation.

Temptation's most dangerous guise is not that of the common and the vulgar. It is when the best that is within us presents itself to us in such a form that it goads us on to sin, that we must be most of all on our guard. What was it that could have distressed Paul so? One thing alone. It was the tempter's voice that spoke to Paul. What do the pillars in Jerusalem concern you? You have just as little to do with them as you have with this crew of spies, these false brethren who are sneaking about in every nook and corner, whose one object is to

[1] Gal. ii. 6–9.
[2] Hegesippus in Eusebius' *Eccl. Hist.*, Bk. ii., xxiii. 7.

disturb your congregations and to alienate their affections. You are an apostle of Jesus Christ. He has appeared, and He still appears to you and gives you instruction and guidance. You have been in the third heaven and in Paradise, you have the miraculous gifts of tongues and of healing—are *you* to go, cap in hand, and beg for the praise and the approval of the men with whose consent, directly or indirectly, these spies are creeping about here? But the other voice said: You are always preaching about love, long-suffering and unity. Now practise as you preach. You keep your body under, add yet one more mortification. Submit and go up to Jerusalem. Would you really venture to rend the body of Christ? And do not those pillars really know more about Him whom you preach than you do? And after all, it may very well be that they will not exact the sacrifice of your freedom, or call upon you to lead your people back again into bondage. It may very well turn out that these men here are not rightly informed. At any rate there is one thing you ought to do. As long as you can, you ought to go and hold out the right hand of peace. It was a severe struggle within Paul's soul, and it ended in a revelation. The apostle went up to Jerusalem.[1]

But not as a subordinate, nor as one resolved to make every concession. He took Barnabas with him, his old friend and companion, a man who was held in great esteem by the twelve, and at the same time shared the principles on which his missionary work rested. He took Titus with him, a young uncircumcised Greek, a living symbol of his Gentile Church.

[1] Gal. ii. 2.

THE STRUGGLE FOR FREEDOM 225

He found in Jerusalem more than he expected, even though we must subtract a little from the glamour with which the editor of the Acts has invested the original facts, for this famous fifteenth chapter shows more clearly than anywhere else the influence of a later Catholic revision. The meeting of the apostles has been turned into a solemn council which issues a decree, the main portion beginning as follows: "It seemed good to the Holy Ghost and to us. . . ." And yet Paul knows nothing whatever about this decree. What we gather from Paul's own account is as follows. He met his opponents—the men who had worked all the mischief in his Syrian and Cilician congregations. They came forward and accused him in the most violent language. They demanded that Titus should be circumcised. The position of the twelve was somewhat different. Peter seems to have been the freest. He believes, like Paul—it is Paul himself who expressly tells us so[1]—that through faith in Jesus, the Christ, we are saved, and not through the works of the law. He was ready therefore to give up the law. But it was Paul's speech, it was the facts of his mission, which carried away the whole assembly. This was the first occasion on which the power of his personality was revealed to those whom he had formerly persecuted. They felt that they were listening to a man that was mighty both in deeds and in words. Then they recognised that the Gospel to the Gentiles had been entrusted to him as that to the Jews had been given to Peter, and that the same God who had granted to Peter wonderful gifts for his mission among the Jews, had endowed

[1] Gal. ii. 16.

Paul with the same gifts for his work amongst the Gentiles. And Peter and James and John, who were counted as the pillars, recognised the grace that had been given him, and held out to him and to Barnabas the right hand of fellowship ; and they settled that Paul and Barnabas should go to the Gentiles, while they themselves turned to the Jews. But the brethren among the Gentiles were not to forget the poor in Jerusalem, but were to gather alms for their support.[1] Such was the concordat at Jerusalem. We cannot follow the account in the Acts,[2] which flatly contradicts Paul's own words in making Peter an apostle to the Gentiles "a good while ago."

After an excited meeting, in which Paul did not give way to the false brethren for a single moment, he appears to have prevailed. In reality the result was a compromise. As is always the case in similar circumstances, those who took part in the debate shut their eyes to the whole difficulty of the problem, which was solved in a different manner by each of the opposing parties, and James said nothing, carried away perhaps for a moment by Paul's personal influence. All disagreement seemed to be at an end, but the hard facts of life were destined to try the compromise too severely.

The fact was, that the expression, "to go to the Gentiles," was ambiguous. Paul always understands the words in a geographical sense. So he writes, Rom. i. 5, including the Romans "among all nations," and yet we see from chap. vii. that there were Jewish Christians at Rome. By "Gentiles" he therefore understood the Gentile world. His Gospel was

[1] Gal. ii. 7–10.   [2] Acts. xv. 7.

THE STRUGGLE FOR FREEDOM 227

intended for all congregations in the Gentile world. We have no means of knowing now what the twelve at first understood by the expression. But one thing is certain, that they soon afterwards interpreted it in an entirely different sense. They wanted to have the law maintained in all Jewish Christian congregations at least, even if they were ready to concede a greater liberty to purely Gentile churches. In actual life, however, it was very hard to carry out this theory. For a Jew who kept the law strictly was not allowed to eat with any one who was not a Jew. How was this commandment to be carried out in mixed Christian congregations? Was not their greatest act of worship a common meal? And, as a matter of fact, this was the difficulty which not long afterwards wrecked the Jerusalem concordat.

It was Peter, a good, kind-hearted man, easily roused to enthusiasm but lacking in resolution, who was the occasion of the new conflict which henceforth embittered the whole of Paul's life and added the heaviest care of all to the anxieties with which he was already burdened.

Soon after the meeting at Jerusalem, Peter travelled down to Antioch in Syria, the centre of the new mission to the Gentiles. According to the Acts, a Christian congregation had been established in this important commercial city, with its great export trade to the west, some time before Paul's arrival, by a few brethren who had found their way thither during the Jewish persecution. The little church had rapidly increased in numbers, and Peter found all the members living in the full freedom of the Pauline communities; Jewish customs had been abandoned, and all partook of the Lord's Supper together without feeling any scruples. Peter did as the others without any hesitation. He eat that which, according to Jewish ideas, was unclean, with men that were unclean, just because he was convinced that not the keeping of the law, but faith in Jesus, the Messiah, saves and makes clean. This did not last long however. Once again messengers came from Jerusalem, despatched by James, to stop this increasing disregard of the law once for all. Such had not been his intention when he held out the right hand of fellowship to Paul. It had never entered into his head that the Jews, too, should live without the law. They were to consider themselves bound by the law —irrevocably bound. There was to be no faltering on this point, even at the cost of the unity of Christendom. James was more powerfully influenced by old instincts and inherited customs than by the new spirit. He shuddered at the thought of eating things strangled, or blood, or the flesh of swine. James' unbending resolution made a great impression upon Peter. Weak natures are always inclined to go back to the old when their attempts at compromise fail in face of the stern requirements of actual life. And this was what Peter did in the present instance. He withdrew himself, and no longer took part in the Lord's Supper. But his example was attended by very important consequences. All the Jewish Christians, and even Barnabas, followed him. Paul was left alone with his Gentiles.

Then came a sudden outburst of wrath. His life-work was now at stake, and he was not inclined to risk all that he had done for the sake of the peace of mind of a man who either did not know or did not want to know the real meaning of his actions. Whether Paul really called Peter and Barnabas hypocrites before the assembled congregation, we do not know. He does so in the Epistle to the Galatians, and says that he told Peter before them all, in order to bring home to him the full meaning of what he had done: "If you who are a Jew live (as you have been doing all this time) after the manner of the Gentiles and not as the Jews, how can you compel the Gentiles to live as do the Jews?" What Peter had done was really tantamount to the exercise of compulsion; for his refusal to eat any longer with Gentile Christians was equivalent to saying that he would in future only consider them as fellow-Christians when they conformed to the law. And surely, said Paul, that contradicts Peter's inmost convictions: "We are by nature Jews, and not 'sinners of the Gentiles'; but as we have recognised that a man is justified not by works of the law, but by faith in Christ Jesus, so we too have believed in Christ Jesus, that we might be justified by faith in Christ, and not by the works of the law, for by the works of the law 'shall no flesh be justified.'"

Paul means, if the law were necessary, they might just as well have remained Jews; but it was just because they had recognised the insufficiency of the law for salvation that they had come to believe. But if they were now to set up the law again as the measure of a man's Christianity, then they would actually make Jesus to be an agent of "sin" in the legal sense: "If, while we seek to be justified by Christ, we ourselves were found to be 'sinners' (and if this legal sense of sin were the right one), would not Christ be an agent of sin? God forbid: (and yet I should be forced to accept this conclusion). For if I rebuild the very things I pulled down, I prove myself a 'transgressor' (in my former actions).

"Through the law I became dead to the law in order to live for God. I have been crucified with Christ. So it is no longer I that live: it is Christ that lives in me. But so far as I still live in the flesh, I live by faith in the Son of God who loved me and gave Himself for me.

"I do not set aside the grace of God. Why, if righteousness could come through the law, then Christ died for nothing."[1]

So entirely was Paul carried away by his own words, that he forgot the situation from which they arose, and has not recorded Peter's answer to this accusation, inspired at once by pain and anger, but full also of the victorious certainty of faith, nor do we know the further consequences. We can only conjecture that one such must have been the breach between Paul and Barnabas. At least Paul went on his way alone henceforth. The Acts does, it is true, account for the separation between the two companions by a quarrel about Barnabas's nephew,[2] just as great questions of principle are to this day transformed into petty personal disputes in the Roman Catholic Church. It seems to us to be not only true to fact, but more honourable, to suppose that their old connection was sundered because of some vital difference of opinion rather than on account of some trivial personality.

[1] Gal. ii. 11–21.   [2] Acts xv. 35–39.

THE STRUGGLE FOR FREEDOM 231

But henceforth Paul turned his steps in another direction. He took, as we have already seen, the road to Europe. And henceforth his opponents dogged his steps in order to alienate his converts. He had to fight a double action. The enemy attacked him from within and from without.

To pursue this struggle in detail would mean transcribing the greater part of the apostle's letters; there is scarce a page without some note of attack or defence. One point remains uncertain to the end, and that is the part played by the twelve in this contest. There is of course the party of Peter at Corinth,[1] but there is nothing to justify us in identifying it with Paul's outspoken opponents, who systematically endeavoured to undermine his reputation. Nor is it any more certain whether Paul is thinking of the disciples of Jesus when he sarcastically speaks on one occasion of certain "eminent apostles."[2] It does not appear to me to be even probable. What is certain is that the apostle's opponents, who plotted and caballed in all his congregations, managed somehow or other to cover themselves with the name of the twelve, and referred—and thus far at least with perfect justice—to James as their authority. Of this we have abundant proof both in the Epistle to the Galatians[3] and in both Epistles to the Corinthians.

The position of affairs was critical. In Galatia part of the congregation had suffered themselves to be circumcised and had begun to observe festivals. At Corinth the Judaisers sowed an evil seed of mistrust between the apostle and his congregation. The complete rupture often appeared to be merely a

[1] 1 Cor. i. 12. [2] 2 Cor. xi. 5. [3] Gal. ii. 6.

question of time. To the very end, even during his captivity, they tried to upset his work. In as late a letter as that to the Philippians, Paul is roused to an angry outburst against the dogs who trust in their flesh, *i.e.* their circumcision, "their concision,"[1] their mutilation. He has to complain too that they appear indeed as preachers of the Gospel,[2] but their motives are not single, they are animated by party-spirit, their aim is to render his bonds more galling and to estrange his converts from him even while he himself is a prisoner.[3] It was on some such occasion that Paul uttered the well-known words: " In one way or another, either with or without a pretext, Christ is being made known, and thereat I rejoice."[4] Those are not the words, however, of a mild and placable temper, they are hard words of the severest condemnation, and are altogether in harmony with the tone which he usually employs towards these people.

On both sides the contest was pursued in an extremely bitter spirit: neither of the two parties understood his opponent's true motives, neither tried to do the other justice. It was not of the Judaisers but of the Jews that Paul said, "They are eager for God's honour, but their knowledge is not equal to their zeal."[5] Of the Judaisers he spoke very differently. He called them liars and slanderers, workers of mischief, going about to ensnare men's souls. It must be owned that their manner of action, especially at Corinth, was characterised by subterfuge and deceit. And the apostle's faults—the volcanic outbursts of his violent temper—however blamable they

---

[1] Phil. iii. 2 *seq.*; iii. 19. [2] Phil. i. 15; iii. 2.
[3] Phil. i. 17. [4] Phil. i. 18. [5] Rom. x. 2.

may be, can be more easily supported than the low and crafty wiles of his opponents. But the whole controversy proves that, with all its greatness, with all its true heroism, the earliest age of Christianity was just as little the ideal age of the new religion as was any other epoch if Christianity is really the religion of love.

In one direction Paul had gone too far, that is, with regard to the twelve. He now repaired his mistake. At Antioch he had called Peter a hypocrite —if not in so many words, at least he made his meaning clear. Later, too, hard words about the "pillars" escaped him when he had been sore wounded by the hatred of the people who referred to them as their authority. And yet he never wearied in collecting money for the poor at Jerusalem; nor were the slanderous accusations which his opponents directed against him because of this very thing, of any avail in turning him from his purpose. He was always ready to acknowledge the precedency of the mother church and its apostles in religious matters, and asked his congregations to think of that church with reverence and with love.[1] And finally, he staked his life and lost it for the sake of peace with the apostles and to obtain their support. For he went up again to Jerusalem not only to hand over the collection, but surely also to consult with them once more. One of his companions has described this journey for us, and tells us [2] how at Tyre and in Cæsarea, Christian prophets tried to induce Paul, in the name of the Holy Ghost, not to go up to Jerusalem. Paul then stayed seven days at Tyre. And after all he went

[1] 2 Cor. viii. 14.   [2] Acts xxi.

up again, as he had done eleven years before. He knew what awaited him.

But one thing he did not know. The twelve had in the meantime issued a decree annulling the concordat of Jerusalem. They laid down certain conditions regulating the intercourse of Jewish Christains with Gentiles. They were to abstain from meat offered to idols, from things strangled, from blood (*i.e.* from the meat of beasts not killed in accordance with Jewish rites), and from fornication. It was only now that Paul heard of this decree.[1] Are we to understand the word "fornication" of sexual immorality? If so, the apostle was grossly insulted. It might certainly signify marriage within the prohibited degrees, and it is perhaps more natural to take it in this sense when we observe that all the other prohibitions regard the ceremonial and not the moral law. Or we can suppose the apostles to have intended both things at once, for this is the meaning of the Old Testament passage, of which they were probably thinking when they wrote.[2] But in this case, and it is the most probable, moral and ceremonial wrongdoing are again placed side by side, "fornication" and "blood." Did not the twelve thereby appear to give colour to his adversaries' constant accusation that in opposing Judaism he taught the licentiousness of heathenism?

In reality this decree was just another attempt at compromise. The apostles had so far kept to the concordat—they had said nothing of circumcision or the keeping of the whole law. All that they asked for apparently was just a little concession.

[1] Acts xxi. 25. [2] Levit. xviii.

THE STRUGGLE FOR FREEDOM 235

But for all that a great stride back to Judaism had been taken. Now that the decree had been issued, no longer that man was pure who had a pure heart, but he who eat no meat sacrificed to idols or things strangled: the weak had won a victory in a matter of principle too, and had dragged down Christianity in this point—as they do wherever they triumph—to the level of the earlier development of religion.

If everything happened as the Acts continues to narrate—and it is our only source—then Paul submitted without saying a word, he even took upon himself a Nazarite vow and sacrifices[1] in order that all Judaisers might know that they had been misinformed about him, and that he himself walked in accordance with the law.[2] If he did that, and if while doing so he was seized in the temple, then his end was in truth a tragic one, and he died not without his own fault in the highest sense of the word. If he did that, then once again he had wished to become a Jew unto the Jews,[3] from a false love of peace and in order to save his work. But this was no longer the time for compromise. If, on the other hand, we refuse to believe the apostle capable of such weakness, then we can dispute the authenticity of the passage on historical or literary grounds. The Acts is no source of the highest order.

One thing is certain. The Paul who stood before the altar at Jerusalem with shorn locks and the offerings of the Nazarite in his hands, is not the man who influenced the course of history. The

[1] Numb. vi.   [2] Acts xxi. 24.   [3] 1 Cor. ix. 20.

Paul who lives in history is he who, eleven years earlier, won a victory in this same town for freedom from the law and for the Christ in us, who henceforth proclaimed the religion of the pure heart and the new birth. It is he who has made his way from victory unto victory throughout the world, after saving Christianity in that decisive hour: for by carrying the twelve away with him, and moving them to acknowledge his Gentile Christians as true Christians, and to forego insisting upon circumcision and the observance of the law, he hindered the new religion from descending to the stage of the old natural legal religion, and preserved it from absorption into Judaism. However urgently rigorous Judaists might insist upon circumcision and the law, they were annulled for the great body of Christendom, and so they remained. Some uncertainty still attached to the lawfulness of certain articles of food, and it was only gradually overcome, and not everywhere in the same manner. Here, as in the sacraments and dogmas of the Church, a postern gate remained open by which the earlier religion would enter in. But we owe so much to this controversy with the Judaisers, that we ought still to be grateful for it to this day. By their attacks Paul was compelled to write his clearest, his most important epistles, such as those to the Galatians and Romans, he was forced to describe himself and his life in the second Epistle to the Corinthians as he would never have done otherwise.

To this controversy alone we are indebted for the clear picture that we get of Paul in history. Still more, if Christianity again and again finds weapons in Paul's words wherewith to fight for its freedom against every kind of legality, works or dogmas, then it has to thank this same controversy for them. Nor must we forget a by-product of the struggle—the introduction of Christianity into Europe.

THE FOUNDER OF THE CHURCH.

CHAPTER XVI.

FREEDOM AND SCRUPULOSITY.

NEVER did Paul treat the Judaisers as "weak brethren," that is, as men who were unable to rise to the true conception of Christian freedom merely from scrupulosity and timid fear. They never pretended to be such either. They prided themselves on the privileges they had inherited from the fathers, on the law and circumcision. And yet there can be no doubt that amongst them too there was a certain admixture of scrupulosity. They shuddered at the thought of eating the flesh of swine or "blood.' It was a revulsion which had become natural by an abstention which had lasted for centuries. But here Paul felt only too clearly that the question at stake was the reversion of Christianity to the stage of the old religion, with all its attendant train of misery. Hence he remained firm and resolute until perhaps those days before his imprisonment at Jerusalem.

His attitude towards another group in his congregations was somewhat different. These were the people who, for reasons of conscience, abstained from meat offered to idols, or indeed from meat in general. The decree of the twelve forbade the use of meat offered to idols; but if we examine the passages in the first Epistle to the Corinthians, in which Paul treats of this question, we shall find that it was not a Judaising scruple with which he was there dealing. The reason of the abstention of the "weaker brethren" was the sacramental conception of the sacrifice as of a blood-bond with the deity: they were afraid of entering into a mysterious but real relation with the demons, of becoming their "fellows," and thus submitting body and soul to their influence. "There are some who, by reason of their previous custom, still eat meat offered to idols as such, and their conscience being weak, is thereby defiled."[1]

There are other "weak brethren" whom we meet with in Rome.[2] They eat vegetables, *i.e.* they eat no meat and they drink no wine. To eat meat or to drink wine is to put a stumbling-block in their way. They are strict vegetarians. Here, too, they observe certain festivals as holidays.

Asceticism of every kind — sexual abstinence, vegetarianism, and teetotalism — is probably as old as humanity, as old as the pleasures of which it is the negation. There are times, however, in which it becomes a very mighty power. They are not the healthiest times in the history of humanity. Whenever reactionary ascetic tendencies set in with primeval power, you will be sure to find that it is an age of the most unbridled pleasure-seeking in which the seeds of decadence are being sown. Such times, in which old landmarks are shifted and the faith of a former generation abandoned, in which the lust for enjoyment seizes mankind like a kind of frenzy, and

[1] 1 Cor. viii. 7.   [2] Rom. xiv.

in which those sections of society which set the example to the rest fling themselves headlong into the delirious pursuit of luxury, are always characterised by that almost morbid craving for purity and that passive rapture of the soul which are the products of asceticism and its constant attendant mysticism. It is a difficult matter at such times to keep to the path of a healthy natural life. Not only whole nations, but individuals too, are enticed from the narrow way over into the magic gardens of pleasure or into the mysterious deserts of asceticism. It is a matter of comparative indifference how people justify asceticism in any particular age, compared with the physiological and psychological conditions which are its real source.

The age of the Roman Empire was a time in which the magic plant of asceticism and mysticism was bound to flourish more magnificently than ever before, for scarcely ever had mankind lived more consciously in and for luxury than during that epoch. A violent ascetic tendency seized hold of Christianity at a very early date—mystic it had already been ever since the day of Pentecost, since the "Resurrection" of Jesus.

Paul himself was unmarried, and held a decided belief in the superior purity of the single state, though his feelings were natural enough for him to recommend a man to marry[1] who found that celibacy involved a hard struggle. He never noticed that by taking up this position he was placing himself on exactly the same footing as the people whom he elsewhere calls the "weak brethren," and he failed to

[1] 1 Cor. vii. 7 *seq.*

notice it, because what presented itself in the first instance as scrupulosity, appeared in his own case as a special gift of God. But this frame of mind, this scrupulosity, prevailed to a very great extent in the earliest age of Christianity, and those who were affected by it were the very last people to look upon it as such. To them it meant holiness, purity, and power. It was only in the case of abstinence from meat that they themselves possibly gave as their reason the fear of polluting themselves with the soul of the animal which they might eat with the meat. However strange it may appear to us, the Jewish custom of eating only the meat of such animals as had been killed in accordance with ritual prescriptions—meat that is entirely without blood— may be traced back to the belief that the blood is the soul or contains the soul. And to eat the souls of other creatures causes a man to be "possessed" by these souls, to be polluted spiritually. So at bottom vegetarianism was at that time based upon the same idea that led men to abstain from eating meat offered to idols and "blood." Wine too, according to ancient ideas, is the dwelling-place of the god of wine, who makes a man to be "full of the god" in intoxication; with this god one is polluted when one quaffs one's wine, and in drinking one becomes his servant. Such are the thoughts which justified asceticism at that time—at present its justification is sought elsewhere: but its real foundation lies in those psychical conditions which we have just examined. For a proof that we have rightly described the thoughts and feelings of that age, we need but turn to the description of John the Baptist in St Luke,[1] and to the account of James the Just in Hegesippus, to which we have already alluded, and which runs as follows: "This man was holy from his mother's womb. He drank no wine nor [other] strong drink, nor did he eat anything that lives [*i.e.* meat]. No razor came upon his head, nor did he anoint himself with oil nor use the bath [his horror of civilisation goes so far that he condones dirt]. He alone was allowed to enter into the temple [at Jerusalem] for he wore no woollen, but linen garments only. And he was wont to go into the temple alone, and used to be found prostrate on his knees, and asking forgiveness for the people, so that his knees grew hard and worn like a camel's, because he was ever kneeling and worshipping God and asking forgiveness for the people." Even if this picture drawn of St James's life does not entirely correspond with reality, it shows us the ideal of the Christian life which prevailed in certain sections, and on what it was founded. Here we have the roots of monasticism.

These ascetic tendencies were neither so pronounced nor so vigorous in Paul's time—neither at Corinth, where they abstained only from meat offered to idols, nor at Rome, where they eat no meat at all—as they came to be in a later age: but they constituted a serious danger for the peace and the unity of the Church. For the ascetics were opposed by just as strong a party which did not intend to be robbed of its freedom. These people took their stand on the right principle that nothing external, no food or drink, can make a man

[1] Luke i. 15.

clean or unclean. But they imagined themselves to be justified thereby not only in calling the others the "weaker brethren," but also in despising them because of their weakness. They felt themselves to be those who "had knowledge," they were "the free." On the other hand, the "weak brethren" were not only "caused to stumble," *i.e.* they did not only run the risk of falling away again from Christianity because it seemed to them to mean licence and to involve fellowship with demons and the souls of brutes, but they "judged" the strong and thereby only made the breach the worse. The weaker brethren were to a certain extent justified, not merely by the beliefs of the age, but also by the fact that the sacrificial feasts were not altogether models of propriety. Their religious scruples were, therefore, fortified by moral considerations. The "strong" naturally wanted to show that they could remain strong in the worst surroundings and amid the severest temptations. It was only in the second century that the danger of a schism in Christianity, in consequence of these two conflicting tendencies, really became urgent. Paul, however, clearly foresaw the danger, and tried to avert it with a firm hand without pressing too hardly upon the people to whom it was due.

As a matter of principle he is on the side of the strong, who have the right knowledge. He knows that there are no gods, and that therefore the meat offered to them is as other meat. In spite of this theory he did of course waver on this point, together with all his contemporaries. The gods and their idols are, he says, nothing, *i.e.* they are impotent spirits. And yet he believed that behind the idols there were the demons to whom the sacrifice was really offered, and with whom one came into contact through the sacrifice. That is why he absolutely forbade participation in the sacrifices themselves—for fear of the demons. But in other respects he had overcome this fear, and in the first Epistle to the Corinthians he quotes the Old Testament passage, "The earth is the Lord's, and all that is in it," to quiet the consciences of those who were afraid of defilement; and in the Epistle to the Romans he has that fine saying, inspired by the true spirit of freedom: "I know and am persuaded in the Lord Jesus that nothing is unclean in itself."[1] Here we have a clear recognition of the new Christian conception of holiness and a distinct expression of our right relation to nature and all the life of nature.

And yet Paul demands the renunciation of this freedom for the sake of the weak. It never entered into his mind that a limit could be drawn here as in the case of the Judaisers. In the course of his argument we come across many sentences that enable us to realise very clearly how deeply pious a man Paul was, and what a fine moral sense he possessed. He even ventured to enunciate the principle that was fraught with so many consequences: "If what I eat makes my brother run the risk of losing his faith, I will never eat meat again." The only demands Paul made upon the weak brethren were that they should not judge uncharitably or consider their brother as lost because he exercised his freedom. Evidently he believed that it would be an easier matter to

[1] Rom. xiv. 14.

get the strong to forego their liberty than to obtain from the weak a gradual expansion into the freedom of the strong.

He bases his demands upon a series of religious thoughts. God is the judge of all Christians. One brother is not to judge the other. Christ alone is our Lord. One brother is not to wish to be lord of another's conscience. But again, let no one put a stumbling-block in the way of another's faith, for Christ died for the believer. You have been bought with a price, you dare not go through the world in light-hearted indifference. And finally: the Kingdom of God, the Christian's foremost care, is more than the question of meat and drink, of enjoyment or asceticism, of vegetarianism or abstinence, it is righteousness and peace and joy in the Holy Ghost.[1]

He supports his argument by moral considerations. Love comes before "knowledge." Knowledge—by itself—puffeth up. Love edifieth, builds up the character of a man and improves his surroundings.[2] He that does not "know that," has no real "knowledge" as yet. True, all things are lawful, but all things are not expedient; it is not everything that edifies. Let no man seek his own good, but that of his neighbour.

There is already a strong ecclesiastical flavour in some of these admonitions. Give none offence, neither to Jews nor Greeks.[3] Have the honour of your church at heart. But as yet the harsh note of ecclesiasticism is softened by the religious accompaniment: It is God's honour which is concerned with your thus living without giving offence,[4] and it

---

[1] Rom. xiv. 17.   [2] 1 Cor. viii. 1 *seq.*
[3] 1 Cor. x. 32.   [4] 1 Cor. x. 31.

is for your brothers' good, that they may not be lost. And above all it is important to notice, in view of the origin of the church, that just as the twelve did in his absence, so now Paul imposes an ecclesiastical regulation concerning food upon his congregations, and so he becomes the originator of an ecclesiastical custom. In doing so he makes no mention of the supposed decree of Jerusalem which, according to Acts xv., was already in existence—a new proof that that chapter does not give us a true account of what actually took place at that conference. Paul regulates his converts' life quite independently. No one is to take part in a sacrificial feast, *i.e.* in the heathen sacrifice itself. But as to the eating of meat in general, he says: "Eat anything that is sold in the meat market without making inquiries [where the meat has come from] 'for conscience' sake' [as the scrupulous say], 'for the earth is the Lord's, and the fulness thereof.' If one who is not a Christian invites you to his house and you care to go, eat all that is put before you without asking questions [as to whether it is meat offered to idols], 'for conscience' sake.' But if anyone should say to you: 'This has been offered in sacrifice to an idol,' then do not eat it, both for the sake of him who calls your attention to the fact [whether he be a heathen who wants to see what you will do, as a Christian, or a weak brother who wants to keep you from sin] and for conscience' sake. I do not mean your own conscience, but that of the other."[1]

In drawing up these regulations, the apostle appears to have been moved by three considerations:

[1] 1 Cor. x. 25–29.

1. The church is to respect the individual's personal convictions. Paul does not wish to pass an Act of Uniformity. No Christian is to be oppressed by any law, he is to have liberty of conscience. But the new law of love is to make a man ready to give up his freedom for the sake of his brother or the church's honour.

2. Paul will have a strong barrier put up against the old religion. There is to be a hard and fast line separating Christians from heathen festivals.

3. But at the same time he wishes to avoid every unnecessary breach, in the case of invitations, *e.g.* and unnecessary talk about the matter, and to enable his converts to enjoy the society of their friends and social intercourse as before. A quiet, peaceable life in the world, that was the thought which inspired Paul's action in the present instance, and it has been the mainspring of much ecclesiastical policy at all times.

Paul's regulations for his church were exceedingly broad and liberal. But unfortunately he failed to see that, just as the Judaisers had done, so now these "weaker brethren" threatened to degrade Christianity to a lower stage of religious development, in which the mark of true Christianity would no longer be the clean heart but "clean food." He did not set himself against the "judging" of the brothers decidedly enough, and his demand for an unconditioned renunciation of freedom for the sake of the weak brother goes too far. In the end it is equivalent to an abandonment of Christianity itself.

One of the most interesting conflicts in the early church centred round this question. The solution arrived at by the church, which was exposed more and more to the ascetic tendencies of imperial Rome, was a very imperfect one. The "weaker brethren" became holy monks, and the "strong" second-rate Christians, who continued to live in the world. After all, the "judging" of the weak has turned out to be stronger in the long run than the strong.

Things were only set right when Luther came.

CHAPTER XVII.

ENTHUSIASM AND APOSTOLICAL WORSHIP.

FAR greater dangers than those which arose from the contrast between the "strong" and the "weak" brethren threatened the young church from the "Holy Ghost" Himself, her founder. The strong, no doubt, ascribed their strength and their freedom to the Holy Ghost, and the weak justified their striving after purity and holiness by the fact that they were called to be His vessels. But the Holy Spirit's chief sphere of action in the eyes of the new converts was divine worship.

Unless he were already familiar with the scene, the visitor to an early Christian service can scarcely fail to have been powerfully affected. He must have been carried away by much that he saw, but much must have struck him as strange and unusual. The people in that bare room, some standing, others on their knees, were evidently deeply stirred. You could see that something was fermenting and working in them—something living that wished to come to the light. You could see that every one of those assembled "had a psalm, a teaching, a revelation, a 'tongue,' an interpretation."[1] And whereof the heart was full the mouth bubbled over in sighs and hallelujahs, in singing and in speaking, in admonition, in consolation, and in prayer. Now and again the scene was one of wildest ecstasy. "They are full of new wine": it was not mockers alone who thus described it.[2] "A stranger would think you were all mad": such is Paul's own comment[3] on an assembly where all spoke with tongues.

Some indeed there are, souls in tune with the mighty hidden forces in man, greater than his conscious life, stronger than inborn feelings of shame and the natural shrinking from open, public profession and confession; such will be deeply moved by the stammering words, the broken exultation, by the amens and hallelujahs which merely inspire others with feelings of mocking and aversion. Paul understood these feelings of antipathy as well, and therefore he warned his congregations not to practise the speaking of tongues too often or in too great numbers; they should rather exercise the gift of prophecy, the gift of inspiring, intelligible speech. Even strangers, and those who entirely lacked miraculous gifts, would be mightily moved and affected by such prophecy if they entered the assembly. Standing there full of expectation, they would listen to the clear and powerful words uttered with the instinctive certainty of men that had suffered and wrestled and yearned, the deepest secrets of their hearts would be laid bare, and then they would fall prostrate and confess, "Truly, God is in you."[4] That was no mere empty phrase. Paul spoke from

[1] 1 Cor. xiv. 26.
[2] Acts ii. 13.
[3] 1 Cor. xiv. 23.
[4] 1 Cor. xiv. 24.

his own experience. Just as certainly as some said, mocking, "They are full of new wine," so others confessed "They are full of God." It is the answer of the human soul to the powerful impressions made by such an early Christian service.

But this mighty enthusiasm, this certain conviction that they were immediate instruments of the Holy Ghost, that they were able to proclaim and to interpret revelations of God, and that irresistible impulse to confession, praise, and prophecy, implied two distinct categories of dangers, caused alike by the contents and the outer form of these services.

The first danger was this, that Christian worship should degenerate into bacchanalian orgies. It was incalculable what would take place in the ecstatic frenzy of the speaking with tongues. Was not Paul obliged to declare expressly, in answer to a question of the Corinthians, that if any one called out "Cursed be Jesus," the Holy Ghost was no longer present, but some demon was at work.[1] If words such as these were uttered, what else cannot have taken place? And that such curses on Jesus can have been pronounced, no one will doubt who knows how, in ecstatic states and in dreams, it is just the subterranean, the forcibly repressed life of the soul, that breaks forth in mighty surges. But even supposing that merely something similar took place, it implied a terrible state of things, and the danger was great enough. Nor were the dangers for the moral life involved in these spiritual gifts less great: hence came vanity and squabbles between those that wanted to speak; hence the exaggerated importance

[1] 1 Cor. xii. 3.

attached to the channels of the religious life, the modes of its manifestation, and the depreciation of simple morality. These are features which are commonly found in all forms of revivalism. Paul's congregations at Corinth and elsewhere formed no exception.

The second category of dangers is connected with the first, only it depends rather on the contents of the new religion. These "perfectionists," the "spiritual" in the special sense, did not only divide the church into parties, but caused Christianity to incur the danger of losing its Founder. Parties began to be formed at Corinth named after Paul, Apollos, and Peter; we have traces of the use of the name of Christ as the watchword of a fourth party.[1]

As the corrective of both dangers, Paul emphasised the supremacy of Jesus. Whoever in an ecstatic state no longer calls Jesus his Master, is possessed by a devil. Whoever divides the body of Christ, making either Paul himself or any other apostle the head of a faction, sins against the Church of God, the body of Christ, the temple of the Holy Ghost: "Know ye not that ye are God's temple, and the Spirit of God dwelleth in you. If anyone destroys the temple of God [through strife or party-faction] him will God destroy. For the temple of God is holy, and that is what you are. . . . Let no one then boast in men, for all things are yours: Paul, Apollos, Kephas, the world, life, death, the present, the future —all are yours, but ye are Christ's, and Christ is God's."[2] Even the apostles, who unite all spiritual gifts in themselves, are but teachers and servants of

[1] 1 Cor. i. 12.   [2] 1 Cor. iii. 16-23.

God's people, they are there for the good of the Church, they are stewards of God's mysteries. But Jesus Christ is much more; He is the foundation of the whole building, the foundation laid once for all that abides for ever.[1] Jesus, the Lord, and the Church of God; these are the two great rocks against which the waves of an enthusiastic "perfectionism," which engulfs all else, shall dash in vain.

In another place the apostle goes beyond the unity of the Church of God and founds his argument on the unity of its great spiritual possessions, in order to show the baselessness of this strife and disorder amongst the possessors of spiritual gifts. "There are diversities of gifts, but there is one and the same Spirit; there are diversities of ministries, but one and the same Lord; there are differences of effects, but one and the same God, who worketh all in all."[2]

And then he sets himself sternly against every form of pride, every kind of boasting about especial gifts. The several limbs in the body of Christ are not to exalt themselves the one above the other, or think little of each other; each is of equal importance, and therefore each is to render its meed of service.

From this he turns to the deepest and tenderest thoughts in the course of his argument against that arrogant reliance on an extraordinary piety, a pretended perfectness. Higher than all the gifts of the Spirit is the highest gift of all—Love. To love he then sings his Song of Songs in the thirteenth chapter. First in sharp contrast with the extraordinary gifts: If I could speak with the tongues of men and of angels, if I had prophecy and faith so that I could

[1] 1 Cor. iii. 5–15.   [2] 1 Cor. xii. 4 *seq.*

remove mountains, if my religious enthusiasm extended to the complete sacrifice of all my goods, even of life itself—and I had not simple, loyal love, it were all nothing. Religion without morality is the most refined form of selfishness known on earth. And then, after contrasting love, Paul describes it with its claims at once small and yet almighty, so that everyone must confess: He that can so love, so bear and endure, so work and rejoice, must really possess the Holy Ghost, that new great power of the soul in all its plentitude. Love must verily be the greatest of all spiritual gifts, for it demands the greatest strength of all in the petty details of daily life. It was of the utmost importance for the Christianity of all ages that Paul was enabled to state this thought and to drive it home so impressively. Religious selfishness can find no foothold in him. Fanaticism and perfectionism are no true children of his. The thirteenth chapter of the first Epistle to the Corinthians is of the highest importance in the history of the Church; it is the Magna Charta of a true Christian Church which shall possess no other creed but active well-doing, and shall know no greater religious power than that of love to God and man. We need not point out how entirely Paul here speaks after the mind of Jesus.

From this standpoint he determined the aims and objects of public worship, and did all he could to further them. All that was said and sung should conduce to edification. By "edification" he does not mean a mystical or æsthetical state of exaltation, but moral growth. He once quite simply calls it by a name which we are not allowed to use in order to describe preaching — instruction.¹ He, the great mystic, who speaks more than they all with tongues, who knows all the transports of ecstasy, and has learned all the raptures of worship—he would rather speak in the assembly five words, with the understanding, than pour forth a whole flood of ecstatic incomprehensibility. Wouldst thou speak with God? —then go into thy chamber. That is the foundation of his personal religion too, though it lacked the childlike purity of Jesus' simple and austere character.

By the side of these moral principles, Paul laid down certain ecclesiastical regulations—the beginnings of a liturgy. They are based upon this thought: that God is a moral being, and therefore a God of order; therefore let everything be done decently and in order.² During a service not more than two or three speakers with tongues are to come forward, and one of them is afterwards to interpret their unintelligible stammering, their singing and their cries of rapture, in plain, clear speech. Of the prophets too only two or three are to speak at once, the others are to sit silent and discern the meaning and value of the prophecies. And that there be no confusion, if, whilst one of the prophets is speaking, another feels driven to speak, the first speaker is to sit down at once and be silent. This rule appears at first sight rather hard and strange, but it is easily explicable, as it was supposed that the same Spirit spoke in all His prophets, and that therefore when He chose a new instrument it was a sign that the first had to cease to play. It might be

[1] 1 Cor. xiv. 19.   [2] 1 Cor. xiv. 32–40.

objected that the speaker who was told to sit down felt that he still had something to say. Paul answers: "The spirits of the prophets, those 'dividings'[1] of the Holy Ghost, are subject to the prophets, and God is a God of order."

This chapter would be incomplete if no mention were made of the Holy Communion, or, as it was then called, the Lord's Supper. It was not excessive enthusiasm which here caused disorder, strife, and jealousy. They were due to the natural passions and the deeply rooted vices of the new Christians. But if we examine the case a little more closely, we shall find that these causes are not mutually exclusive, and that at bottom the same psychical causes produced the same effects. For enthusiasm in itself is no virtue, as Paul observed and stated (1 Cor. xiii.), enthusiasm is sanctified only by the object towards which it is directed. And the apostle had to address the same reproach to the "spiritualists"—who would not serve in love, but wished to be the lords of others and the objects of their admiration—as he had to those who turned the Lord's Supper into a scene of licence and wild disorder. Only that here he speaks far more sternly, for in this case old vices, pride and drunkenness, were displayed much more openly, though perhaps not quite consciously or altogether without excuse.

How was this possible? In order to understand how it came about, we must remember that the Lord's Supper had become a sacramental meal. It had always been a real meal, as the name "supper" indicates, the chief meal of the day, taken towards

[1] Heb. ii. 4.

ENTHUSIASM & APOSTOLICAL WORSHIP 257

evening. But it must have entirely lost the character of a memorial of the death of Jesus at a very early date. The Acts—perhaps it is even a passage from an older document—says that " the bread was broken at home . . . with joy."[1] The words of institution had, in fact, as we have already seen, been so changed by the time of Paul, that they could be repeated without thinking of the death of Jesus. The passage in which Paul speaks of the Lord's Supper is in many respects so important that we must examine it a little more attentively. It runs as follows: " To begin with, I hear that when you meet in assembly, divisions exist among you, and to some extent I believe it; for there must be sects among you in order to test those who are really good. When you meet therefore it is not possible to celebrate a [true] Lord's Supper; for as you eat, each of you makes sure of his own supper first, and so one has too little to eat whilst the other has too much to drink. Why, surely you are not without houses in which you can eat and drink? Or are you trying to show your contempt for the church of God and to put the poor to shame? What shall I say to you? Shall I praise you? In this matter I cannot. *For* I had from the Lord the account which I have handed on to you, that our Lord Jesus, *in the night in which He surrendered Himself to death* [perhaps: when he was betrayed] took a loaf, and after he had given thanks, he broke it and said: 'This is my body which is [intended] for you. Do this in memory of me.' Likewise also the cup after supper with the words: 'This cup is the new covenant in my blood: do this as oft as ye drink

[1] Acts ii. 46.

it in memory of me.' For as often as ye eat this bread and drink this cup you proclaim the Lord's death until He comes [= comes again]. Therefore whosoever eats the bread or drinks the Lord's cup unworthily, is guilty of a sin against the body and blood of the Lord. But let a man examine himself, and then let him eat of the bread and drink of the cup. For those who eat and drink, eat and drink a judgment upon themselves [a judgment of God such as Paul sees in the fact he proceeds to refer to, that some members of his church at Corinth had fallen ill and some had perished] if they do not distinguish the body [from an ordinary meal]."[1]

We see clearly from this passage that Paul had already given the Corinthians the words of institution, and yet they continued celebrating the Supper as though it were a glad festival, without thinking of the death of Jesus. In the words of institution the reference is to the body and blood of the ascended Lord, the heavenly being, in which one mystically participates, and to the new covenant, a member of which one thus becomes. Paul's only reference to the death of Jesus is when he says: " Remember that Jesus uttered these words in the most solemn moment of His life, in the night before His death, therefore your frame of mind should be a serious one." All that comes after the words "the night when He was betrayed" is mere repetition, and no emphasis is laid upon it. Therefore Paul begins again with a " for," which is exactly parallel to the first and has caused the commentators a great deal of trouble, just because they read a reference to the death of Jesus into the

[1] 1 Cor. xi. 28-29.

words of institution, whereas Paul simply says: " I cannot praise you : for (1) Jesus uttered these words in that terrible night . . . ; for (2) in the Lord's Supper you proclaim the death of Jesus."

Now in this passage Paul imparted a new character to the Lord's Supper: it is no longer, or no longer exclusively, the enjoyment of the heavenly food in glad exultation, but a solemn memorial of the death of Jesus and a solemn reception of the holy food. It is in this connection that we should read the notorious sentence about unworthy participation of the Lord's Supper, which, from its mistaken application in confirmation classes and preparation services, has kept away in the past more people from the Lord's Table than all the scepticism in the world. It turned the Holy Communion into " the dreadful sacrifice," something gruesome, something awful, especially for many childlike souls. It is surely high time that the text should be understood in its original simple sense, and that all perverted dogmatic interpretations should be left on one side. The unworthy participation of the Lord's Supper in St Paul's sense is, as is clearly evident from the context, solely and simply that wild licence that had gradually crept in at Corinth, so that the rich and well-to-do did not wait for the poor and the slaves in order to share with them, but eat for themselves, and even went so far as to turn the feast into a senseless orgy, becoming guilty of drunkenness and not distinguishing the Lord's body from an ordinary meal. This is a desecration which the mere change in the form of celebration renders impossible to-day.

It is Paul again who took the first steps which resulted in this change and created the first liturgical forms. For these are the rules which he finally lays down as to the method of celebrating the Lord's Supper: "Therefore, my brothers, when you meet together to eat the Lord's Supper, wait for each other. If a man is hungry, let him eat at home, so that your meetings may not bring a judgment upon you."[1] The Lord's Supper is still a supper, but the supper, the feast, is no longer the most important part: the meaning of the whole ceremony, the solemn words that are spoken, force it into the background.

Here too, therefore, we have our first rubrics by the side of the principles which are to regulate the conduct of divine worship; though, as in the rest of the service, everything is still very vague, and in the future more was required to meet the demand for an orderly and solemn ceremonial. Centuries, however, were still required for the slow development of those great liturgies which are still used in the Roman Catholic Church, of which, after all, the liturgies of our reformed churches are merely more or less successful modifications. But though a long time was needed for the development of a complete liturgy, we find a more or less fixed order of service at a comparatively early date as a counterpoise to the disintegrating tendencies of gnosticism. As early as the year 150, the Christian apologist, Justin Martyr, gives the Roman emperors a description of divine service which he says is widely extended among the Christians. In this we no longer find any trace of the unhampered speech and action of the congregation as distinct from the office-bearers. Every kind

[1] 1 Cor. xi. 33.

of disorder was henceforth guarded against, but the bold trust in the spirit of order had been abandoned. Law and custom reigned supreme again. The heavy cloud of bureaucracy had settled down upon the freest and most spontaneous elements in the Church. Gradually the voice of the Spirit came to be no more heard in divine worship, but gave way, as once before in Judaism, to a holy and venerable liturgy and a sacred book. One little compensation was left for all the rich and varied life that had vanished—the sermon of the priest; and that was but a poor compensation, for it was quite exceptional that the ordination which, in later times, made the priest, imparted the prophet's gift as well. The want of this gift can, it is true, be concealed to a certain extent by practice and training: we can never make up for it entirely. Prophet and priest have always been opposed to each other, and the history of the Christian Church proves no exception to the rule. The priest can only reign where he has killed or gagged the prophet.

Even where, as in our reformed churches, sacerdotalism has been purged out, except for a few insignificant relics, we have not yet recovered the free spontaneous utterance of the heart; save possibly amongst the despised "sects." The minister, the "official," has taken over a great part of the "priest's" work. The "congregation" is for the most part a mere figment of the imagination, for the individual member has been deprived of the rights of a full-grown Christian. Our ecclesiastical polity is sick, not merely because we have not yet entirely rid ourselves of the remnants of the sacramental conception, such as "ordination," the clerical dress, and the ethics which, in part at least, are supposed to go with the dress, but still more because of the spirit of the "official," the ecclesiastical bureaucracy, from which, with the best will in the world, we do not seem to be able to emerge.

THE FOUNDER OF THE CHURCH.

CHAPTER XVIII.

THE FAITH AND THE WORLD.

THE greatest danger finally arose for the young faith and the new fellowship from the innermost essence of its piety. Primitive Christianity is at heart mysticism and apocalyptic: life in God, in Christ, in the Spirit, in the beyond, in the future, not in this present world. From this there arises, if not in every case a revolutionary, yet certainly an anarchical state of mind, a hostility, or at least an absolute contempt for "the world," its goods and its values, its fellowships and organisations. The apocalyptic dreamer has no positive interest in anything in this mundane life; he is eager as zealous missionary, only he wants to conquer the world as missionary of the kingdom that is to come. "For the time that remains to us is short; meanwhile, let those who have wives live as though they had none; those that weep, as though they wept not; those that rejoice, as though they rejoiced not. Whoever buys anything, let him do so with the conviction that it will not long be his; those who use the world, as using it sparingly. For the fashion of this world is passing away."[1]

[1] 1 Cor. vii. 29.

With the sure instinct of self-preservation, the Roman State opposed itself to the anarchy of the new religion, which found a plain symbolical expression in the refusal to adore the emperor. He who would feel the full glow of the anarchical hopes of primitive Christianity, must read the first sacred book this religion produced, the Revelation of John, the book that once registered the pulse of Christian piety, that is nowadays obsolete and forgotten in the Church, that has become the book of interpretation of dreams to the sectarian and an eagerly handled subject of learned research. Let us steep ourselves in the marvellous imagery in which this book contrasts the State and the young faith with each other: Yonder the beast that has power over tribes and peoples and tongues and nations, worshipped by the whole world and marking the whole world in forehead and hand with its mark—and here the Lamb on the Mount Zion, with the hundred and forty and four thousand sealed, guileless souls, who know no lie, virgins who have not defiled themselves with women; there, the earth from Asia to Rome strewn with the bleeding bodies of the enemies of God—here, the heavenly Jerusalem with its golden streets and gates of pearl, where the saints walk in blissful peace. And their God shall be their light.

Christianity was all one huge rebellion against the State—the State of antiquity, the Roman State; it was an anarchy of opinion. Down-trodden humanity voiced itself in Christianity with an appeal for deliverance from this State, its wars, and its law. We must not make a mistake here. Learned opinion is entirely right in attributing such apocalyptic notions to Jewish inheritance, but we must not misunderstand or underrate the real though hidden foundation of these very ideas. Because life under the State drove men to desperation, they became anarchists; and because they were respectable people, because their criticism of the "world," *i.e.* the State, had its origin in their love for the suffering, they did not become anarchists in outward deed, anarchists of terrorism, but anarchists of faith and hope—apocalyptic anarchists. The State was to die. . . .

And the State must needs die, if even the bare principles of the apostle were to be maintained: not to marry any longer, not to go to law, because they were above the law.[1] . . . It is the same passive attitude to which Tatian in the second century, in his "speech to the Greeks" (11), has thus given a typical expression: " I will not rule; I do not wish to get rich; I disdain to be an official functionary; I have learned to hate unchastity, I am no pirate, I take no trouble in striving for a crown, I have put away the thirst for glory; death I despise, I feel superior to every sort of infirmity, grief does not agitate my soul." On the rock of such an attitude, when it persists unto martyrdom and is sincere, the State must needs be wrecked as soon as it succeeds in seizing the majority of its citizens. Tolstoy has quite rightly seen this, just as the Roman emperors and functionaries were conscious of it.

But all anarchy wrecks itself. The force of organisation is invariably the stronger of the two; it will break anarchy sooner than anarchy will break it. For in the long run, anarchy either ends

[1] 1 Cor. vii. 1; vi. 1–11.

in martyrdom or it persists beyond martyrdom and unto revolution—and in open fight it is always the weaker. Moreover, man's need of marriage and the family, and need of protection for these by a superior power—a need that created the State in the first instance—is so ineradicable, that no cloistral faith and no loathing of its abuse can ever rid the world of it.

How far primitive Christianity may have actively worked in its radical negation of things as they were, we can now no longer grasp completely, as these tendencies are known to us only vaguely through the descriptions and the measures of their opponents. Among these Paul stands in the front rank. With his unerring perception of the powers in humanity that make for life and moral value, in spite of all his radicalism in principle, he combated these manifold currents keenly and openly, as they threatened to end by destroying the very life of the community.

But the presence of the heathen world, into which the young religion found its way, was yet another factor that made for the opposite influence. This world did not alone provoke a radical opposition, but effected also a gradual accommodating of the new religion to the habits, standards, and aims that had hitherto been prevalent. However much the converts might feel themselves to be new creatures, they still bore very evident traces of the old Adam about with them; and not only did they look for their sacraments and their redemption in the new religion, but their former habits of other kinds, and their pre-Christian justice or morality, was for ever

THE FAITH AND THE WORLD 267

bringing their new life into the danger of becoming lax and inert.

In a survey of the various departments of social life and of the measures promoted therein by Paul, we shall constantly meet with the same underlying convictions upon which the apostle's organisation rested.

The foundation of all social life—marriage—was regarded by Paul, in accordance with the ascetic tendencies of his day, if not as something to be absolutely rejected, yet certainly as of secondary importance. "It is good for a man not to touch a woman."[1] It was not only the expectation of the approaching end of the age, and his belief that those who married would have trouble in the flesh in the time of suffering close at hand,[2] that impelled him to this general sentence. No; he looks on marriage in general only from the sexual point of view, and admits that "because of fornication," *i.e.* in order to avoid it, each man shall have his own wife and each wife her own husband.[3] With him there is no intrinsic appreciation of marriage. Still, he was sternly and decidedly opposed to every extravagance of asceticism, particularly to all *tours de force*, such as were already beginning to be practised in Christendom.

Thus in the first place he strongly advised all those who were trying to live ascetically, but who did not possess the special gift of grace which Paul was enabled to attribute to himself in this matter,[4] and were "burning" in abstinence — rather to marry

[1] 1 Cor. vii. 1.   [2] 1 Cor. vii. 26-28.
[3] 1 Cor. vii. 2.   [4] 1 Cor. vii. 7.

than to continue the exhausting struggle and so perhaps fall into immorality from very exaggeration of self-control. Such a danger was indeed specially imminent, in cases where the trial of strength in sexual abstinence had already begun with the sham marriage. The rather vague passage, 1 Cor. vii. 36-8, appears to point to the fact that such trials of strength, which were of quite common occurrence later, were already known to the apostolic age: young men lived together with virgins in the most intimate intercourse, yet without all sexual enjoyment, trying thereby to put to the proof the strength of their morality and to tread Satan under foot. Paul attempted to avert the perils of such unions, not by enforcing the commandment, but by permitting marriage. Yet he never for one moment withheld his opinion, that to lead the chaste life in companionship was the higher thing, and that marriage was only a makeshift; in such a sense marriage was "good," but the other life was "better."[1]

Things were in a similar state in cases of already contracted marriage. Here ascetic tendencies urged people to turn the marriages into such as were not really consummated, and consequently either the same dangers arose, only in lesser degree, *i.e.*, without the risk of public scandal, or strife and hatred were engendered where perhaps only one of the contracted couple had adopted such ascetic views. It was for these reasons that Paul conceded the ascetic life in marriage for a season only,[2] and only with mutual amicable consent, and that he granted one consort a moral claim on the other.[3] The conditions were

[1] 1 Cor. vii. 38.   [2] 1 Cor. vii. 5.   [3] 1 Cor. vii. 3 *seq.*

rather different in mixed marriage, but Paul applied the same point of view to them. He simply forbids the Christian consort to divorce. And yet there were abundant religious scruples. Could that most intimate communion in which the two become "one body," as Paul says also,[1] be allowed to subsist with a person over whom the demons had power? Must not the Christian contract "defilement," must not saints become "unclean" through intercourse with the "unclean"? It is only necessary to recall to mind how strong these ancient animistic associations of holiness in sacrifice and sacrament still were, in order to enter fully into the horror which the Christian consort might feel for the unchristian. Paul's attack is based on these feelings, and on the natural love to one's children, and not on the thought of loyal love: "If any brother hath an unbelieving wife, and she is content to dwell with him, let him not leave her. And likewise, if the woman hath an unbelieving husband, and he is content to dwell with her, let her not leave him. For the unbelieving husband is sanctified in the wife, and the unbelieving wife is sanctified in the brother; else were your children unclean, and now are they holy."[2] Here Paul states that the power of the holy is greater than the power of the unclean, both terms being understood in the sense of natural holiness—as men believed in pre-Christian religions. But this basis of his opinion was not, after all, the real motive that moved him to command continuance in the marriage state as a duty, for then indeed it would have been tantamount to an approval of mixed

[1] 1 Cor. vi. 16.   [2] 1 Cor. vii. 12 *seq.*

marriages generally. This approval, however, Paul withheld: a widow may marry "only in the Lord,"[1] *i.e.* a believer. Moreover, he commanded the Christian consort to yield instant assent to a divorce proposal from the unbeliever; he did this even in opposition to the justifiable missionary zeal of the Christian consort, who might still be hoping to win the other for the new faith. And here we get at last to the ultimate reason upon which all his counsels rest. If the unbeliever wishes to separate, let him or her do so. The brother or sister, *i.e.*, believers, are not bound in such a case; God has called us that we should live in peace. "How do you know, O wife, if you will save your husband? or how do you know, O husband, if you will save your wife?" In fact it is only when we have recognised his need of peace and quietness, of a peaceable accommodation to the world with all possible avoidance of strife and open conflict—a moral need, but still more an ecclesiastical necessity—it is only when we have recognised all this, I say, that we have the key to the inner harmony of the commandments of this first Christian legislator. And we are amazed to find that the very man who is hoping so ardently for the end of the age, is able to fit himself to that age so diplomatically. Yet very likely—and in this we judge from the general tone of all the apostle's letters — very likely his ground motive was not worldly wisdom at all, but rather scorn of the world, a feeling that it was not worth the trouble to enter the lists for such reasons. The progress of the enemy was precisely furthered by this attitude of indifference;

---

[1] 1 Cor. vii. 39.

it is an experience we have only too much occasion to verify.

In his effort to maintain " peace," Paul finally went so far in this matter as even to put on one side the Master's words which forbade all divorce. Just as Matthew, yielding to a "human" impulse, afterwards added to the Master's prohibition the further words, "except it be for adultery," so Paul, with a still greater indulgence for the weakness of his church members or for their ascetic leanings, not only tolerated divorce where the separating consort was an unbeliever, but in fact merely required that those who were separated should remain unmarried.[1] This concession also was granted, as we can readily understand, in the interests of " peace." Jesus made His appeal with a bold confidence in two hard hearts who might fancy they could not agree, demanding from them repentance and love. And so the transcendent morality of Jesus already becomes in Paul possible ecclesiastical custom, and a practicable ecclesiastical law.

Only later did the Church, again under the pressure of strong ascetic and legal tendencies, bring forward and carry through Jesus' prohibition of divorce. But, in turning this from a moral claim into a law of ecclesiastical right, the Church committed herself to the greatest of falsehoods. For since, in as far as she is the Church, *i.e.* a compromise, she is constantly obliged to allow for the "hardness of your hearts,"[2] so she is also committed to the untruth of declaring invalid, *i.e.* never truly contracted, any marriage whose divorce seems to her to be necessary on social,

[1] 1 Cor. vii. 10 *seq.*   [2] Mark x. 5.

ecclesiastical, or moral grounds. And thereby the Church has plunged marriage into a monstrous insecurity, however high a value she may pretend to put upon it as a sacrament; for no one can be assured of the validity of a marriage, *i.e.* sure of the sacramental consecration of the marriage in this church which, whenever it seems good to her, can not divorce, but declare the marriage never to have been contracted. Here, as everywhere else in matters of ecclesiastical law, we need a radical change. Ecclesiastical law is all made up of one big lie—for it affects to enforce and protect morality by means of legislation and thus confounds the two, while legislation and Christian morals stand on opposite planes. It is one of the supremest deserts of the Reformation at the hands of humanity, that it recognised this truth.

Jesus claimed from His disciples renunciation of their rights in regard to worldly possessions: " If any man would go to law with thee and take away thy tunic, let him have thy cloak also,"—as well as with regard to their honour: " Whosoever smiteth thee on thy right cheek, turn to him the other also." A commandment which in its consequences would lift the whole "world" out of its hinges, for the world up to now has enough to do with the preliminary process of securing and protecting man in his rights. Already in Corinth Paul had to struggle with the old-established legal instincts, although the waves of enthusiasm beat high: lawsuits about meum and tuum were already afoot between members of the Chnrch. Paul here certainly did in theory uphold the standpoint of Jesus, but he did so in the same attenuated form which our contemporary preachers

THE FAITH AND THE WORLD 273

also use: "Nay, already it is altogether a defect in you that ye have lawsuits one with another. Why not rather let yourselves be wronged? Why not rather be defrauded? Instead of this you wrong and defraud others yourselves—yes, even 'brothers!'"[1] Yet we almost see the apostle's significant shrug, we almost hear his big "But!" and we understand his consideration for their human "weakness" with which he refrains from demanding a renunciation of their rights seriously and with a firm regard for principle. Here again he is the great founder of the Church: "Yes, *even* brothers!" and he merely bids Christians not to go to law "before the *heathen*"—and bids them be their own judges. They, so soon to judge angels, how should they not be able to decide between meum and tuum![2] To him the worst of all is this, and this must be set right at once: the infringement of the honour of the Church: "Brother goeth to law with brothers, *and that before unbelievers!*"[3] We understand the apostle, the motives of his concession, and his "at the very least," very well. But in here adapting himself again to circumstances, he lays the foundation on which later that huge monument of ecclesiastical law, with all its marvellously fine ramifications, was built, which conjured up all those countless conflicts between State and Church, in which the two contending parties were not morality and law, but one law against another. And one of these laws coming forward with the claim of the Eternal and the Divine, must perforce stand in far more startling contrast to morality than merely "worldly" law, which latter very slowly indeed, but

[1] 1 Cor. vi. 7 *seq*.   [2] 1 Cor. vi. 1-5.   [3] 1 Cor. vi. 6.

still surely, follows the development of morality and allows itself to be transformed by it just because it can always remain conscious of its human limitations and incompleteness, its ministerial character.

Midway between legislation and the social question stood the problems of the emancipation of slaves and the emancipation of woman. The later centuries before Christ were in Greece and Italy filled with party struggles, which took the shape of fierce revolts among the enslaved classes and the proletariat. Social, democratic, revolutionary, and anarchical tendencies, the outcome of economic depression, made themselves universally felt and prepared the ground for the approaching religions of deliverance, more especially too for Christianity, with its mighty social activities—which latter, however, had their source in no motives of modern spread of culture, but rather in contempt of the world. And it is precisely from this same source that the peculiar passive position of the young religion springs—above all, that of its great apostle—in the face of these problems.

Within the congregation indeed, in as far as it regarded itself from a religious point of view, there was "neither Jew nor Greek, neither bond nor free, no male and female; all are one in Christ."[1] The ecclesia is *one being, one body*. And these were not hollow words, as they have since become to our ears. Paul addresses a very sharp reproof to the rich people in Corinth, who kept themselves aloof at the eating of the Lord's Supper, finishing their portion rapidly, before the poor and the slaves could arrive from their daily work.[2] "Despise ye the church of God, or

[1] Gal. iii. 28.   [2] 1 Cor. xi. 22.

will ye put to shame them that have nothing!" Here in very deed all were equal, all were brothers.

But again, if you were about to deduce a revolutionary claim from such a faith, Paul sternly cut short such radicalism with the words: " Let each man abide in that calling wherein he was called."[1] Not for one moment did or would Paul ever represent to himself the position of moral and religious danger in which the slave found himself. Like the Stoics he declared, a slave was after the inner man— in his language, in Christ—free: as if this were true in fact, and not in very many cases a mere self-deception! For the slave was really after all a thing without any will of his own, whose conscience was simply his master's conscience, who did what he was told.

Clearly as we can everywhere trace a radical socialistic revolutionary party in the first centuries of Christianity who aimed at freedom for the slave, it is admirable to observe how the men of the early church invariably managed to prevent the monstrous contrast between the religious standing of the slave and his actual position, from coming to complete manifestation in an open rebellion. We can only understand this if we take into account the enthusiasm which lay in the renunciation of "this world." The proletariat had left off hoping for anything from political revolution and social struggles: their souls were wholly fixed on the inward life. They had learned, the greatest foe to their happiness lay hidden in their own hearts, and all their earthly desires were swallowed up in the blissful satisfaction of his defeat.

[1] 1 Cor. vii. 24.

It was an easier fight for the position of woman. Here too Paul's attitude was very conciliatory, and he really tried to make his words, "here is no male nor female," a fact for his congregation. He permitted women, as they wished, to speak in church, to pray and to prophesy, when the Spirit came upon them; only in so doing they might not lay aside the thick veil which concealed the face entirely. The reasons adduced for this are of a quite peculiar kind. His real reason was a matter of feeling—it appeared to him unseemly for a woman to take off her veil;[1] and probably besides this, he dreaded calumnious reports about the church assemblies, such as became the vogue at a later date. But the reason which he reproduces from the Scriptural account of creation, namely, that the woman who unveils dishonours her head, her husband for whom she was created[2]—and the other reason, "because of the angels," probably in order not to be a temptation for them, or not to risk falling a prey to their "authority," she was to wear "authority" or a counter-charm on her head[3]—all this, with its rabbinical flavour, makes a very singular impression. And Paul was apparently himself conscious that his feeling had more to do with this than his logic, and thus in conclusion he cuts short every objection with abrupt reprimand; "We have no such custom, nor have the churches of God."[4]

But when, in another passage of the same epistle, we meet with the categorical prohibition: "As in all the assemblies of the saints, so too with you, let

[1] 1 Cor. xi. 5.
[2] 1 Cor. xi. 7 f.
[3] 1 Cor. xi. 10 *seq.*
[4] 1 Cor. xi. 16.

THE FAITH AND THE WORLD 277

the women keep silence,"[1] we may perhaps assume interpolation by a later hand, and have not to attempt an artificial harmony between this blunt pronouncement and its opposite a few chapters earlier. We must not be surprised at such later additions. For we know that throughout subsequent centuries an embittered fight was fought all over Christendom about the right of woman to speak in public worship. And the ecclesiastics who, for peace' sake and to avoid all evil reputation, continually diminished the woman's religious equality, and in thus subordinating her lowered themselves again to the "world's" level—were not afraid either of calumniating their enemies or of applying "emendations" to ancient Scriptures. Both these things they did with an easy conscience: for the heretics "must needs" be wicked people, and the holy apostles "could" not have written with such freedom—such was and is a naïve ecclesiastical belief. Precisely in reference to the woman's question we have a drastic example of this in the two different texts of the book of the Acts. According to one tradition, wherever the couple Priscilla and Aquilas appear, it is always the wife who comes prominently forward as the real motive power, while the other account places her completely in the shadow of her husband. Thus the addition in 1 Cor. xiv. is quite comprehensible, as also the first Epistle to Timothy, written indeed under the apostle's name but in reality belonging to a much later period, which states roundly: "I permit not a woman to teach!"[2] Around the State itself the waves of radical enthusi-

[1] 1 Cor. xiv. 34.   [2] 1 Tim. ii. 12.

asm likewise surged high. The most ardent hope was, we know, that the State, the Roman dominion, might pass away and God's Kingdom come, that the king in Rome might be thrust from his throne and the King of Kings, "Our Lord," come at length to take unto Himself the power and the kingdom and the glory: it belonged in truth to Him, and not to the devilish usurper, the beast from the pit. The struggle with a radical tendency that was ready to help on the tardy arm of God, is to be traced throughout the whole of primitive Christian literature. To mention only one or two examples: Matthew makes Jesus say: "Put up thy sword into the sheath, for all they that take the sword shall perish with the sword."[1] Prayer for the emperor is constantly being enforced, and in St Clement's first letter one such prayer is preserved for us, full of subtle reminder that it is God who gave the emperors their authority, and full of fervent petition for insight and goodness to be granted to the representatives of this authority. Paul's detailed discussion in the celebrated thirteenth chapter of the Epistle to the Romans is to be placed under the illumination of the above-mentioned passages. The vehement manner in which Paul here places the "higher powers" under the protection and authority of God, indicates plainly, that more than one radical tendency and opinion lay below the surface and might grow dangerous. We have already seen that Paul indeed, with his nation, believed that all the powers—the angels as the guardians of men, and their representatives on earth — were ordained by God; but he

[1] Matt. xxvi. 52.

THE FAITH AND THE WORLD   279

believed no less that these angels meantime had fallen away and ensnared the nations in ignorance, angel-worship, and immorality.[1] Have they not plainly proved their nature, become hostile to God by crucifying the Lord of Glory? But in Rom. xiii., just as if nothing had happened, Paul refers to their appointment by God, and clings to the remnants of their administrative activity in order to prove their divine nature: the sword of judgment! And a few years later this same sword of judgment had been directed against himself! Was it indeed a power "that was a terror to the evil work only"[2] of which one could say: "Do that which is good, and thou shalt have praise"? And what is it the apostle demands? "Custom and tribute, fear and honour."[3] It is clear, that if Paul has to support these elementary demands by such strong and express exaltation of the "authority," there must have been a strong opposition and negation. For the same reason that led Luther into such violent invective against the peasants, Paul used the strong expressions which in times of reaction have always been supposed to justify the doctrine of the limited intelligence of the subject: his object was to keep the cause of religion and the revolution, social and political, distinctly apart from each other. It is fear that thus loses sight of all proportion in distributing praise.

No words in the New Testament admit of less immediate application to the needs of our own day than the passages concerning the Roman State. Wherever to-day the preacher implies that Rom. xiii. is a valid

[1] 1 Cor. ii. 6–8; Gal. iv. 9; Rom. i. 21 *seq.*
[2] Rom. xiii. 3.   [3] Rom. xiii. 7.

pronouncement for all time on the Christian's relation to the State, he has misunderstood the difference in the position of the world entirely. And the Scripture lesson that still has these verses recited by heart as if they had a present-day application—is a mere gerund grinding. A " Christian power " and a power in which all citizens have a share, as is the case in every constitutional state, must judge itself according to quite different standards from the words with which Paul made a heathen government—one entirely beyond their influence—acceptable to his congregations.

Marriage and the State—the foundations of all social life — threatened dissolution in the fiery radical enthusiasm of the new religion; even the organisation of labour was broken up by it. If the end of the age was at hand, why, then! all labour was superfluous that was not saving of souls. True, the announcement of the world's end has never yet in the history of the world spread over the whole of a civilised community in a manner sufficient to entail famine and death as results. Only an isolated few have hitherto let their enthusiasm thus degenerate. And here is exactly the greatest danger for the moral life of these isolated few, however noble their enthusiasm may be. It was so too in Thessalonica, where men had drawn the natural conclusions from the announcement of the approaching end. A dreamy laziness crept in, that could not exist for long without forcing Christians who, to begin with, were not rich, into downright beggary. In Jerusalem the enthusiasm that gave up everything had already impoverished the congregation and obliged them to sue for help from Gentile brothers. When the same danger began to threaten in Thessalonica, Paul had preached against it energetically, although indeed in very tender words of praise: "Concerning love of the brethren, ye have no need that one write unto you: for you yourselves are taught of God to love one another, and ye indeed do prove it toward all the brethren, who are in Macedonia. But we exhort you, brethren, that ye abound more and more, and that ye study to be quiet and to do your own business, and to work with your hands even as we charged you; that ye may walk honestly toward them that are without, and may have need of nothing."[1]

We see, even such a noble and high commandment of enthusiasm as Jesus gave: Go ye and sell what ye have, and give to the poor! could not maintain the Church. Give and give up—yes, but within the limits of one's work and calling as a citizen. Thus Paul had to interpret Jesus. "And if I give all my goods to feed the poor, and have not love"—in the case of this experience too the road of morality leads from enthusiasm to the Church. And here again Paul appeals to church honour: "honestly toward them that are without."

In every direction in which the Church has developed itself out of the high unworldly gospel—we find Paul. With tremendous energy he tried to stem the rising tide of the very enthusiasm he had himself let loose, opposing himself fearlessly to the apparent or actual consequences of the young religion, in order to save it from perishing in a revolution.

Everywhere there is the same energetic moral will, a clear appreciation of the danger of religion to

[1] 1 Thess. iv. 9-12.

morality, a clear perception also of the danger of the new morality itself, in its immediate entrance into a world so alien to it, an unwearying patience that tries to further peace and kindness, a strenuous life and growth in the world, so that all great catastrophes may be averted as long as possible. And withal the apostle does not want to make a sharp line of separation from the world for his churches, and thus risk strife and anger which might arise as a consequence. When the Corinthians have misunderstood in this sense some expression of the apostle in a letter to them, which we no longer possess, he explains himself with absolute clearness: "I told you in my letter not to associate with immoral persons. I did not exactly refer to men of the world who are immoral, or who are covetous and grasping, or who worship idols—for then you must needs go out of the world altogether."[1]

Yet this morality—grave and reasonable, pure and kind as it is—is already beginning to accommodate itself to the world. Everywhere angles are rounded which might have given occasion for conflict. Paul certainly does not want to surrender any particle of the gravity of the Christian ideal, yet, as far as we know, he is the first to practise with worldly-wise shrewdness the delicate art of policy, the art of "the possible." He knew he must make concessions to his churches, that he could not lay down as law for all alike the Absolute that he required from himself: he was more pedagogical than Jesus. But with that he took the first steps on the road that leads in the end to the Church: which is as much as to say that

[1] 1 Cor. v. 9 *seq.*

THE FAITH AND THE WORLD 283

he indirectly revived the very "world" that both Jesus and he had discarded, he decorated the powers of antiquity with Christian emblems: at best it was an alloy of antiquity and Christianity.

Certainly the Church itself was what saved religion. The new manhood which Jesus perceived and incarnated could not at once prevail wholly and entirely; it was necessary that a milder environment, made up of elements from the old world and the new life, should first be formed—that then in it real Christianity, the religion of Jesus, might become a vital force.

Without this milder environment the young life must in each case have fallen a prey to a speedy death, just as did its prototype. But the Church is nothing more than this slightly modified world, this milder form of the ancient order of things.

Luther felt this deeply, when he had rediscovered the central point of Christian religion. It was his point of departure when he began to demolish the Church; he held that the world was sufficiently Christian for him to entrust much, yea, everything, to it. But the makeshift churches which originated in Reformation times are in many respects a still poorer compromise between antique morality, Roman law, and the spirit of Jesus; and the Christianity of the Reformation churches seeks and gropes its way darkly to a new fashion of overcoming the world, after having laid aside the church forms. Many people who have settled down into the makeshift tabernacles that date from those Reformation days, still imagine everything is right and plain. But at the present moment the knowledge is everywhere awakening that this is not true. And so many are standing at their narrow windows and gazing yearningly back across the years at the towering old cathedral church in which our fathers found rest to their souls, and are thinking within themselves, "If only we could retrace the way, or if only we might build as well!" But others, who are fired by the ardour of youth that burned in the soul of Jesus, have dreams of future days when men will worship God in spirit and in truth, days when "the world" itself will have come to nought, when we shall make no more pacts with her and no longer sacrifice our best and highest possessions for the sake of peace and quietness—when it will be possible to recognise on every countenance the clear reflection of the divine sonship, of the new manhood, when there will be no more church, but a Kingdom of God upon earth.

He indeed whose heart is as full of golden visions for his fellows as were once the hearts of Jesus and of Paul—such a one will not let himself become a dreamer merely, but he must be a worker. The new way upwards must be sought in slow and painful labours and in many individual resolves. This was the way Paul was seeking when he took the first deliberate steps towards the Church.

And here one thing is necessary above all else: there must be no disguisement of the aim. Christianity did not come in order to bolster up old relics and obsolete ways of salvation. It is the message of the redeeming love of God and of men, it does not exist in order to "hand the sword to authority," or to wage "righteous" war, or to establish church rights, or to tolerate everything, and put up with everything that was ever good and great in the world before. If we cannot yet do away with all that contradicts Christianity, because that would mean a widening of men's wounds and not a healing, yet we must not study the evil art of making a good thing out of a bad one. Human life is no child's play and no bed of ease; and he who dares not take guilt upon himself, let him vegetate. But to call the guilt of humanity and its hard-heartedness *good*, to call those things Christian to destroy which Jesus laid down His life—this is blindness or a lie. And these two things have never been life-giving; but a sense of guilt and an upward, striving will—this creates life!

THE THEOLOGIAN.

CHAPTER XIX.

The Beginning of Dogma. Justification by Faith.

The life which Paul the prophet experienced, which the missionary spread abroad and the founder of the Church fostered, that the teacher cast into a definite mould; and out of this complex whole he created a doctrinal system which, from that day to this, has exercised a decisive influence on the thought of the Church. So decisive has this influence been, that former generations have looked upon the great apostle and ecclesiastical organiser merely from the point of view of his teaching, even of his dogmatic system. And yet one might almost as well envisage Frederick the Great merely as an historian. But modern realistic theology has worked a beneficial change. It has freed itself from the superstition that the succession of theological systems forms the history of the Church. It has left the stifling atmosphere of the study. It looks upon a great man in the light of his holy life with God and his ethical influence on his fellows: and so it has found the right criterium for the apostle's true greatness; that still abides

THE BEGINNING OF DOGMA

even though we no longer feel ourselves at home in his doctrinal system.

There are three reasons why St Paul's teaching has dominated the whole of Christian dogmatics and still dominates it, in its outlines at least, with the exception of Schleiermacher's system. First, there is a perfectly simple external reason: the Epistle to the Romans is the only portion in all the sacred Scriptures of the Christian faith which contains a summary, a compendium of Christian teaching. It is of course only in appearance that it does so, and we are compelled to abandon this belief when we examine the letter a little more attentively: it is in reality an apology for the apostle's missionary preaching. But there is at first sight something that looks like a regular dogmatical system. The letter does in reality treat of man's creation and destination, of his fall and his redemption, of his new life, and of the end of all things, the final consummation. And that is the scheme which the Church teaches and which we all of us have learnt.

There was another reason, however, why not merely the form, but the contents of the teaching, exercised so widespread an influence in the early ages of the Church. These ideas were in a great measure not Paul's peculiar property at all, but Saul's inheritance. They were a complex of thoughts characteristic of the Hellenistic age, thoughts which had been germinating in the heads of thousands, and not of Jesus alone. In Greece and Italy too, men believed in paradise and hell, in God and the demons, in rites and sacraments. In the first part of this book we have seen how great the inheritance was. We have traces of this Jewish-Hellenistic inheritance in Christian dogmas of all ages, and in spite of all advance in historical knowledge, there are still people who look upon this inheritance as that which is really Christian in Christianity, just because they cannot forget their dogmatics.

However great the influence of this inheritance, it does not diminish the importance of the third of our reasons. The effect of Paulinism was great, because Paul was really a great theologian. Not that you can compare him to a subtle book, or that he was a learned scholar. His theology does not form a systematic whole, nor was it devised in order to present a systematic unity in the conception of the universe. It is apologetic, a defence of his religious experience against the attacks of new doubts and ancient sanctities. But has not all "true theology" at all times been apologetic in the end? Has it not been an attempt to harmonise religious experience with the ideas and conceptions of the age? That is why theology is something ever new. Nor can progress in theology ever be arrested, either by subscription to articles or by an ecclesiastical censorship. And that is why Paul was a great theologian. He was not only a keen and practised thinker, but the centre of his theology was that point which ought to be the centre of all theology—personal religious experience,—its purpose being to defend this experience against destructive criticism and to clarify one's thoughts. For this purpose Paul employed the means with which his old theology supplied him, in the shape of juridical conceptions and biblical passages. It was the "Spirit" that told him that he was a child and an inheritor of God, the Spirit that cried " Abba, Father," within him. But men are never content with the subjective proof. They want conceptions, conclusions, theories, and texts.

In attempting to give a sketch of the principal features of the apostle's theology, we begin therefore by leaving on one side all that was not Paul's theology, but merely a part of the contemporary conception of the universe, as well as all that belonged to the common body of Christian or Jewish missionary preaching. Our concern is with such of the ideas of this first theologian as were peculiar to himself. And firstly, the doctrine of justification by faith, which forms the core and centre of his theology even though not in that isolation in which it has become the "material cause of Protestantism."

Justification by Faith and the Descent from Abraham.

The fundamental question of religion is: What must I do to be saved? Paul's theology starts from this question. It works at first with the presuppositions which Saul inherited. As to what constituted the everlasting blessedness, the Christian and the Jew thought alike, or at most the Christian added to the traditional blessings—salvation from God's wrath, peace with God, the glory of Heaven and everlasting life,[1] this new one "to be with Christ."[2] It cannot of course be decided how much sentiment lies in this word and how much of the old hope in the Messianic glory. But it is a new element and one that might well become the outer vehicle of an inward and

[1] Rom. v. 3, 9, 18; i. 16, etc.   [2] Phil. i. 23; 1 Thess. iv. 17.

spiritual faith. Now Paul still knows, as did Saul before him, two roads whereby to attain to this salvation: the descent from Abraham and "righteousness."

The promises belong to all the children of Abraham. Such was the national faith inherited from early days, a faith against which the prophets are never weary of declaiming: "Are ye not as children of the Ethiopian unto me?" Such the bitter question Amos had once put in his God's lips: "God is able of these stones to raise up children unto Abraham," so the last of the prophets, John the Baptist, had again exclaimed. Not birth, but one's own righteousness,[1] that was the answer given by the legal religion of Israel, shaped by the influence of the prophets. On the day of judgment God will examine the deeds of every man, and will either "set him forth as righteous," *i.e.* acquit him if his deeds are good, or even if the sum of his good deeds exceeds that of the bad, or God will declare him guilty if he deserves it. This is "justification." The word "justification" has become an almost unintelligible formula. We can best understand it if we always substitute for it some such word as "acquittal." For that word suggests to us, as did the Hebrew "Hisdîq" to the Jews, the heavenly court of justice in which God passes sentence. The Jew then thinks of a future verdict of the Supreme Judge. Paul too employs the word fairly frequently with reference to the future.

The two roads to salvation are therefore descent from Abraham and justification. It is on the latter

[1] Rom. x. 3.

JUSTIFICATION BY FAITH

that Paul's theology starts, for it was the thought of righteousness that had filled the mind of the Pharisee, the strict believer in the law, not the natural ideal of the divine childhood. Now the experience of his life showed him that the road of righteousness was an impossible one. No one can acquire so much righteousness of his own as to be quite sure of God's acquittal. Rather all men are sinners, Gentiles as well as Jews, and both are condemned by the law itself, the former by the law which is written in their own hearts, the latter by the detailed written laws of Moses. All are sinners, and all therefore come short of the heavenly glory of God.[1] Such are the main contents of the first part of the Epistle to the Romans, i. 18, iii. 20. There is no righteous man; no, not one.[2] Neither amongst the Gentiles nor among the children of Abraham. All alike deserve to go to hell.

Then God determined to grant righteousness "freely," to acquit men even without the works of the law, in spite of their sins. For this purpose He sent His Son, the heavenly Christ, not, as the Jews imagine, to be a great earthly king who will conquer all the heathen, but to become a man, a Jew, and to be crucified. Why that was necessary, why God could not at once acquit sinners and grant them salvation, is to be explained later. We here turn back to the first series of thoughts, which treats not of God but of men, but which we had to leave, following exactly in Paul's steps (Rom. iii. 21). Thus over against man's righteousness, to which the Jews hoped to attain through the law, but in vain, God

---

[1] Rom. iii. 23.   [2] Rom. iii. 10.

set the divine righteousness which He "gives," bestows as a present, which assures man of His "grace" (grace is χάρις, and to bestow as a present is χαρίζεσθαι), Rom. iii. 21–24. Of course this righteousness which God grants is not that of which mention was made first. Paul has changed the original conception into its exact opposite. It is just those that are not righteous that God calls righteous and acquits, and it is sinners whom He regards as guiltless for His Son's sake.

What?—all sinners? No, only such as believe; only those that accept His Son's work in faith, who, acknowledging that this Jesus was the Christ, the Son of God, that He died for their sins on the cross and for the sake of their "righteousness" was raised from the dead,[1] base their lives on this faith. To them "God reckons" their faith as righteousness,[2] their sins He does not reckon to them.[3] "In His eye" they are righteous;[4] through Jesus they are "set down"[5] as righteous.[6]

How can "faith" have so great a power, how can it take the place of good works? No, faith is to take the place of nothing else, but God has withdrawn all claim to good works. He grants righteousness as a free gift, but it is faith that takes hold of righteousness, *i.e.* the believer *dares to believe* that God imputes no guilt to him, because he has come to the faith that Jesus is the Son of God and has risen from the dead, that He has died for sinners, and that therefore God is no longer wroth with

---

[1] Rom. iv. 25. [2] Rom. iv. 3, 5, 9, 22; Gal. iii. 6.
[3] 2 Cor. v. 19. [4] Rom. ii. 13. [5] Rom. v. 19.
[6] Rom. x. 9, iv. 25; Gal. ii. 20, etc.

sinners. In order to understand this fully we must bear two things in mind. First, that by "faith" Paul always means a conviction of the resurrection of Jesus and of His propitiatory death out of love for us; and secondly, that he had himself given up the law as the way of salvation at the very moment that he yielded and looked upon Jesus as the risen Christ. Hence his conclusion that faith in the risen Lord, and not the way of the law, was the way of salvation. Whosoever is won over by the preaching from which comes faith, and by the testimony of the apostles, so that he can look upon Jesus as the Christ crucified for our sins and raised from the dead, he has at the same time won the conviction that God will pardon sinners.

Paul's doctrine of faith is to be understood from a purely psychological and religious point of view. Faith is not the discharge of a duty which is looked upon as a good work, it is not a man that is "righteous" because of his faith that God acquits, but a sinner who ventures to believe. And because this faith is already experienced and sealed in baptism, Paul can say that the believer *is* already acquitted,[1] not merely that he will be. The mention of the Spirit shows us that this juridical theory of acquittal is simply a systematisation of the experience of conversion.

St Paul's treatment of the second train of ideas —the promise of blessedness was given to all the children of Abraham—exactly resembles that of the first. Here too he has altered the thought so as to harmonise it with his conversion; nor does he assign less importance to it than to the doctrine of justi-

[1] Rom. vi. 8.

fication, whereas in the teaching of the reformed churches it has come to occupy quite a secondary place. Hence the third chapter of the Epistle to the Romans is immediately succeeded by the proof that the Christians alone are the true children of Abraham, internal and external evidence being brought forward in an interesting manner. Here too we must of course disentangle the various threads and examine each separately if we would understand the whole. First of all we have the attempt to prove Abraham to be the true father of all Christians, in so far as his experience exactly resembles theirs. Of him too we read in Holy Scripture: " He believed God, and it was counted unto him for righteousness"; so, says Paul, he was "justified" not by works but by faith. " Now wages are reckoned to those who work not as a favour but as a debt; only [of] him who works not but believes on him who justifies (acquits) the ungodly [can one say that to him] his faith is 'reckoned as righteousness'; so, *e.g.* David describes the blessedness of the man to whom God reckons righteousness without works, Ps. xxii. 1 *seq.*"[1] Paul here employs a philological argument. He refers to the usage of the Old Testament in order to prove that where the word "reckon" ($\lambda o \gamma i \zeta \epsilon \sigma \theta a \iota$) occurs, it is always a reckoning as a present and not a payment for services rendered that is meant. For in the above-quoted Psalm we read, "Blessed are they whose iniquities are forgiven and whose sins are covered. Blessed is the man to whom the Lord does not reckon sin." In reality it is rather the contrary that is here proved, for the passage speaks of God's forbearance to reckon

[1] Rom. iv. 4–8.

JUSTIFICATION BY FAITH

something that does as a matter of fact exist, a negative "service rendered." So too the passage about Abraham in the book of Genesis bears exactly the opposite interpretation. Faith is there reckoned to Abraham as a good work, as righteousness; it is not that God draws a veil, as it were, over the lacking righteousness as He does in the case of Christians, according to Paul's theology, and demands faith instead of the good work.

It is nearer the truth when the Christians are declared to be the "true seed," the true children of Abraham, because they are the children of his faith, and he their true father because he, like them, has believed "against hope in hope," taking his stand upon his faith [1] against all human expectation. Here Paul has indeed discovered the essence of the paradox which lies in every act of faith. Unfortunately he immediately changes this general statement into a rabbinical quibble: as Christians believe in Him who raises from the dead, so Abraham too believed. "Though he was nearly a hundred years old, yet his faith did not fail him, even when he saw that his body was dead (worn out from age) and the deadness of Sarah's womb. Yet he doubted not in God's promises through unbelief, but was strong in faith, and he praised God in the firm conviction that what God has promised He is able also to carry out. And that is why it was said of his faith that it was reckoned to him as righteousness." [2]

Other trains of thought cross these whose aim it is to prove the inner likeness and therefore relationship of Abraham to the Christians. He is not

[1] Rom. iv. 16 *seq.* [2] Rom. iv. 19–21.

slow to point out that Abraham was yet uncircumcised when he received the promise. He is a living proof, therefore, that the blessedness which the promise holds out is for the uncircumcised as well, *i.e.* for his Gentile Christians. And he very boldly deprives the Jew himself of his distinctive sign and sacrament. Abraham received it merely as the seal of the righteousness which he had by faith, for the promise stands in Gen. xv., his circumcision in Gen. xvii. So then Abraham is the father of all "those who walk in the steps of that faith which he had being yet uncircumcised."[1]

Finally, Paul draws attention to the fact—this is his *ceterum censeo*—that the promises generally were void if they were attached to the fulfilment of the law. The end of the law is not mercy, only "wrath," the wrath of God against transgressors, and all must transgress it.[2]

We see what trouble Paul took to make his proof complete. In the Epistle to the Galatians also we have an exhaustive treatment of the same subject. Here again the Sonship stands in the foreground, and it is based upon the same faith.[3] Those who are of faith are the children of Abraham;[4] and the promise extends to all the heathen,[5] for it runs "in thee shall all nations be blessed." In the religious vocabulary of Jews and Christians we find the same word for "nations" and "heathen."[6]

Then we come to a somewhat confused maze of arguments — less surprising in this letter to the Galatians, which was written under the influence of

[1] Rom. iv. 9–12. [2] Rom. iv. 13–16. [3] Gal. iii. 6.
[4] Gal. iii. 7. [5] Gen. xviii. 8. [6] Rom. iii. 8 *seq.*

JUSTIFICATION BY FAITH

the strongest emotions, than in the somewhat less entangled fourth chapter of the Epistle to the Romans. We will only allude to the scattered thoughts which belong to our argument. Wherever the promise is made to Abraham, the book of Genesis uses the expression "thy seed" in the singular. In Hebrew the word is a collective noun, and means descendants, but Paul simply clutches hold of the strictly grammatical form and maintains that the promise can be understood only of one being, *i.e.* of Christ, to whom, according to the faith of that age, all this referred.[1] Now as all Christians are mystically "one in Christ," one being, so they are all together the one promised seed of Abraham, and therefore heirs according to the promise.[2]

Finally, in the fourth chapter, St Paul produces that strange allegory of Sarah and Hagar, to which we have already referred. Abraham had two sons, one of the slave-woman (Ishmael), and one of the free (Isaac). The son of the slave-woman was born in the ordinary course of nature, the son of the freewoman was born through promise:[3] which things are an allegory, the women stand for the two covenants. The one given from Mount Sinai, whose children become slaves, *i.e.* Hagar. Now he likewise discovers, as pointing in the same direction, that Hagar is an Arabian and must stand for Mount Sinai in Arabia, and for this reason alone signifies the covenant of Sinai and can be compared to the Jerusalem that now is, and not merely because she is in slavery (of the law) with her children. "But the Jerusalem which is above is free, and it is she who is

---
[1] Gal. iii. 16.   [2] Rom. iii. 28.   [3] Gen. xv. 14.

our mother,"—through Paul's great mission she has a numerous family of children. Finally, there is a third point of resemblance: just as Ishmael, the son born after the flesh (in the ordinary course of nature), persecuted Isaac, the son born after the Spirit (supernaturally), so the Jews now persecute the Christians. But they shall have their reward: the son of the slave-woman shall not inherit together with the son of the free-woman, neither in the one case nor in the other.[1]

However clever and even convincing these arguments may have appeared to St Paul's contemporaries, for us they are nothing but a forced employment of texts which mean something quite different; and the whole theory of justification, with its forensic formulas, is, after all, a very imperfect expression of the deep, transparent feeling which characterises the intense and fervent religious life which it is intended to defend and justify. What a different note Paul strikes when he exclaims:

"O ye foolish Galatians! Who hath bewitched you? Has not Jesus Christ been *depicted* before your very eyes as crucified? This one thing I wish to know of you: Did you receive the Spirit by the works of the law or by the hearing of faith? You are still so foolish. . . . So many things you have received in vain! Was it really in vain? He therefore that gives you the Spirit and worketh miracles among you, does he do it by the works of the law or by the hearing of faith?"[2]

Or when he passes from the descent from Abraham to speak of the Divine Fatherhood in the beautiful

[1] Gal. iv. 21–31.   [2] Gal. iii. 1–5.

words: "But because ye are sons, God sent forth the Spirit of his Son into our hearts, crying, Abba, Father. So that thou art no longer a slave, but a son; and if a son, then an heir through God."[1]

Or when he tells us of that which stirs the depths of his heart: "As many as are led by the Spirit of God, these are sons of God [and here is the proof thereof]. For ye received not the spirit of bondage again unto fear. No, ye received the spirit of a son, whereby we cry, Abba, Father. The Spirit Himself beareth witness with our spirit that we are children of God. But if children, then we are also heirs, heirs of God, joint-heirs with Christ, if only we suffer with Him, that we may be also glorified with Him [in the glory of heaven]. For I reckon that the sufferings of this present time are not worthy to be compared with the glory which shall be revealed and conferred upon us."[2]

Wherever Paul speaks of the Spirit, we can feel the quick pulse of his own religion. The theories of justification and descent from Abraham are juridical and theological formulæ. But the formula is not to be despised. After all, in its abrupt, paradoxical fashion, it expresses the very essence of Christianity as opposed to every legal religion, Jewish or Catholic.

[1] Gal. iv. 6 *seq.*   [2] Rom. viii. 14–18.

THE THEOLOGIAN.

CHAPTER XX.

THE SIGNIFICANCE OF THE DEATH OF CHRIST.

WE have separated one question from the rest of the doctrine of justification, that which characterises it objectively, the question as to the necessity of the Messiah's death. Why had the Messiah to become man, to become a Jew, to die, and, above all, to die on the cross? These are all questions which are included in the first.

It is a question which played a great part in St Paul's thought, and a no less important one in his teaching; not that he especially needed it for his new life—that drew its supply of strength from the spirit and the resurrection of the Messiah—but because His death, the shameful death of Jesus on the Cross, had been the stumbling-block, the great hindrance that had prevented him from believing that this Jesus was the Messiah who had come down from heaven. That hour on the road to Damascus had shown him that the crucified Jesus was the Messiah for all that, that His death was not caused by any guilt of His own therefore, but had to be undergone, as the disciples taught, because of the sins of men.

This experience is the starting-point of Paul's

dogmatic thinking. Not that he would not often have been more than satisfied with the first simple conclusion. On the contrary, in the majority of cases he goes no further than the simple statement of fact, without giving any explanation.

"He was delivered up for our trespasses, and was raised for our justification."[1] "He gave Himself for our sins, that He might deliver us out of this present evil world, according to the will of our God and Father."[2] "The Son of God loved me and gave Himself up for me."[3] "For while we were yet weak, in due season Christ died for the ungodly."[4] "But God puts His own love for us beyond doubt by the fact that Christ died on our behalf while we were yet sinners."[5] "We are justified by His blood."[6] "Through the obedience of one man (Jesus) shall many be made righteous."[7]

All these statements—and there are many others to a similar effect—contain as yet no dogmatic theory. They only state the fact. They do not explain *how* the death of Jesus was able to save. But Paul, the thinker and the theologian, was bound to go beyond this statement of fact which was common to all early Christian teaching.[8] He was bound to try and discover a reason for this death.

He had his choice amongst several lines of thought in order to find an explanation.

For a man of the ancient world, the most obvious was, no doubt, to be found in the idea of a sacrifice. Jesus Himself had used this picture to make His

[1] Rom. iv. 25.   [2] Gal. i. 4.   [3] Gal. ii. 20.
[4] Rom. v. 6.   [5] Rom. v. 8.   [6] Rom. v. 9.
[7] Rom. v. 19.   [8] 1 Cor. xv. 3.

death comprehensible to Himself and His disciples. It is not the saying about the ransom (Mark x. 35) —the genuineness of which might besides be called in question—but the words at the Last Supper that contain the thought of a sacrifice, with their reference to the shedding of blood. And so, when Paul speaks of blood, as he does in one of the above-quoted passages, the death of Jesus is regarded more especially as a sacrifice. For at that time almost the only thought connected with sacrifice was that of a propitiatory rite accompanied by the shedding of blood. The picture then is founded on the thought which was expressed more clearly in the Epistle to the Hebrews: A better means was needed to purge away our sins than the blood of beasts, even the blood of the Messiah, "the lamb without blemish, without spot."[1] The conviction on which these thoughts are based is that sin needs blood for its expiation. In Jesus' use of the word the thought is entirely overshadowed by the picture: He sees His dead body, broken and torn—as was the bread that He held in His hand—by the stones of the multitude; He sees the blood flow from His wounds, and so He explains His death: as the blood flowed of old in the first covenant, so it must now again flow in the new. The thought of expiation is here thrust entirely into the background. Later, however, all the more emphasis was laid upon it in this passage, when it came to be needed for the defence of Jesus' Messiahship, and when greater importance was throughout attached to this idea, and to sacramental conceptions. And that is why so much stress

[1] 1 Pet. i. 19.

was laid upon the blood of Jesus, although no blood was shed at Jesus' death. It is only the fourth Gospel[1] that supplied the want by the invention or popularisation of the story of the spear-thrust.

In some passages St Paul too retains the thought of a sacrifice as a mere picture. It is nothing more than such a symbol when he says that Jesus was the Christians' " Paschal Lamb,"[2] which thought probably induced the fourth Evangelist to transfer Jesus' hour of death to the day on which the paschal lamb was sacrificed.

There are two passages, however, in which St Paul has more minutely described the sacrificial death of Jesus, both as to its effects and its necessity. Unfortunately both passages are so obscure that a completely satisfactory explanation can be given of neither of them. The first is Romans viii. 1 *seq.*, which I would translate as follows: " There is therefore now no condemnation to them that are in Christ Jesus. For the law of the spirit of life freed you in Christ Jesus from the law of sin and of death. For what the law could not do in that it was weak through the flesh, God, sending His own Son in the likeness of sinful flesh, and because of sin (cp. above, Gal. i. 4), condemned sin in the flesh, in order that the acquittal of the law might be fulfilled in us, who walk no more after the flesh but after the Spirit." In the dependent sentence, which contains the most important statement, there is an aposiopesis, as is often the case in Paul's writings, and it is hard to say how he really meant to continue. There remains the further question : Did God, accord-

[1] John xix. 35.   [2] 1 Cor. v. 7.

ing to Paul, "condemn sin" in the mortal body in which His Son was incarnate by causing this body to die, or was it because His Son lived without sin? In the first case we should have a thought parallel to that which we shall have to mention shortly, the thought of the curse of the law, the sentence passed upon the law, which takes effect in the body of Jesus and is thereby invalidated. This explanation would harmonise with the beginning of the passage, according to which the sentence of death of the law cannot touch those who are "in Christ." The second interpretation, that Christ condemned sin through His sinless life in the body of sin, fits in better with what follows, where the apostle speaks of those "who are in Christ," and can no longer walk after the flesh. This train of ideas we shall likewise meet with again.

The second passage, the exegesis of which is very hard, forms the climax of the first part of the Epistle to the Romans (iii. 23-26), and is one of the most disputed passages in the whole Bible. It runs as follows: "All have sinned and fall short of the heavenly glory of God; justified freely through His grace by means of the redemption in Christ Jesus. Him God set forth as ἱλαστήριον, through faith in His blood, as a proof of His righteousness because of the passing over of the sins which had been committed before in God's time of rest, as a proof of His righteousness at the present time, so that He might be (and show Himself as) the Just and justify (acquit) him that is 'of the faith' in Jesus."

The sense of the latter half of this sentence is much disputed (as is the rest of the passage), but it seems to me there can be no doubt it has the

THE DEATH OF CHRIST 305

following meaning: God had of old time, in the time of His "rest" let men sin without punishing them. But now the time has come for this to stop: God wished at length to show Himself as the righteous God. He would not, however, do this by destroying men, as He would in reality have been compelled to do had He followed strict justice. He *wished to show mercy*. But that He could only do after His justness had been established beyond all doubt by the death of Jesus: and for this purpose "He set forth Jesus openly (or set before Himself, regarded) as ἱλαστήριον." But what is the meaning of the word which has not been translated, and in what connection are the words, "through faith in His blood," to be taken? For these few words there are quite a number of possible interpretations. ἱλαστήριον can be: (1) Masculine (*a*) propitiating God; (*b*) propitiating sin; or (2) Neuter (*a*) reconciling God, propitiating sin, whereby again we can take that which reconciles or propitiates, as (α) a sacrifice, (β) a present or a memorial such as was then erected in a temple in the shape of a column or a statue. The words, "through faith in His blood," can furthermore be explained as follows: (1) God set Him forth in His blood or through His blood as a propitiation, etc., through faith (*i.e.* He has become for us a propitiation through faith); or (2) God set Him forth as a propitiation through faith in His blood. Of all the many interpretations which are rendered possible through the manifold meanings which are borne by the words and the compressed style of the sentence, it seems to me that the following translation is still the best: "Whom God chose as a propitiatory (sacrifice) through His blood by means of faith." That is to say: God's character is indeed love and compassion. He shows His love to us in that "while we were still sinners Christ died for us."[1] He loves men: though, were He to regard their actual condition, they must be "enemies" to Him, *i.e.* hated,[2] "vessels of His wrath" and not of His love. But His love wished to help them and reconcile them to Himself. Simple forgiveness of sins was not, however, possible for God. He was bound to show His justice, which mankind might begin to doubt, since for so long a time He had sent no flood upon sinners, but had apparently looked on at sin unmoved. This justice could be satisfied either by punishment or by a propitiation: God's love would not admit of punishment; a propitiation was therefore the only possible alternative. So then God's beloved Son, who abode with Him in heaven, the Messiah destined to reign upon earth in glory, was "purposed" by Him for a propitiation. That is what "προέθετο" usually means, not "set forth," and there is no reason why we should give up the usual meaning of the word. Before the second advent in glory, God sent His Son then from heaven to earth, as a man and a Jew, to save, to redeem, to bring an atonement for those that were born of women and were groaning under the oppression of the law. There is a further reason why the word ἱλαστήριον is probably to be taken in the sense of a propitiatory sacrifice, for propitiatory memorials or presents are naturally only offered by people as a propitiation for their own sin. The clever paradox which would

[1] Rom. v. 8.   [2] Rom. v. 10; xi. 28.

have been introduced into the sentence if we accept this exegesis, would have made it all the harder of comprehension.

I have endeavoured to give an instance—in a very rapid and superficial manner—of the minute attention to details which is a necessary feature of theological exegesis, in order to show with what difficulties we often have to contend, and how very uncertain the interpretation of such well-known dogmatic passages is more especially. Their obscurity and succinctness also afford us the best proof that Paul was not greatly concerned if they were not accurately understood. He writes with perfect distinctness and intelligibility on such subjects as the veiling of women and the arrangements for the collection of alms.

In both these difficult passages we can therefore contest the idea of sacrifice, and can substitute in Rom. viii. "the life of Jesus," and in Rom. iii., "Jesus as propitiatory memorial." If we try, however, to imagine a concrete instance of the abstract noun "propitiation," it must be confessed that the idea of sacrifice is the most natural in the latter passage. And besides, all these attempts to eliminate the conception of sacrifice from St Paul's theology are open to the very grave suspicion that the wish to find his own theology in St Paul has inspired the exegesis of the modern inquirer.

Besides the idea of sacrifice, there is another which explains not merely the death of the Messiah, but also His death upon the cross. There is none more distinctive of St Paul's thought. The starting-point is the law. The curse of the law overtakes all transgressors of the law, and this curse, this sentence of the law, is called death.¹ No one can fulfil the law; therefore all who are under the law are under its curse, are condemned to death. Christ has taken this curse upon Himself: He obeyed God when He ordered Him to become man, and to be born "under the law," *i.e.* as a Jew.² But then He died of His own free will upon the cross, and thereby He literally placed Himself under the law's curse, for it is written in the book of the law, Accursed is he that is hanged on a cross. So the curse spent itself on Him, the innocent, that knew no sin,³ and thereby it is done away. All they that were "under the curse" have now been redeemed by Him.⁴ This is the clearest, the most consequent theory that St Paul advances of the death of Jesus. But just like the belief in sacrifice, it rests upon a strange idea of primitive man, upon his conception of the curse, upon its objective reality, so to speak. Just as Isaac's blessing works itself out, because it is uttered, and neither God nor Isaac can alter it in anywise, so this curse of the law must also spend itself on someone. Now if it lights on one who was not doomed to die through his own guilt, then it has "worked itself out," its force is spent, for it has put itself in the wrong. And so the curse being removed, God's mercy has free play.

Finally, we have a third line of thought which is closely connected with St Paul's experience on the road to Damascus. This derives redemption from the risen Lord, and is St Paul's own teaching, even though some deny it altogether, and others put it into the background because it is not as well furnished

---

¹ Rom. v. 16.　　² Gal. iv. 4.　　³ 2 Cor. v. 21.
⁴ Gal. iii. 10–13 ; 1 Cor. vi. 20, vii. 23.

THE DEATH OF CHRIST 309

with proofs as the other theories, which were better adapted for apologetic purposes. All believed in sacrifices, and the doctrine of the curse of the law was, in the eyes of St Paul's contemporaries, strictly logical and proved by passages of Scripture. This last idea, however, only those could appreciate who had had St Paul's experience. For here again the key to all lies in the mystical communion with Christ. Christ must needs die that all men might die in and with Him who enter into communion with Him through faith and the Spirit. In that hour before Damascus, St Paul died in Christ, so do all Christians. There is therefore now no more condemnation to those that have died with Him. Such is the connection between Rom. vi. and viii., chap. vii. being merely a parenthesis. This thought finds its typical expression in 2 Cor. v. One died for all, *therefore all died.* " Wherefore, if any man is in Christ, he is a new creature: the old things are passed away; behold, they are become new. But all things are of God, who reconciled us to Himself through Christ, and gave unto us the ministry of reconciliation; (the apostleship which comes to all men with the message). God was reconciling in Christ the world unto Himself, not reckoning unto them their trespasses, and having committed unto us the word of reconciliation. We are ambassadors therefore on behalf of Christ, as though God were intreating by us: We beseech you, on behalf of Christ, be ye reconciled to God. Him who knew no sin, He made to be sin on our behalf: that we might become the righteousness of God *in Him.*"[1] He that is "in Him" is "righteousness,"

[1] 2 Cor. v. 17–21.

just as He was before "sin," and became man that all who were received in Him might become "righteous." "In Him" God reconciled the world, in its attitude of hostility, unto Himself.

The mode of expression in Rom. vi. is somewhat different. Here and there are ethical trains of thought, and all is connected with baptism. But the following sentences certainly belong to the idea we are considering. "Our old man was crucified with Jesus, that the body of sin might be done away, that so we should no longer be in bondage to sin; for he that hath died is *acquitted* (justified) from sin."[1] In that Christ died therefore, all Christians have died, the sentence of death has indeed taken effect upon them, the mystical body of Christ. They *are dead*, they have died once for all. Now eternal life awaits them: "But if we died with Christ, we shall also live with him: so we believe."[2] We meet with the same thoughts in Rom. v. 10 and 1 Thess. v. 10. If this theory is not put forward as often as the others, it is the real source of their strength. It harmonises with the sublimest passages in the apostle's letters, as in Rom. vi. and viii., passages which breathe a spirit of the deepest piety.

All these theories as to the death of Jesus start from a problem which was a burning question for the disciples: Can one say of a dead man that he was the Messiah? And if so, *why* had the immortal, the Messiah, to die? He was a heavenly, an eternal being, and He had done no sin, whose wages is death. These theories are, *ipso facto*, non-existent therefore for those to whom Jesus is not the Jewish Messiah,

---
[1] Rom. vi. 6 *seq*.   [2] Rom. vi. 8.

THE DEATH OF CHRIST 311

and who do not look upon the death of Jesus as a still greater miracle than His resurrection, as a miracle which needs another than a historical explanation.

The orthodox theories of the atonement can rightly appeal to St Paul as their authority. He was their originator, even though his doctrine harmonised neither with Anselm's theory nor with the teaching of the Reformers, nor with the theories of our articles and confessions, where they are rather presupposed than elaborated dogmatically. He was their originator because he first thought that he could prove logically the necessity of the death of Jesus, and because for this very purpose he limited the love of God by the necessity by which God Himself was bound of satisfying His justice, that is, of demanding some condition without which His love could not have been realised. Yet the later doctrines of the atonement do not explain the death upon the cross. They get as far as the death of the God-man, but no further. These modern doctrines—including most of those which claim to be orthodox—are only very pale and shamefaced copies of these old theories: for none of them ventures to accept the two presuppositions of all these dogmas:

1. That it is permissible to presuppose juridical or forensic measures of any kind as determining the relations of God to man.

2. The idea of the propitiatory sacrifice of the blood of the Messiah in its genuine ancient form.

And for this reason they have "all fallen away" from orthodox doctrine, and only a miserable appearance of it is maintained, more in words and in strong attacks upon "the unorthodox" than through any inherent truth. But we reject all such theories as to the death of Jesus not shamefacedly but consciously. Not because of their logical insufficiency, however rightly this may be insisted upon, but above all because they contain an unchristian, a less than Christian, conception of God and His relation to man. The "Father" of Jesus does not need to establish or to prove His "righteousness" by suffering an innocent man to die for sinners: a strange kind of righteousness! He does not wish to be just, but He is Love. Holy love of course, but not such as needs first to be propitiated. And there is no "holy" blood, no holy things in the religion of Jesus, no propitiatory sacrifices with which sin can be "washed away." All these thoughts, which are taken from the animistic religion, are pre-christian and unchristian, whether they be founded on the blood of bulls or on the blood of Christ. The ethical change, renovation and sanctification, is degraded into something external and sacramental; instead of faith we have mystical miracles, which are to have natural effects.

Jesus' death does not lose one whit of its significance for our own life with God and our following in the Master's footsteps, if we cease to fancy that we can forcibly apply such theories to it. He who cannot be moved to repentance by God's goodness and a man's surrender unto death, even the death upon the cross, will listen in vain to systems of sacrifice and theories of propitiation which are intended to establish God's "righteousness" palpably.

THE THEOLOGIAN.

CHAPTER XXI.

· THE CHRIST AND JESUS.

BY the side of the doctrines of justification by faith and of the atoning death of Jesus, the most contested dogma of Christianity is that of the divine nature in Jesus. Of this doctrine too we find the earliest and clearest traces in St Paul. We have already examined the roots from which the mighty tree of later christological dogma grew up.

This dogma already existed in all essential particulars before Jesus was born. Jewish Messianic speculations had already imagined a picture for the completion of which really nothing was wanting but the Nicene dogma that the Father and the Son were of the same substance. We have already brought together these features in Paul's picture of Christ. (p. 45 *seq.*) Even the statement that the world was created by the Son of God was as current an opinion among the Jews as everything else that Paul tells us of Christ's life from the beginning of the world until His second advent in judgment.

And by the side of this Jewish inheritance the apostle's Christology is rooted in his experience before Damascus, as it was interpreted by him with the help of the picture of the heavenly Christ. It seemed to him that he had now the same kind of proof as the disciples had acquired through the Resurrection. He now knew, from his own experience, that that heavenly being in whom his people believed existed as an actual matter of fact. He was identical with Jesus. The apostle had "looked upon" a bright light or a form in heavenly glory, so Christ lived, so the man Jesus continued to live as Son of God, declared to be the Son of God with power.[1]

Having declared Jesus to be the Christ, Paul, like the first disciples, ascribed to Him all that the Jews had hitherto believed or expected of the Messiah. An immediate consequence of this belief was that an aureole surrounded the young carpenter and peasant of Nazareth, and that His simple and yet all-powerful features threatened to disappear beneath this nimbus.

Paul's sole merit herein is that he did not quite conceal the man Jesus beneath the heavenly being, for, as we have already seen, he always maintained the connection with the twelve; and even in a critical hour of his life he overcame the temptation once for all to break the tie between his congregations and the tradition of Jerusalem and thereby to separate them from Jesus. But he himself attached no value whatever to Christ according to the "flesh," to the man Jesus, nor would he know any one according to the flesh, not even Jesus.[2] Indeed Jesus can scarcely be said to have existed for him as a human being. What interested him in Jesus is simply His present life in the believer and His death. Even where he holds up His life

[1] Rom. i. 3.   [2] 2 Cor. v. 16.

THE CHRIST AND JESUS

as an ethical pattern, he mentions, it is true, a number of features which we have learned to value likewise in the man Jesus, because we find them in the gospels; but as a matter of fact they are for him simply and solely the deeds of the Divine Son of God. He was obedient, in that He died;[1] He lived not to please Himself, in taking upon Himself reproaches and suffering;[2] His great act of love was His death.[3] Paul only once speaks of His gentleness and sweet reasonableness in general,[4] and that in such a way that one might imagine him to be alluding to the now living, exalted Lord; and the same remark applies to the apostle's references to the love[5] and truth[6] of Christ. If besides the death he mentions any special incident in the life of Christ, then it is the incarnation of the Son of God when He became "poor"[7] and "emptied Himself"[8] of His divinity in the glad zeal for sacrifice and in humility. "Let the spirit of Christ Jesus be yours also. Though He was in the form of God, He did not look upon equality with God as a prize to be clutched at (*i.e.* He did not wish to win it as did Satan and Adam of old, by forcible means). But He emptied Himself, taking the form of a servant, and appeared in the likeness of men. And being found in fashion as a man, He humbled Himself, becoming obedient unto death—yes, death on the cross. And that is why, too, God so highly exalted Him, and gave Him the name which is above every

---

[1] Rom. v. 19.
[2] Rom. xv. 3 *seq.*
[3] Gal. ii. 20; 2 Cor. v. 14 *seq.*
[4] 2 Cor. x. 1.
[5] Rom. viii. 35 *seq.*; 2 Cor. v. 14.
[6] 2 Cor. xi. 10.
[7] 2 Cor. viii. 9.
[8] Phil. ii. 6.

name—that at the name of Jesus every knee should bow, of things in heaven and things on earth and things under the earth, and that every tongue should confess that 'Jesus Christ is Lord,' to the glory of God the Father."

This passage from the Epistle to the Philippians is especially instructive. It shows us how the whole human life of Jesus vanished in the spiritual being. If Paul had wished, he could easily have found examples of Christ's humility, love, subjection and self-sacrifice in the life of Jesus. There was no need for him to seek his pattern in the heavenly being. Probably, then as now, it made a greater impression on the mass of men that so high, divine, and all-powerful a being should divest himself of his power, and humble himself, than that a man should sacrifice himself. And yet, if we would arrive at a right moral judgment, it is an exceedingly difficult matter to decide whether these acts of the Divine Being have any ethical value whatever for us when they are held up as patterns for our imitation. In any case, the death of Jesus, as of a person in the Trinity, loses all the religious value that it might have as the death of a struggling yet believing human being.

We must not, however, suppose that Paul knew nothing of Jesus. On the contrary, his letters contain so much about Jesus that he is our best and surest witness in the controversy that has just been started afresh about the historicity of the person of Jesus, and we would have to dispute the authenticity of all his letters if we wished to set aside this testimony. For, according to his own words, he became acquainted with the outlines of the life of

THE CHRIST AND JESUS

Jesus from the disciples themselves; and though his religion is everywhere in touch with the risen, living Lord, yet we find clear traces everywhere of his acquaintance with those memoirs of Jesus which afterwards assumed a definite shape in our gospels.

Paul clearly testifies [1] that the Messiah became man, born like every other man, "of a woman," and like every Jew, "made under the law." The traditional exegesis fancied that in these words it had discovered a reference to the supernatural birth of Jesus because nothing was said of the "man," but it simply read the exact opposite of St Paul's real meaning into the passage. Nothing can be more certain than that Paul here wishes to emphasise the true human birth of Jesus. So too he says that Jesus was "born of the seed of David,"[2] that is, if we take the words in the sense they bear everywhere else, of a *father* who was, or was considered to be, a descendant of David. Again, Paul speaks of the brothers of the Lord [3] without any qualification: it is only Catholic exegesis that made cousins of Jesus out of these brothers, with the sure instinct for that which was an ecclesiastical necessity. Paul himself knew as yet of no story concerning the virgin-birth, although he already looked upon Jesus as more than a man, viz., as an incarnate heavenly spirit.

The features which, as we have already seen, Paul emphasised in the character of this heavenly being, either before or after incarnation, will probably not have been contradicted, in his opinion, by anything that He did as man. And in this way St Paul's

[1] Gal. iv. 4; cp. Rom. ix. 3 *seq.*   [2] Rom. i. 3.
[3] Gal. i. 19; 1 Cor. ix. 5.

dogmatic assertion, that Jesus knew no sin[1]—resting as it indubitably does upon the impression which the person of Jesus made upon the disciples—acquires a fuller and clearer meaning. It cannot have been purity alone which shone forth from the form of the prophet of Nazareth, but goodness also, and love, self-surrender, and the power of self-sacrifice.

Again, when St Paul says that the Son of God became poor,[2] he is thinking, primarily, no doubt, of the laying aside of His divine glory. But his words only acquire their full meaning when we remember that Jesus as man too belonged to the poor and humble in the land. Here St Paul once again confirms the picture of Jesus given us in the gospels. St Paul tells us too, quite clearly, that Jesus came forward as a prophet with a definite message, that He made definite claims on men, and even Himself gave them certain definite commandments. There are also in St Paul's writings not merely allusions to sayings of Jesus—one or two such are actually quoted. The most noteworthy passage of this kind is the section describing the institution of the Lord's Supper.[3] If we compare St Paul's with St Mark's account, we can plainly see that both are derived from the same traditional source, without any sign, however, of literary interdependence: on the contrary, the words had already begun to be changed, and that, very curiously, in the process of oral tradition. So too St Paul introduces his quotation of Jesus' prohibition of divorce with the words, "Unto the married I command—no, not I, but the Lord."[4] And

[1] 2 Cor. v. 21.
[2] 2 Cor. viii. 9.
[3] 1 Cor. xi. 23 *seq.*
[4] 1 Cor. vii. 10.

THE CHRIST AND JESUS 319

a few verses further he says, "Even so the Lord appointed that they which proclaim the gospel should live of the gospel."[1] The passage in the second Epistle to the Corinthians, in which Paul solemnly assures his readers that his word was not "yea and nay" at the same time, appears also to refer to a well-known saying of Jesus: "For the Son of God, Jesus Christ, who was preached among you by us . . . was not yea and nay, but in Him has been yea, for all the promises of God in Him are yea."[2] There is of course no direct connection between the words and Jesus' prohibition of oaths, "Let your yea be yea, and your nay, nay,"[3] but it seems to me that we may very possibly have a clever adaptation here by St Paul of the words in the Sermon on the Mount. Elsewhere, on the contrary, St Paul says that he has received no command from the Lord.[4]

Yet he did not look upon the "law of Christ" as a law in the Old Testament sense. The meaning he attached to it was far broader and more liberal. In two of the above-quoted passages he permitted deviations from the law to be made. Especially he reserved to himself the liberty to decide whether he should or should not, as a matter of conscience, receive support from his congregations. The "law of Christ," after all, meant something very different to him from the dull, literal accomplishment of His commands: "Bear ye one another's burdens, and so fulfil the law of Christ."[5] To serve Christ is to have righteousness and peace and joy in the Holy Ghost,[6]

[1] 1 Cor. ix. 14. [2] 2 Cor. i. 19. [3] Matt. v. 37; James v. 12.
[4] 1 Cor. vii. 12, 25, perhaps vii. 6; 2 Cor. viii. 8.
[5] Gal. vi. 2, *cp.* 1 Cor. ix. 21.   [6] Rom. xiv. 18.

to be seeking to please God,[1] not men. So it becomes exceedingly probable that where Paul once speaks of love as the fulfilment of the law[2]—which is quite contrary to his habitual usage—he is thinking of the fulfilment of the law in love. Herein too he seems to have been a genuine disciple of Jesus—none more so—that the true mark of Christianity for him was not the ecstastic form of religion, but its transformation into a power of warmest love.[3] For in Christ Jesus neither Jewish nor Gentile natural pride is accounted anything but faith which works through love.[4] Paul did not make Jesus into a "law" either, but he understood that, in order to fulfil the law of Christ, one must measure oneself, one's whole being, by the standard of Christ's character. Thus on one occasion when he was forced by continued slanders to dwell upon his achievements on behalf of Christianity, he says expressly that this, his "self-praise," is not "after the Lord,"[5] not in accordance with His character—his boasting is foolish, but he is forced to do it in self-defence. The total impression of the person of Jesus which we derive from the Synoptists was already a living reality for Paul, and determined his action.

I expressly say the Synoptists, for, in the fourth gospel, that of John, we have a version—or perversion—of the Master's life by a disciple who has portrayed Him not in His self-sacrificing love, which sought not its own, but as the mighty, superhuman being demanding recognition of the Divine Sonship and Messianic glory.

[1] Gal. i. 10.   [2] Rom. xiii. 10.   [3] 1 Cor. xiii.
[4] Gal. v. 6.   [5] 2 Cor. xi. 17.

THE CHRIST AND JESUS 321

But the remarkable point in Paul is this. Although he has already heaped upon Jesus all the speculations of Judaism about the Messiah and the Son of God, and himself lived altogether in the "Risen Lord," he has yet preserved the picture of Jesus for us very clearly and distinctly in the few references that he makes to Him. Here again we have an instance of his true inner greatness. He always makes straight for the heart of the matter, for the essential, the universal. And we have an instance too of the vigour and delicacy of his style. Clumsy as it is in expression, it is still so plastic and significant that even quite brief indications are charged with much meaning.

How high in the heavenly hierarchy did Paul place the spiritual being incarnate in Jesus? Was he already acquainted with the later theological conception of the divinity of Christ and of the Trinity? Those who answer these questions in the affirmative, quote above all the passage we have already translated (see p. 315) from the Epistle to the Philippians, especially the words, "although He was in the form of God," and they emphasise the fact that it is at least said of Christ that He became "equal" to God, not by forcible means, but by humility and self-abasement, for which God rewarded Him in that He "highly exalted" Him and gave Him "the name which is above every name." But the words, "form of God," can only be used in contradistinction to "form of a servant," *i.e.* to that which is human generally, and all that we can conclude from it is that Jesus' nature was divine, not that He was God Himself. Paul states explicitly a little lower down what he means by the "name above every other name"; it is "Lord," and in it there is certainly included the idea of equality with God in glory and power, but only relatively to this present world. Another passage is also quoted. We have already noticed it as well. It is that enumeration of the high privileges of Israel which thus continues after the mention of the name of Christ: "From them (the Jews) is Christ as concerning the flesh, He that is over all (ruling) God blessed for ever: Amen."[1] If we take the last words in apposition to Christ, then He would here be clearly designated as God Himself. But this translation is improbable, because it is not the heavenly being that is here in question, but Christ, as man, who sprang from the Jews. It is much better to put a colon at "flesh" and take the last words as referring to God Himself. As in other places, so here[2] Paul ends his chapter with a doxology: The God that rules over all things be blessed for ever. These are the only two passages in which we could possibly understand the apostle as speaking of Jesus as God. It is only later writings that do so, and they mostly in the form that a Christian would call Jesus "his God"[3] in his prayers and in acts of adoration.

On the whole Jesus still stands for Paul below God. God has sent Him, His Son. He became obedient unto the Father until death. God raised Him up, exalted Him, and gave Him power. It is God from whom the Son has all things. And even though the Son is now equal to God and "above all things," when all enemies, men, and devils have been

---

[1] Rom. ix. 5.   [2] *E.g.* Rom. xi. 36; Gal. i. 5; Rom. xvi. 27.
[3] *E.g.* John xx. 28.

overcome, He shall deliver up the Kingdom again to the Father, and subject Himself that the Father may be "all in all."[1] There are two separate beings: "God" that rules, now evermore Almighty; and subordinate to Him "the Son," who has been called into life and endowed with power by Him for the creation and redemption of mankind and the destruction of devils.

But how are we to understand the title "Son of God"? When the title was transferred later from the Jews to the Greeks, the Semitic use of the word "son" was misunderstood, and it was taken in the sense that this heavenly being was not created, but had proceeded in some mysterious manner from the Father's inmost being; or it was even supposed to refer to the miraculous birth of Jesus. In the Semitic languages the word "son" is used in a number of secondary applications. Instead of the disciples of the Pharisee, we find, "sons of the Pharisees";[2] instead of subjects, "sons of the kingdom."[3] Worldly-minded people are "sons of this world,"[4] men doomed to hell are "sons of hell,"[5] those led astray by the devil, the possessed, are "sons of the devil."[6] The words "God's son" and "God's sons" (or, as A.V., children) may therefore mean all kind of things, they certainly imply belonging to God. Thus in the Old Testament the "sons of God" are the angels,[7] the Jews as chosen people are called "God's sons," and, above all, the chosen ruler of the future kingdom, the Messiah, is called by

[1] 1 Cor. xv. 28.   [2] Matt. xii. 27.
[3] Matt. viii. 12; xiii. 37.   [4] Luke xvi. 8.
[5] Matt. xxiii. 15.   [6] Matt. xiii. 38.   [7] Gen. vi. 1-4.

this title. There is a complete absence of all later speculations as to the relation of this " Son " to the Father. The name merely implies that Christ belongs to God, stands to Him in a special relation.

It is hard to determine what special meaning Paul attached to the words " Son of God." For the most part he only employs it where the turn of the sentence suggests it to him, when he has to declare the relation of God to Jesus or the Christ.[1] There is a certain solemnity too in the expression. With scarcely an exception it is only used in such portions of the letters as are marked by an especial elevation of style. So in the first chapter to the Epistle to the Romans,[2] in the fifth and eighth chapters and other places[3] where he reaches the height of his great argument; in the introduction to the first Epistle to the Corinthians;[4] in the passage just quoted from the fifteenth chapter describing the end of the world, in a very important explanation (2 Cor. i. 19); in the Epistle to the Galatians, in the narrative of his conversion[5] and in the exultant conclusion of the first part[6]—three times he calls God by the same solemn title, " The God and Father of our Lord Jesus Christ."[7] Scarcely anywhere can we determine exactly whether by " Son of God " Paul would designate the high and heavenly origin of the Messiah or the special relation of love in which the Christ stands to God. The latter is, however, plainly the meaning in some cases. So when Paul says God spared not His own Son,[8]

---

[1] Except in Rom. i. 4; Gal. ii. 20; 2 Cor. i. 19.
[2] Rom. i. 3, 4, 9.   [3] Rom. v. 10; viii. 3, 29, 32.
[4] 1 Cor. i. 9.   [5] Gal. i. 16; ii. 20.   [6] Gal. iv. 6 *seq.*
[7] Rom. xv. 6; 2 Cor. i. 3, xi. 31.   [8] Rom. viii. 32.

THE CHRIST AND JESUS 325

that He sent Him.¹ Very often, however, the word stands without any such expression of feeling, simply as a name for the Divine Being of the Messiah. But Paul, like Jesus, applies exactly the same word to Christians too, whom God has "accepted" to be His sons. They are His sons because they have been accepted in Christ, "adopted" by God.² Yet Paul's declarations on this point are not very clear, for in another place he speaks of the sending of the Spirit into the heart simply as a consequence of adoption, *i.e.* this latter is merely a declaratory act corresponding to justification (acquittal): "Because ye are sons, God sent forth the spirit of His Son into your hearts, crying, Abba, Father."³ And so too he mentions the Spirit not only as the cause of, but as the witness to the Divine Fatherhood in the Epistle to the Romans. Here are the two sentences side by side: "As many as are led by the Spirit of God, these are sons of God," and "the Spirit beareth witness with our spirit that we are children of God."⁴ In both cases, however, as well with regard to the Christians as to Christ Himself, the emphasis is on the high divine claim which the sons of God can make as beings of another world on the "inheritance" which is reserved for them. That is what Paul intends by the title "Son of God." There are no dogmatic speculations about the "divinity of Christ" in Paul.

Thus Paul never forgot the barrier between the Christ, even if He is the Son of God—yes, just because He is His Son—and God Himself. On the

¹ Gal. iv. 4; Rom. viii. 3. ² Gal. iii. 26; iv. 5 *seq.*
³ Gal. iv. 6. ⁴ Rom. viii. 14, 16, *cp.* viii. 19, 21.

other hand, he could not clearly distinguish the Son from the Holy Ghost. We have already seen the reason for this. The experiences which came to him as a vision of Christ are exactly the same as those which were ascribed to the Holy Ghost. He can say indifferently, "in Christ" or "in the Spirit." Indeed, for his contemporaries the Spirit of God and God, the Spirit of Christ and Christ, can no longer be distinguished.

The expression "Spirit of God" comes down to us from that primitive age in which God was pictured in the semblance of a man, and in which it was therefore as natural to speak of His Spirit as it was to speak of His foot, eye, and ear. In that early age God walked in the cool of the evening in the garden of Eden.[1] He shut the door of the ark behind Noah,[2] and had to descend from heaven in order to see what strange thing the children of men were building upon earth.[3] At that time every form of sickness, the loss of consciousness, ecstasies and visions, were explained as a kind of possession by ghostly beings, by the souls of the living and the dead, by devils and angels, and by the Spirit of God. If God were both body and spirit, then His Spirit could "pass over" into a man, "seize" him—could speak and act through him. Such were the beliefs and thoughts of Israel of old. But when its faith became more elevated and less gross, when its old anthropomorphic conception of God—when Jahwe—was transformed into the creator of heaven and earth, then there was really no room left for the Spirit of God. "God is Spirit," a pure spiritual being, not tied down to any

[1] Gen. iii. 8. [2] Gen. vii. 16. [3] Gen. xi. 5.

one spot where alone He can be worshipped.[1] But the things experienced remained, and so the word remained too. "The Spirit of God" works miracles and cures, causes ecstasies and visions. So men believed in Paul's day. Nor did the word connote then more than it does now. Only men's faith then was more living and more powerful, and so too were their experiences which came to them again and again as effects of the Spirit of God.

Since similar effects were also ascribed to the risen Lord, these two heavenly beings were naturally no longer clearly distinguished. Such is the chaotic condition in which we find Paul's views. On one occasion he even says quite explicitly, "The Lord is the Spirit."[2] This, however, must not be pressed. He can and does distinguish the two beings elsewhere.

Far less right have we to try and find any traces of Trinitarian doctrine in these expressions. It is just an old-inherited conception, a traditional usage combined with a new experience, which brings the Christ and the Spirit in such close connection. The doctrine of the Trinity is compelled to distinguish the three persons of the Godhead—especially in their effects—as distinctly as it has to endeavour to maintain the unity of substance. But in Paul the state of things is this. Christ and the Spirit—the Spirit of God and the Spirit of Christ—are merged indistinctly into each other, so that the same effects are ascribed to both, and God is sharply distinguished from both. After all He remains the highest, He is all in all.

It is true of course that Paul already uses phrases in which God, Christ, and the Holy Ghost are named

[1] John iv. 24.   [2] 2 Cor. iii. 17.

in succession with a solemn liturgical rhythm. The completest of these we find in the second Epistle to the Corinthians, which we use every morning and evening in our services:

"The grace of our Lord Jesus Christ, and the love of God, and the communion of the Holy Ghost, be with you all."

Even here, however, we can see that the three beings do not stand on the same level. God and Christ give, the Holy Ghost is received in common by all.

In the first Epistle to the Corinthians,[1] St Paul uses the same formula to urge the Christians to unity:

> There are diversities of gifts,
>   But there is one and the same Spirit.
> There are diversities of ministrations,
>   But there is one and the same Lord.
> There are diversities of workings,
>   But there is one and the same God
> Who worketh all things in all.

The unity of all the gifts, and the possibility of employing them in well-organised work for the edification of character, is based upon the unity, not of the three beings together, but of each in and by itself. We may go so far as to say that, if Paul had already believed that these three beings together formed the one Almighty God, he would have said so here. For it would have formed the natural conclusion to his argument had he been able to say: "And these three are one." But as yet no one in Christendom had thought of that.

[1] 1 Cor. xii. 4 *seq.*

THE THEOLOGIAN.

CHAPTER XXII.

THE PAULINE ETHICS. FOUNDATION OF ETHICS.

WE have already seen that St Paul must be counted as one of the great discoverers in the domain of ethics. He made two discoveries in the course of his attempt to base his morality on the foundation of a law that contained the unknown will of God. Try as hard as he would, brace his will as much as he could, he found it impossible to lead a truly moral life on the basis of the categorical imperative; a new element was needed, a religious transformation of the whole man who begins his life afresh in reliance on the loving Father of all men. And the second discovery, which was connected with the first, was this: that morality cannot even be presented in the shape of a law, but is something entirely individual, something that has always to be created afresh by every single man from his own heart.

Yet Paul was compelled to become an ethical legislator and to form a regular system of ethics, creating new laws, and in the end forming new customs. The new man, conversion, love—these were not enough. He had to go further, he had to go into details, and he had to attempt to find a new basis for the demands of ethics.

We have already seen how the daily needs of his congregations forced him to elaborate a kind of sociology. It is not a true system of social ethics which Paul has left us. Nowhere did he face the question as to the moral significance of these communities and their right organisation. For him the only question is this: How can his church of God, the body of Christ, be preserved from party strife and schism, from revolution and from anarchy? He is guided in his inquiry by an immediate ethical feeling for the value of the "natural" human groups, husband and wife, the family, society and the State—but he does not examine them as a moral philosopher. It is not, after all, a system of social ethics, in the proper sense of the word, that St Paul has left us.

St Paul's point of view is so exclusively religious that morality has no independent significance in his theory. All faith, all religion, is nothing to him if it be not transmuted into love. And yet, if we look a little more closely, we see that morality for St Paul has no other aim than to keep the community and the individual in a condition of purity and of faith. As he goes forth not in order to help the poor and the wretched by works of love, but in order to save their souls through conversion, so the object of all works of love that they can do themselves is, according to his theory, simply to prevent their souls being lost again,—for "no unrighteous man can inherit the Kingdom of God." Paul is no reformer, but a missionary: this did not of course prevent the new morality from effecting reforms. It did

THE PAULINE ETHICS

so by building up a church, and so moulding custom. But what the apostle has before his eyes is not a world ethically organised, a moral civilisation, but a world doomed to destruction, in which individuals saved by religion keep themselves pure and unspotted.

Herein lie the greatness and the limitations of his ethic in so far as it is presented in a series of single demands. But he was compelled to go into the minutest details not only because of the position of the infant church in the midst of a hostile world, but because of the character of his converts—these children of God and saints. It was impossible simply to tell them to follow the dictates of their conscience. A new conscience had slowly to be formed by a gradual transformation of the old. So they needed a great deal of "law" as yet. Paul was disciplinarian enough too to see that. He was so great from an ethical point of view that he was not afraid of being misunderstood and accused of inconsistency. So he wrote no letter without its practical ethical part. The contents of the first part of each letter may be very varied—there are theoretical discussions, there are personal matters—but he never concluded a letter without giving some ethical instruction in a short summary. This he does even in the Epistle to the Romans, though he himself afterwards feels that it was likely to make a strange impression on readers with whom he was personally unacquainted, and so in this place he expressly excuses himself.[1]

But it is very noteworthy with what fine art and with what vigorous concentration he maintains

[1] Rom. xv. 14.

his fundamental principles while dealing with minutiæ. He always sets up some one general principle or ideal in connection with the context, and then from that he derives his detailed regulations. This is his method even when he is employing materials that are not his own, for the purposes of moral admonition, even when he recurs to the Old Testament law. We have already seen how he thus sets up the idea of the "reasonable service" in Rom. xii. A little later, plainly alluding to Jesus' word about the greatest commandment, he summed up everything under the point of view of love in which "the rest of the law" is fulfilled, a point of view which does not, it is true, harmonise very well with the rest of his teaching about the law, and is best explained by the influence of the oral gospel. "Love is the fulfilment of the law," *i.e.* all the demands of the law can be included in the one commandment of love, it "fills up" the whole law, constitutes its contents—that would be the best translation.[1]

In the Epistle to the Galatians, Paul expresses a similar thought negatively. He does not, it is true, in face of the arrogant claims for the law which some of his readers made, say here that love is the fulfilment of the law, but that the law "does not forbid"[2] those virtues which he taught as the right manner of action. Here again he sums up the single commandments—freedom, the Spirit, the fruit of the Spirit. These are here the unifying principles; and so it is everywhere else. Thus Paul shows himself to have really been a theologian, who consciously maintained his great inner experience

[1] Rom. xiii. 8–15 *seq.*   [2] Gal. v. 23.

and knew how to enunciate it in clear definitions, differing here too from Jesus, who has far less of the theologian about Him.

An examination of St Paul's ethical system in detail leaves us with very mixed feelings, besides the two impressions which we have already noticed — the renunciation of the world and the purely religious nature of these ethics.

Even though, as we have seen, the absoluteness of Jesus' ethical enthusiasm had been toned down in some particulars for the sake of a peaceable compromise with the old ethics "of the world," Paul's demands still make an impression of imposing greatness upon us. It is true, the command to keep peace is no longer unconditioned, its edge is blunted by the concessions, "as much as in you lies,"[1] "as far as possible," and the command of love begins almost imperceptibly to be confined to the brotherhood: "Let us do good to all men, especially to them that are of the household of faith."[2] It is very natural and yet, for that very reason, it is not quite in the spirit of the parable of the Good Samaritan, who does good to the wounded man though he belongs to another nation and is of another creed. So too we have shown, in many other places in the preceding chapter, how, again and again, the *via media* of compromise is sought after. Yet as a whole the prevailing impression which St Paul's moral demands make upon one is still that of a loftiness which cannot be exceeded, and, like Jesus' words, wherever they are read and understood in their true sense, they contain a judgment upon our

[1] Rom. xii. 18.   [2] Gal. vi. 10.

present "Christian" ethics: the Christian is to be ready to make every sacrifice, he is to abhor every act of violence, his only weapons wherewith to conquer the world are to be the loving heart and deed: overcome evil with good — a principle which no present system of Christian ethics carries out in all its consequences.

In politics above all the application of the maxim of "might is right" is considered to be morally justifiable and even necessary. There is no doubt that Jesus and Paul would have rejected it. One of the marks of the fellowship of His disciples, Jesus has told us, was precisely that they would *not* so act.[1] But this is just the point where we perceive a second limitation of early Christian ethics, a limitation which has hitherto prevented the satisfactory solution of the problem. Even Jesus' moral teaching turns away from social life; it is individual in its tendency. But Paul's is altogether cut off from a national life; his ethical system is that of anarchism without and of a conventicle within. The vices and the virtues with which it is concerned are those of a tiny circle of believers, absolutely cut off from the rest of the world. It does not move along with the full stream of a broad life, in touch with the world at every point, nor has it to do with people who either could or would acquire any influence in the shaping of society or the State. That is why its characteristics are for the most part strongly negative. Read from this point of view, *e.g.* the wonderful panegyric of love in 1 Cor. xiii., even the positive commands have a negative character if you

[1] Mark x. 42.

look at their contents. Love is long-suffering (not quick to punish) and kind, rejoices in the truth, covereth all things, believeth all things, hopeth all things, suffereth all things. Even Rom. xii. leaves quite the same impression upon us. If one bears in mind this character of the early Christian ethics, it is easy to understand how Christianity has been confounded with the compassionate ethics of Buddhism. For all that it *is* a confusion and is founded upon ignorance.

One fact, however, is of supreme importance for the later development of Christian ethics—that is, the limited space which Paul's ethics covered. There are wide domains of human activity which lie untouched, unnoticed by it. And that is why all manner of wild ethical ideas—pre-christian for the most part in their origin—have taken possession of these places and have covered them. What then is the sphere to which Paul's moral admonitions apply? Listen to a summary, *e.g.* from first Thessalonians, where he develops it under the comprehensive title, " How one ought to walk and to please God."

" This is the will of God, your sanctification : (1) Ye shall abstain from fornication; each shall make one woman his wife, purely and honourably, not for the mere gratification of his passions, like the heathen who know not God. (2) Ye shall not overreach or take advantage of your brethren in business. For the Lord takes vengeance upon all who do such things. . . . (3) Concerning love to the brethren, ye have no need that one write unto you. . . . (4) Everyone is to live quietly and attend to his own business. [Here is the passage which is directed against dreamy idleness].[1] Sexual purity, commercial morality—the "brother" only is mentioned, but non-Christians are probably not meant to be excluded—and brotherly love—such are the virtues St Paul insists upon. And the impression we gain from those passages, where the admonition is founded upon the catalogues of virtues and vices, is much the same. In Rom. i. the "vile passions," the sensual, come first; then follow again dishonesty in trade; and then the list: "envy, murder, strife, lying, deceit, backbiting, enmity to God, insolence, haughtiness, boastfulness, disobedience to parents, senselessness and untrustworthiness, hard-heartedness, unmercifulness." In 1 Cor. v. 11 *seq.* we have sexual immorality, dishonesty, idolatry, abusiveness, drunkenness, extortion; and in 1 Cor. vi. 9 *seq.* the same vices in rather more detail; in Gal. v. 19 *seq.*, unchastity, impurity, indecency, idolatry, sorcery, quarrels, strife, jealousy, outbursts of passion, acts of rivalry, dissensions, divisions, envy, drunkenness, revelry. It is evident from an examination of these passages not only that St Paul's eye was fixed upon a definite, restricted sphere of human life, but that he was here following a customary practice in his preaching, and possibly he had actual copies before him. These catalogues of vices in fact exactly correspond to the enumeration of sins which were then very common in Greek and Jewish popular literature—even the conclusion is the same, "and the like."[2] Paul will have copied these lists not only because he needed a definite framework for his moral exhortations, but also because he knew that the ground was here best prepared in the con-

[1] 1 Thess. iv. 1–12.   [2] Gal. v. 21.

sciences of his readers, and that they were ready to receive his teaching on these points. We must not therefore make the apostle and his peculiar circumstances alone answerable for this limitation of his ethical horizon to the vices and virtues we have quoted, but we must realise that the morality of early Christianity as a whole was not simply an indigenous growth. In spite of all Paul's polemics against the law—even in Rom. xiii. 8-10, where his attitude is a different one, he merely quotes from the ten commandments those prohibitions which are found in the catalogues of vices—it forced its way in again by means of these Hellenistic-Jewish ethical instructions.

In drawing up the lists of virtues, St Paul is probably less dependent on the work of others, and that is why he writes more freshly. Such a list we find in Gal. v. 22. The fruit of the Spirit is love, joy, peace, forbearance, kindness, generosity, trustfulness, gentleness, self-control. Here too therefore the ideal is that of a gentle, meditative, passive rather than active, and creative type of morality. Paul said more of the militant virtues when he spoke of his own life, or when he thought of the individual's struggle against the devil. On another occasion too we find him addressing these words of comfort to his converts at Philippi, in the midst of their manifold trials and sufferings:

" Let the life of the congregation be worthy of the gospel of Christ: that, whether I come and see you or be absent, I may hear of your state; that ye stand fast in *one* spirit, striving together with *one* soul for the faith of the Gospel, in nothing affrighted by the adversaries ; to them a proof of their (everlasting) ruin, to you of your salvation, and that from God. For to you it hath been granted not only to believe in Christ, but to suffer for Him. So you are now engaged in the same struggle, which you saw in me and which you hear I am still maintaining."[1] Those are bold and brave words. And surely we may apply to St Paul's life, and to the lives of his converts, Lessing's wise observation, that we speak least of those virtues which are our surest possession. Nor need we imagine that a morality which lays greater emphasis on passive endurance, while it comparatively disregards the active virtues, demands a less great effort of the will or is in any way easier: on the contrary. It is not only in actual warfare that the easiest method of defence is a lively and vigorous attack.

Though he enjoins renunciation of the world, the apostle's claims are not ascetic. He nowhere makes morality to consist in celibacy, vegetarianism, or total abstinence. We have already examined this point at some length; it is only necessary therefore to remind ourselves here once more, that the only way in which asceticism enters into the apostle's life or teaching is as a sacrifice peculiar to a special calling, it is a temporary service of love. Here too St Paul and Jesus agree.

Still further removed from St Paul's teaching than the monastic ideal—excepting the one point of celibacy—is the Buddhistic conception of asceticism—that redemption for man consists in withdrawing oneself from the things of this world. St Paul's religion is

[1] Phil. i. 27–30.

THE FOUNDATIONS OF ETHICS 339

not lassitude or a yearning for death, but peace and joy in the Holy Spirit; and where the Spirit is, there is freedom and strength, new, eternal life that never wearies.

THE FOUNDATIONS OF ETHICS.

However little St Paul succeeded in establishing a satisfactory basis for each ethical command taken separately, he proved himself to be a theologian of vigorous thought, with a perfect command of expression in his derivation of morality as a whole from its religious presuppositions.

As Nietzsche has rightly observed, you must always see the "for" in an ethical system, and that not only because of the formal reason which we have just noticed, but in order to understand its character thoroughly. We must of course learn to judge cautiously. In Jesus even more than in St Paul, the new "for" which is peculiar to both does not stand out clearly from the old message of threats and penalties of the prophets to which they attach themselves. In St Paul as well as in Jesus the claims of morality are still supported by the sanctions of divine rewards and punishments. In St Paul, the theologian, a progress is however perceptible. In him the idea of rewards and the true inner sanction of morality are about equally balanced, and the thoughts of reward are more frequently expressed in an individual manner. So he puts an old picture to a new use when he says, speaking of his fellow-labourers without mentioning their names, "whose names are written in the Book of Life."[1] On the other hand, it

[1] Phil. iv. 3.

is quite in the popular style—just as Jesus would have said—and opposed to his own usage when he adds to a catalogue of vices the threat: "They that do such things will not inherit the kingdom of God."[1] Because of the promises his Corinthian converts "cleanse themselves from all defilement of the flesh and (Holy) Spirit, perfecting holiness in the fear of God."[2] Elsewhere St Paul has given a profounder and more peculiar expression to the usual apocalyptic thoughts derived from his early piety: "Wherefore we faint not: but though our outward man is decaying, yet our inward man is renewed day by day. For our light affliction, which is for the moment, worketh for us beyond all expectation an eternal treasure of glory, while we look, not at the things which are seen, but at the things which are not seen; for the things which are seen are temporal, but the things which are not seen are eternal."[3] In sentences such as these the idea of reward vanishes in a yearning which crowds all petty motives out of sight, filling the whole heart, and awaiting the heavenly treasure but as a wonderful gift, for the sake of which patient endurance in the misery of this life certainly carries its reward.

But not even in this form does the old Jewish thought contain the roots of the Pauline ethics, or even of the theological sanction for the claims of his ethics. We come across this in quite different passages — where St Paul's opponents forced him to defend his doctrine of grace against unwarrantable deductions drawn from it: for here he was compelled to derive morality as something absolutely necessary

---

[1] Gal. v. 21; cp. 2 Cor. v. 10. [2] 2 Cor. vii. 1.
[3] 2 Cor. iv. 16 seq.

from the highest and the best that he possessed—his religion.

The central thought in the whole chain of the argument is the following: The new life that has begun in the Christian through the Holy Ghost, the indwelling Christ, can be no other than moral in correspondence with the nature of the heavenly being. These are the profoundest thoughts St Paul ever uttered (see Rom. vi. and viii.): he is not in reality so much finding a theoretical sanction for his ethical system as giving immediate and positive utterance to his personal religion. We need not therefore do more than quote one or two of the incisive phrases: " We who died to sin, shall we any longer live therein?"[1] " Even so reckon ye also yourselves to be dead unto sin, but alive unto God in Christ Jesus. Let not sin therefore reign in your mortal body, that ye should obey the lusts thereof; neither present your members unto sin as weapons of unrighteousness, but present yourselves to God, as alive from the dead, and your members as weapons of righteousness for God. For sin shall not have dominion over you: for ye are no more under law, but under grace."[2] " Therefore, brethren, we are debtors, not to the flesh, to live after the flesh, for if ye live after the flesh ye will die: but if by the Spirit ye mortify the deeds of the body, ye shall live. For all who are led by the Spirit of God are sons of God."[3] Here we have a "therefore" and a "for" side by side, two separate and distinct sanctions of morality which St Paul has not harmonised. The first—the "therefore"—derives morality as that which is "due" to the redeemed

[1] Rom. vi. 2. [2] Rom. vi. 11 *seq.* [3] Rom. viii. 12 *seq.*

nature, to the possession of the new life; and the second—the "for"—brings forward the old Jewish ideas once more—the reward of everlasting life, the inheritance of the sons of God. So again in the Epistle to the Galatians we have both lines of thought side by side. First, the new, the Christian, wonderfully distinct: "If we live by the Spirit, by the Spirit let us also walk."[1] Then the old: "He that sows to the flesh, shall from the flesh in the course of nature reap corruption; he that sows to the Spirit, shall from the Spirit reap eternal life." Paul did not perceive that two religious systems here jostle each other— the Jewish religion of rewards and a legal righteousness, and the new religion of redemption and of the Spirit; the religion of the second born, that is, in newness of life. But we must draw a sharp dividing line, and say, that in the latter religion alone is the high level of Christianity maintained, for in it alone we get beyond Judaism and every form of legal religion. Surely the theory that finds the sanction for morality in an actually experienced redemption is the only thought that harmonises with the apostle's own great experience.

It is interesting too to notice that man's divine sonship, as a consequence of the possession of this Spirit, enters as an integral factor into St Paul's ethics. And here he touches most closely that sanction of morality which was Jesus' peculiar possession, and yet he does it in such a manner that we see how, starting from his mysticism, he has reached the same end, the same thoughts, by quite a different road. There is an allusion to this train of thought in Rom. viii.,[2]

[1] Gal. v. 25.   [2] Rom. viii. 14.

but St Paul has expressed it most beautifully in Phil. ii. 15: "Do all things without murmurings and disputings, that ye may be blameless and harmless, 'children of God without blemish' in the midst of a 'crooked and perverse generation,' among whom ye shine as stars in the world."

Could these thoughts but be carried out in any one of their manifold forms, we should no longer need to state morality in terms of the categorical imperative, but in the shape of simple statements. The religious man "ought" not to be moral, he is moral—that is a fundamental Christian thought. Nevertheless the categorical imperative has always been needed—in any case it has had a very hardy life—not only now by us who have to educate children, but also in early Christianity, where whole congregations had to be educated. And so Paul wavers not only between the ethics of redemption and of retribution, but also between the assertion that morality is a natural and necessary consequence of religion, and the traditional method, wherein he uses religious ideas as motives, and maintains one must be moral because of one's religion. If we read passages such as Rom. vi. or viii., or even Gal. v., we shall easily perceive this constant vacillation. It is very difficult to decide what Paul really considered the normal Christian life to be. Was it to be perfectly sinless or not? Passages such as, "The flesh lusteth against the (Holy) Spirit and the Spirit against the flesh: they are opposed to each other, so that ye do not what ye would,"[1] do not in any case warrant the statement that Paul believed, like Luther, that a new Adam had to be born daily. For in the

[1] Gal. v. 17.

verse immediately preceding, we read, "Walk by the Spirit, and ye shall certainly not fulfil the lusts of the flesh."[1] And he assures the Corinthians, "God is faithful: He will not suffer you to be tempted above that ye are able, but will with the temptation make also the way of escape, that ye may be able to endure it."[2] So then Paul's ideal will have been sinlessness, but in face of the actual condition of his congregations he could not conceal from himself that they were still very "carnal."[3] And yet he could also use language indicating not only that Christians ought to be sinless, but that they actually were so, and could not be otherwise. Just as "necessity is laid upon him," so he says of others that, being free from sin, they have become "slaves" of righteousness or of God;[4] that having died unto the law, they have become the "property" of Him who was raised from the dead, that they might bring forth fruit unto God.[5] He even speaks of a "law of the spirit of life," which set him free[6] from the other law of sin and of death. It appears as if one form of compulsion had only made room for another, but these strong expressions are all based upon the experience of his conversion. They must always be taken together with those others which correspond more nearly to the facts of daily life—not till then have we the full expression of the morality which is to be characteristic even of the new religion.

But St Paul is not content merely to lay down these central thoughts, just as little when he is establishing the basis of his ethical system as when

[1] Gal. v. 16.   [2] 1 Cor. x. 13.   [3] 1 Cor. iii. 3.
[4] Rom. vi. 18–22.   [5] Rom. vii. 4.   [6] Rom. viii. 2.

he is defending his religious experience. Each doctrinal theory has its practical consequence most skilfully indicated. From the doctrine of justification he infers, "Ye were slaves of sin, but being freed from it, ye have become slaves of righteousness";[1] or, "Ye, brethren, were called for freedom, only use not your freedom as an opportunity for self-indulgence (in selfish misuse) but serve each other in love."[2] And still more distinctly from the theory of redemption he draws this sanction: "Or know ye not that your body is a temple of the Holy Ghost, which is in you, which ye have from God, and that ye are not your own. Ye were bought with a price: glorify God therefore with your body."[3] It is God that accomplished the work; the Christian's duty[4] is therefore to live unto God and to serve Him, to serve God, the Lord, the Redeemer.[5]

There is a slight touch of ecclesiasticism in the expression "worthy of God or the Gospel,"[6] but even so morality is still based upon the centre of religious life, without any thought of reward.

Unlike Luther, St Paul has not made use in this connection of the motive of gratitude to God who has done such great things for His children. But it amounts to very nearly the same thing when Paul speaks of the sacrifice of the body, which is to be rendered to God in memory of His mercy.[7]

In the preceding chapter, we have seen that when St Paul sets up individual ethical demands, he is

---
[1] Rom. vi. 18.   [2] Gal. v. 13.   [3] 1 Cor. vi. 19.
[4] Rom. vi. 11-22, vii. 6; 1 Thess. i. 9.
[5] Rom. xiv. 8; 2 Cor. v. 15.   [6] 1 Thess. ii. 12; Phil. i. 27.
[7] Rom. xii. 1.

dependent upon the law and upon Hellenistic models. His ethical system would only have been complete if he had been able to derive it, in its particular as well as its general outline, from the Christian's great and novel experience. It is not merely a question of the symmetry of his theological system—that is a very subordinate matter—but it would have made all the difference for Christianity if its first theologian could have developed a new ideal of life in the beauty of completeness and in perfect clearness, and derived it from the new contents that life had acquired. This, however, was not done.

Only here and there do we find some few ineffectual attempts to prove that this or that particular rule of morality depends necessarily on the new religion. Thus, above all, St Paul based the great central claim of brotherly love on purely religious grounds—not, primarily at any rate, on the idea that all Christians are God's children, and therefore brethren, though it may have been present to his mind also, but clearly and plainly on that thought to which we have so often referred, on the common possession of the Holy Ghost, of Christ, who makes of all Christendom one great body, so that each individual is a member, whose sufferings must rouse the sympathy of all others, in whose joy all share alike, and who thus serves, and is meant to serve, all others.[1]

Paul made another similar attempt to substantiate the law of chastity. There were already men in the church then, as there were for many long years afterwards, who wished to carry over into the new Christian ethics the popular idea of the morality of

[1] Rom. xii. ; 1 Cor. xii.

THE FOUNDATIONS OF ETHICS

the ancient world: free sexual intercourse was a thing quite outside of the sphere of morality, it was something altogether "natural," just as eating and drinking, and did not affect the inner man, the religious subject. "Everything is lawful," free love just as much as the eating of meat offered to idols; nothing can rob the redeemed, the new-born man, who has the sacrament and thereby everlasting life, of his divine kinship, his life. St Paul set himself sternly against this sense of religious security which rushed to meet half-way the natural instincts of mankind—to which the sacramental conception of religion inevitably leads. He alleges three reasons against it: (1) Eating and drinking cannot be included with sexual licence under the same category of "natural wants." Food only concerns the belly, and will perish with it, as will flesh and blood generally. But sexual intercourse affects the whole "body," and the body belongs to the Lord, who will once raise it up. This is just an evasion. But the other two reasons are not much better: (2) The Christian's body is a member of the Lord; the Christian dare not therefore give this body to another, but in sexual intercourse "the two become one flesh." But this argument would make marriage—especially marriage with a heathen partner — impossible, and Paul expressly allowed such marriages and desired them to continue. (3) He expresses the same thought, substituting, as we might readily expect, the Holy Ghost for Christ: "Or know ye not that your body is a temple of the Holy Spirit that dwelleth in you, which Spirit ye have from God? And ye are not your own, for ye are bought with a price. Glorify God therefore in your body." This third reason appears to our feelings the least unsatisfactory, but that simply because, to start with, we understand by "Holy Ghost" a moral power, and consider chastity to be moral. But in St Paul's case the argument is a religious one, and is really only a repetition of the second reason: As belonging to God and the Spirit, the body may not be given to the woman.[1]

Either the argument goes too far and then marriage is attainted — and certainly Paul only "suffers" marriage—or it does not go far enough. For the apostle, who stood under the influence of the *tradition* of his own people, the free love of the Greeks was something altogether abhorrent and immoral. That was his real reason.

To this day Christian ethics suffer here from a great lacuna. The difficult problems which are raised in this domain by modern inquirers in opposition to the traditional Christian morality are not treated with the earnestness, thoroughness, and openness that they deserve. Through our indolent prudery we have suffered a pestilent bog to be formed in the midst of our people, we have allowed a very upas-tree to grow up which is poisoning our national life. It is high time that theology too should begin to think a little more seriously of these difficult questions on a scientific basis, should try and substantiate better the claims of Christian morality in particular instances, should show why it is necessary to maintain the ideal here if life is to continue, and how the ideal is to be implanted in the minds and hearts of the young. By our ostrich-like procedure with regard to these ques-

[1] 1 Cor. v. 12–20.

tions we actually thrust the young into the bog by leaving them to seek enlightenment in these matters from their corrupted companions or older schoolfellows. This must be changed. Both church and school must learn to meet this all-important question of our social life more openly and more thoroughly than they have done in the past.

But not only here; in almost every domain of ethics the most thorough, and in some respects the most important, work for our present-day Christianity remains to be done. In the face of our modern civilisation, the mass of the unsolved problems that the age of the Reformation has handed down to us becomes very formidable, and the ethics of the conventicle are as little adapted to our wants as the belief that the State is the servant of the Church and the executive of Christian morality. The modern State is no longer that. The State claims to be outside of and above all creeds. What we need, more than anything else, is that our ethics should be based throughout clearly and distinctly on the idea of love. Then we shall have an ideal of life which we shall be able to acknowledge as a symmetrical whole, instead of misunderstood law and obsolete traditional custom.

By the side of this theoretical basis of morality the most important incentive is to be found in the imitation of Christ. Even as early as St Paul, the imitation of Jesus is a constantly recurring demand. Nor do we find it merely in such general thoughts as that which we have already examined, that we should look upon ourselves as dead with Christ, and therefore also as risen with Him to a new moral life,[1] but it is

[1] Rom. vi. 11.

applied to particular cases. Every one is to live so as to please his neighbour, not himself; he is to act for his neighbour's good, for his edification, just as Christ lived not to please Himself, but willingly took upon Himself all suffering and every kind of reproach; as the Scripture says, "The reproaches of them that reproached thee fell upon me."[1] Just as Christ received us by becoming a "minister" of the circumcision, by becoming incarnate and suffering Himself to be circumcised in order to help others, so we should receive each other.[2] The incarnation is frequently employed in this manner, as an ethical pattern, even such a detail as in the case of contributing to the great collection for the poor. Surely you do not forget the goodness of our Lord Jesus Christ! How that for our sake He became poor (incarnate), although He was rich (in the divine glory in heaven), that ye through His poverty might become rich.[3] But above all it is the humility of the Lord from heaven that St Paul holds up to his Philippians with such winning impressiveness: "If therefore there is any encouragement in Christ, if there is any persuasive power in love, if there is any fellowship in the Spirit, if there is any tenderness or pity, then make my happiness complete: be united, have the same love, be of one heart and one soul, do nothing in a spirit of faction or from vanity, but in humility let each look upon the other as better than himself: do not regard your own interests exclusively, but always consult the interests of others as well. Let the spirit of Christ Jesus be yours also. Did He not . . . empty Himself (of His glory) and take upon Himself the form of

[1] Rom. xv. 3. [2] Rom. xv. 7. [3] 2 Cor. viii. 9.

THE FOUNDATIONS OF ETHICS 351

a slave?"[1] Let us notice, by the way, the conception of humility as it appears here and in other passages where Paul praises this virtue. It is not a humility that is incompatible with genuine moral pride, that makes itself cheap and is hypocritical, but it is the child of love and finds its true sphere of work in peacefulness and readiness to serve, in opposition to all factiousness, conceit, and vanity. From the fact that this motive of the imitation of Christ appears so frequently in the apostle's letters, we may infer that it formed an important factor in his preaching. It was of course a good deal easier to understand than the intricate theories upon which morality is usually based.

Paul often expressed this same motive still more simply—Do as I do: "Be ye imitators of me."[2] Here again he did not mean slavish literal copying. Perhaps there was no other way in which his congregations better realised the fact that morality is an *individual* art requiring a delicate appreciation, than when the great contrast between the demands which the apostle made upon himself and those he made upon his converts came home to them. He had to fulfil every claim made by the most fervent enthusiasm. He did not marry: his converts were at least suffered to marry. He had no quiet settled calling: they were ordered to have one. He took no money for his teaching: in the case of the other apostles he finds working for hire perfectly natural. He was always coming into conflict with the State: of his converts he demands the strictest obedience. Indeed to be his true follower one needed to copy

[1] Phil. ii, 1–6. [2] 1 Cor. iv. 16, xi. 1; Phil. iii. 17.

the pattern of his life, not mechanically, but to assimilate it in heart and mind, as "he also" had done that "of Christ."

A man must have a conscience free from reproach and some pride to say, "Be my imitators." Had Paul a right to use such words? Are not his letters full of violent accusations against his enemies? And has not the last great opponent of Christianity painted him in his *Antichrist* as animated by the low and mean instinct of revenge felt by the disinherited for golden Rome? Has he not branded his faith and his hope, his message of love and goodwill, as hidden hatred and the common envy of the Tschandala caste? Whom are we to believe? His old and his new enemies or his words? This question we will endeavour to answer by now finally placing the apostle's picture before us, simply as he was as man, apart from his weighty sayings about the new religion and apart from the work of his calling.

THE MAN.

CHAPTER XXIII.

Dross. The Apostle's Human Greatness. Winning Love.

It is true that even while we were considering the apostle, as he manifested himself outwardly, as he laid bare the supremest hours of his spiritual life, vindicating and defending them as prophet and as theologian, as he proclaimed his faith, won hearts, and welded together his converts with moral earnestness and shrewd common sense in one great fellowship—it was one side of the man Paul that engaged our thoughts and feelings. But we have other, more directly human demands on him. His epistles are the outcome of his great hours when he focussed his experience as a whole—the expression of his highest ideals. But how did he stand himself with regard to these ideals? We certainly are not going to "judge" him. He has pronounced these words which show such deep insight: "To me it is a very small thing that I should be judged by you or by any human court. Indeed I do not even judge myself; for I am conscious of nothing against myself: not that that proves me innocent, but He that judges me is the Lord."[1] A man cannot judge even himself justly, to acquit or condemn; a Higher than he searches the hearts and our capacities and inheritance of faults and virtues from our forefathers and from humanity.

Perhaps, however, it will not appear presumptuous if we refuse to stop short in our study of the man Paul at the results gathered from his achievements in his vocation. Moral and religious prophets have to submit to a closer scrutiny; we want to see how far the ideals they proclaim were realised in themselves; for the influence they exercise upon the souls of men lies in the fact not of their teaching something, but of their living something. Above everything else they must submit to the inquiry, how they transformed and ennobled their natural aptitudes of temperament and endowment according to the ideals which they preached.

Yet, after all, it is not only this legitimate demand for a clear insight into the power of a new faith over a great human heart, but something far more tender and intimate, which impels us to penetrate even to the inner recesses of this heart: even our admiration, and the love that Paul has won from us, if we have rightly understood him as prophet, apostle, teacher, and organiser. Thus, for example it is, to begin with, readily comprehensible that we should wish to know what was the outward appearance of the man whose inner life and energy have been so much in our minds, and have exercised so great an influence upon all the Western world. On this point, however, it is not possible to discover anything more than what we

---

[1] 1 Cor. iv. 3 *seq.*

THE MAN

have already given in the section on Paul as preacher. Neither will we speak here at greater length about his ailment; at various points in the story we have insisted upon its significance in his life. His contemporary Jewish - Christian adversaries, and those who in our own day still hate him for his teaching, imagine they can account for his faith very simply by such terms as disease, insanity, hysteria; but, as we have seen, in doing so they are quite as unjust as if they imagined they could put down Cæsar or Napoleon as madmen likewise because they suffered from a like disease. It is just the men of genius who must needs frequently pay their tribute to the limitations of human greatness by having to endure such a "messenger of Satan." The only influence his malady may have had was on the particular form in which Paul realised his religion, so that with him it broke out in trance and vision. But even this can hardly be ascertained with accuracy, for men who are perfectly healthy can also have visions and fall into trances. Goethe himself, the man that seems to us so unruffled and serene, so self-contained and well-balanced, and who certainly had the soundest of health, was yet not without such visions. For a fair estimate of the apostle, we must not look at this morbid tendency of his, but rather at the clearness of his moral judgment and at the strength of will with which he endured and overcame the "messenger of Satan." His heroic nature, the dominating power of his personality, which he manifested outwardly to others in conversion and "signs," stand out all the more brightly on the sombre background of his infirmity, and the words he once heard in prayer as a response from God, "My strength is made perfect in weakness,"¹ should be written as the motto to Paul's life.

DROSS.

The apostle's vehement temperament was never completely subdued by his ideal: "Peace, joy, love, long-suffering, gentleness."² Even as a Christian he could still hate hotly, damn and curse passionately. True, this man no longer knows personal hatred and individual vengeance, yet even then too, when he launches anathema at the opponents of his sacred cause, we can hardly any longer recognise him. The "woe" of Jesus³ has certainly quite a different sound from His apostle's words, such as these: "Yet even if we, or if an angel from heaven, were to preach to you contrary to what I have preached unto you, may he be accursed! I have said it before and I repeat it now: If anyone preaches another gospel to you, may he be accursed."⁴ Or, when he concludes his first Epistle to the Corinthians with these words: "If any man loveth not the Lord, let him be anathema."⁵ Love and execration side by side, surely not after the same mind as was in Christ Jesus! Just such zeal for the good cause brought forth at a later period that terrible "love" of the Church which paled the heretic to the stake. Paul too wanted to strike a sinner dead by his curse,—true in a case that was "unheard of even among the Gentiles."⁶ As yet it was grave moral delinquencies that were under his consideration, or hypocrisy that only feigned to be Christian, or the defeat of Chris-

---

[1] 2 Cor. xii. 9.   [2] Gal. v. 22.   [3] Matt. xxiii.
[4] Gal. i. 8.   [5] 1 Cor. xvi. 22.   [6] 1 Cor. v. 1.

tianity through the inroads of Judaism,—as yet it is not subtle points of dogma, for the sake of which he calls for a malediction of death or everlasting perdition on the wicked brother: but when once we err from the way of merciful love even to the most worthless, there is no stopping still. Formerly a fanatic, to whom even what was most horrible readily appeared "to the glory of God," he certainly did learn quite a different conduct as a Christian with regard to those who differed from himself in matters of faith; yet now and again the old hard and cruel man breaks out against the "false brother."

Paul stands again in similar violent contrast to Jesus in the matter of his frequent oaths and asservations, so entirely different from the triumphant clearness, candour, and truthfulness of Jesus. How kingly are Jesus' words about the slanders His enemies circulated against Him. They say: "When He goes to visit publicans and sinners, He does so in order to gormandise and indulge Himself." How does He answer them? "Whereunto shall I liken this generation? It is like unto children sitting in the market-places, and calling out to their playmates: We piped unto you, and ye did not dance; we wailed, and ye did not beat your breasts. For John came neither eating nor drinking (living as an ascetic), and they said, He hath a devil! The Son of Man came eating and drinking and they said: Behold, a gluttonous man and a winebibber, a friend of publicans and sinners."[1] Paul is fain to defend himself otherwise. He too can be proud and majestic, but he is always excited and vehement; he does not stand

[1] Matt. xi. 16-19; Luke vii. 31-34.

superior to all reproaches in purity aloof. No, he must passionately plead for credence. Take the second Epistle to the Corinthians, especially the four final chapters, in connection with this point of view, and the difference from Jesus will at once become patent. As we have seen, Paul himself knew this, and felt that what he did was not "after the Lord,"[1] "as the Master would," but he deemed it necessary "to become a fool" because he was jealous for his congregation with a godly jealousy.[2] His nature is not harmonious; passion carries him away, and his speech is not invariably the clear, calm expression of what was best in his character. A certain softness and pliancy in dealing with his personal opponents contributed to strengthen their accusation that he was double-tongued. And then unfortunately he often has recourse to that old weapon of his own and of all peoples—the oath—of which Jesus in His plain way said it came of the evil one;[3] for it is only a compulsory truth-telling, forced from an insincere nature. Paul's oath, "God is my witness," may on many occasions merely have been an old Jewish habit; sometimes he may have used it to strengthen an appeal to his readers' hearts, as when he assures the Romans—calling God to witness—that he always prays for them;[4] for all that it remains a bad habit, and causes a certain repulsion in us, especially when Paul makes use of this expression to assure his congregation of his love.[5] Its use is more pardonable when he has to defend himself against base reproaches;[6] yet even then we feel that it is scarcely

---

[1] 2 Cor. xi. 17.   [2] 2 Cor. xi. 1 *seq.*   [3] Matt. v. 37.
[4] Rom. i. 9 *seq.*   [5] Phil. i. 8.   [6] 1 Thess. ii. 5–10.

worthy of his own better self when he thus defends himself against an almost silly reproach: "I call God to witness against my own soul that it was only to spare you I did not come to Corinth."[1]

We have also seen already that Paul did not always do full justice to his opponents in controversy. He neither appreciated their motives nor the strength of their historical position, which they derived from the essentially more conservative relation of Jesus to the law. But Paul had the spirit of history on his side, and the essence of the Gospel of Jesus as well.

Perhaps it is a law of universal history that wherever a great and new idea is to be realised, its advocates cannot "do justice," cannot see every side of the question, cannot fully understand their adversaries' historical development. On one occasion when Paul had gone too far in a personal dispute— he had been insulted by a Corinthian—he confessed his error and gave way to the decision of the congregation, which was unfavourable to the infliction of that punishment on his opponent which he had desired. At least it is possible to take the passage 2 Cor. ii. 10 in this sense. Or it may be merely this. The majority of his converts at Corinth had acted with great severity towards the offender. The apostle wishes them to take advantage of his own readiness to forgive, and impresses this upon them with a charm of style which he knows well how to employ. The first verse of this somewhat obscure chapter seems to favour this interpretation.

Lastly, we must repeat once again, that his keen

[1] 2 Cor. i. 23.

intellect and his Pharisaic training led him to employ more than one quibble, of which it is hard to imagine that they were more to him than mere means in his controversies about the letter of Scripture.

But having said this, we have exhausted our enumeration of the defects of Paul's great qualities and of those remnants of the old man, due to previous education or to inheritance, which had not yet been " made new."

The Apostle's Human Greatness.

And surely these remnants vanish into infinitesimally small proportions when we compare them with the human, lovable features in the apostle's character. Whoever reads Paul's letters with an open mind and not in search of texts, is sure to be deeply impressed by the force of his character, by the passion of his feelings, and the strength of his will. But such too was the impression he made on all with whom he came into contact during his lifetime. It is not only the tradition about his "miracles" that bears witness to this. We have besides the travel-document of one of his companions, to which we have already referred. It contains for the most part dry entries concerning the places visited and the length of the apostle's stay in each: but interspersed between these are pictures of the apostle's sayings and doings, and in these naïve accounts we can plainly read the awe and the veneration which the writer felt for the great man in whose journeys and sufferings he was permitted to share.

He tells us how at Philippi, a demon of divination, which had entered into a certain maid, met the apostle.

For many days the hysterical girl runs screaming through the streets after the apostle and his companions, until at length the apostle adjures the demon, bidding him come forth: "And the demon came out that very hour."[1] But greater things than these the apostle could do in the eyes of his companions. It was on his journey to Jerusalem that Paul preached at Troas in the upper room of a house till far on into the night. A young man had sat down in the window and had fallen asleep. He moved so that he fell—it was from the third story—and was picked up dead. Paul hurried down, threw himself upon him, embraced him and said: "Be not afraid, his life is in him."[2] So the men related to each other in awed whispers, and all remembered that in like manner the great Elisha had awakened from the dead the son of the Shunammite.[3] All believed that they had here beheld one raised from the dead. It would have seemed to them absurd, and a mark of unbelief, to ask whether the apostle's words did not point to something different, and whether the man had not merely been stunned or had fainted. But the great man did not only do miracles, he was also proof against all dangers which are fatal to other mortals. In the island of Malta, the apostle is placing a bundle of sticks on a fire when a viper crawls out because of the heat and fastens on him. Then his companion gives us a graphic picture how the "barbarians" sit round the fire with horror on their countenances, gazing at the apostle: "No doubt this man is a murderer. He has just escaped from the sea, but justice will not

[1] Acts xvi. 16–18. [2] Acts xx. 7–12. [3] 2 Kings iv. 34.

let him live." But he shook off the beast into the fire, and no harm came to him. They expected the wound to gangrene, or that he would suddenly fall down dead. When they had waited a long time and perceived that nothing amiss happened to him, they changed their minds and said that he was a god. How vividly the story is told! How imperceptibly our attention is drawn to the notoriously poisonous nature of the beast! And yet again, with what art the author omits to tell us whether the serpent bit Paul's hand or not: "it fastened on his hand." It made no difference to him, who admired and revered the apostle. It was only the divine power possessed by his hero that could possibly have miraculously preserved him from certain death from the poisonous serpent.[1]

Such was the atmosphere of the miraculous which surrounded the apostle even during his lifetime—as it does every saint. We realise the power of his personal influence, his strength of will, yet more clearly, however, through the position of authority which he occupies on the sea voyage in the midst of the dangers of shipwreck. As an experienced traveller, he warns the sailors before starting.[2] When the storm bursts upon them, and every one else on board the big, closely packed transport has lost his head, it is Paul again who is alone calm and unconcerned. Still more, when all despair, he, the prisoner, the despised Jew, steps into their midst and says: "Friends, I urge you to be of good heart. For last night an angel of the God to whom I belong and whom I serve came to me and said, 'Fear not, Paul,

[1] Acts xxviii. 1–6.   [2] Acts xxvii. 10.

THE APOSTLE'S HUMAN GREATNESS

thou shalt stand before Cæsar; and behold, God hath granted thee the lives of all thy fellow-travellers.' So do not lose heart, friends. I believe God. It shall be as it was told me. We must be cast upon an island." And when at nightfall they come near to the land and are still in great danger, and the sailors treacherously intend to leave the ship, it is again Paul who calls the attention of the captain of the soldiers to the danger which threatens them all. He advises the exhausted men to take something to eat, and makes so deep an impression on the captain of the cohort, that he saves not only his own, but his fellow-prisoners' lives, when the soldiers would rather kill them than run the risk of their escaping by swimming away.[1]

Such was the apostle as he presented himself to his companions in travel. A man of great trust in God, to whom visions were vouchsafed and who possessed miraculous powers, leading a charmed life in the midst of danger: withal a man wise in council, with a profound knowledge of human nature, quick in action and perfectly fearless, towering above all around him, even in his bonds.

The key to this invincible personal influence was that he himself, as we have seen, had an unshaken confidence in God and his mission. He shared his disciples' belief, felt that he was full of a mysterious, miraculous force, even Christ, and that he was preserved by God in a wonderful manner against all dangers. But a faith like this, firm as a rock, and that moves mountains, never fails to exercise an incomparably powerful influence upon the souls of

[1] Acts xxvii. 31, 33-42 *seq.*

men and multiplies the effect of natural courage and inborn vigour to an infinite degree.

THE APOSTLE'S WINNING LOVE.

But these impressions of heroic strength and energy, of ardent vehemence and glowing passion, form but one side of the apostle's character. As we examine a little more attentively, as we look a little more deeply, there rise slowly, like thin vapours from the heavy masses of these first impressions, yet other facts which point to a tender, delicate, and loving personality and one of a peculiarly winning charm.

Like sweet-smelling flowers, these tender, loving phrases are scattered over the rugged, stony slopes of Paul's letters; and some there are who, as they read them, are at first so surprised that they are rather inclined to attribute them to the apostle's keen intellect than to his inmost being. There can be no doubt that few men in all antiquity had a profounder knowledge of human nature than this man who had himself suffered and experienced so much, who had wrestled for his soul with God and with devils, and had then found in that soul of his an unfathomable well of everlasting truth. The sterner his own wrestling had been, the deeper the wound he had inflicted on himself, the finer was his understanding for others, the more enthralling the power of his words, which he knew how to choose with a nice calculation of their effect.

We have already had occasion to notice many illustrations of this side of the apostle's character, especially in the section on the origin of the Church. Even

THE APOSTLE'S WINNING LOVE 365

in his liturgical prayers we can observe the fineness of his style and the nicety of his psychological calculation. For we are not only to look upon the prayers, with which he commences his letters, as the expression of his own heartfelt piety, they are intended also to open the hearts of his readers to him. Thus he wins over the Romans, who are strangers to him, by forging as it were a double chain of prayer round them and himself. As he begins by assuring them that he prays for them without ceasing, so at the close of the letter he begs them in turn again for their prayers for his ministry.[1] And when he thanks God for the spiritual gifts and the manifestations of the Spirit with which He has blessed the Corinthians,[2] he certainly does not do so without the nicely calculated intention of implanting the belief that he attached no small value to these gifts or to those who possessed them, even though he was afterwards compelled to impose limitations upon them. It was with the same intention that he assured them, in the course of his letter, that he counted himself entirely as one of themselves—yes, he spoke with a tongue more than they all, and yet he put upon himself a greater constraint than he demanded of them;[3] and when he comes to sum up the whole matter, he expressly forbids the speaking with tongues to be entirely discouraged.[4]

Nor is the nicety with which he dispenses his praise less remarkable. He knows that there are no more powerful levers in education than praise administered rarely but with discrimination, and entire trust: *possunt quia posse videntur*. At least he acts

[1] Rom. i. 8 *seq.*; xv. 30 *seq.*
[2] 1 Cor. i. 4–9.
[3] 1 Cor. xiv. 15, 19.
[4] 1 Cor. xiv. 39.

in accordance with these maxims. A specially good illustration of the skill with which he adapts his style to the object in view is to be found in the passages where he urges his converts to contribute to the poor at Jerusalem. Not only does he promise the fulness of God's blessings upon them if they persevere,[1] not only does he reassure the anxious—the good man scatters, yet God ever supplies his needs afresh [2]—but he stimulates them to make fresh exertions by holding up to them the example of other churches. "We want to tell you, brothers, about the goodness God has shown to the churches in Macedonia; how, tried though they were by many a trouble, their overflowing happiness (caused by their new faith) and their deep poverty resulted in a flood of generosity. I can bear witness that, to the full extent of their power, and even beyond it, of their own free will too, they earnestly appealed to us for permission to take a part in this grace and ministry to the saints. And (they gave) not (only as much) as we might have expected—no, they first gave themselves to the Lord and to us in accordance with God's will. This led me to urge upon Titus that, as he had begun this 'grace,' he should also complete it, and that in you."[3] And then he adds, with much delicacy, that no idea of compulsion is present in his mind: "I say this not as a commandment"; nor does he ask them to give beyond their power: "God loveth a cheerful giver."[4] But his most effective argument is the information that he stimulated the Macedonians to make especial efforts by telling them, "Achaia was ready a year ago."

[1] 2 Cor. ix. 6–9.
[2] 2 Cor. ix. 10 *seq.*
[3] 2 Cor. viii. 1–9.
[4] 2 Cor. viii. 8–15; ix. 7.

This is one of those cases where we see clear traces of the diplomatist in Paul. He spurred on the Macedonians by his praise of the Corinthians, and the Corinthians with the praise of the Macedonians. Did both quite deserve it? In any case he is not quite sure of the Corinthians, hence the great stress laid by the apostle on the contribution in his letter, and the mission of Titus and his companions, lest his boast should turn out to be unfounded in case any Macedonians accompanied them.[1]

Very skilful too is his treatment of the factions at Corinth, especially the way in which he is careful never to leave out Apollos, always mentioning him in the same breath as himself, treating him on a perfect footing of equality, and facing the divided church (*i.e.* his own adherents and those of Apollos) hand in hand with "his brother Apollos."[2] In the last chapter too, Apollos, who is staying with the apostle, seems to be quite united with him and opposed to the leaders of his own party at Corinth.[3] If we read chaps. 2–4 of the first Epistle to the Corinthians from this point of view, we shall not fail to admire the delicacy of touch with which every word and every metaphor is inserted in the argument. Paul planted; Apollos watered. Paul laid the foundation; Apollos built upon it. The work of both will be tested, not by the Corinthians, but by God. All that one looks for in stewards is that they be found faithful. Everywhere Paul combines the full and proud consciousness of what he was for the congregation with the most delicate reserve and the nicest discrimination in the use of words. He weighs every expression, for, without

[1] 2 Cor. ix. 2–5.   [2] 1 Cor. iii. and iv.   [3] 1 Cor. xvi. 12.

offending Apollos, he has to show his partisans that they are in the wrong.

Many more illustrations might be given. These few will suffice. One's attention need but be called to the point, and as one reads the letters carefully, one will not fail to notice instances in abundance.

It is quite true then that it is the apostle's keen insight and foresight that make of him such a master of style and enable him to play so cleverly on the souls of men. But it would be altogether a mistake to imagine that cleverness here accounts for everything. On the contrary. Fineness and delicacy of touch are only genuine when they issue from a loving and lovable heart. True charm of manner is inborn; it can be as little acquired as a man can learn to be a gentleman. It is no mere surface quality, like routine and cleverness. You must dig deep down. Such is the apostle's wonderful goodness, the tenderness of his heart, which is ever making its way through all obstacles—just as the sun bursts brightly into sight after a heavy thunderstorm—when his passion has vented itself in fierce anger and bitter resentment and irony with words that wound and terrify.

It is especially in his most passionate letters, *e.g.* that to the Galatians and the last four chapters of the second Epistle to the Corinthians, that the effect is exceedingly surprising and charming when he thus suddenly veers round.

In two passages in the Epistle to the Galatians he interrupts himself, while he is marshalling his heavy array of facts and hurling forth his masses of thoughts with all the weight of his apostolic calling and with all the passion of a heart quivering with anger and with anxious love, in order to appeal to his converts who are forsaking him, by all that is dearest, by their old love for him and their admiration for him. After the unexpectedly abrupt conclusion of the first part—we have already heard these verses (see p. 230)—he begins once more with a cry of pain that pierces to the heart: "O ye foolish Galatians, who hath so bewitched you?" Then he reminds them of the wonderful beginning of their new life, when the Spirit came over them in a whirlwind, when they spoke with tongues and worked wonders. "Was it really all in vain?"[1] And then, after turning aside a second time to a somewhat difficult piece of theoretical reasoning, his warm heart suddenly wells up in these affectionate words: "You remember that illness was the cause of my telling you the good news in the first instance; and as for what must have tried you in my complaint, it did not inspire you with scorn or disgust (lit. spitting out, as one did in superstitious fear, in presence of an epileptic or hysterical case). No, you welcomed me as if I had been an angel of God, as Christ Jesus. What has become of the expressions now with which you then congratulated yourselves? For I can bear witness that, had it been possible, you would then have torn out your eyes and given them to me. Have I become your enemy then by telling you the truth? O they (the Judaisers) are zealously courting your favour, but not honourably. They want to shut you out (stamp you as not yet Christians), so as to make you court their favour (in order to be recognised by them). Zeal is good—in a good cause—always,

[1] Gal. iii. 1–5.

and not only when I am with you, my little children, you for whom I am again enduring a mother's pains until Christ acquire form (and life) in you; I could wish to be with you now, and try once again what I could do in another voice, for I am perplexed about you."[1] Just as the anxious sympathy of his heart breaks out here while he is carried away by the recollection of his converts' early affection, so in the stern, harsh conclusion of the epistle,[2] "see with how large letters I have written this to you."

We have already seen (p. 204) in what loving terms he described the commencement of his labours at Thessalonica. With what delicacy he intimates to the Philippians that he does not need their present, and that he only accepts it out of love for them, so that he almost gives them more than he receives.[3] And again, how delicately he answers the complaint of the Corinthians, that he would accept nothing from them, when his adversaries had sown suspicion in their minds in consequence: "I do not want your money, but you. It is not the duty of children to put by for their parents, but of parents to put by for their children. I will gladly spend—yes, suffer myself to be spent, for your souls. Can it be that the more intensely I love you (*i.e.* receive no money from you), the less I am to be loved?"[4]

It is just when he has to be severe that his love breaks forth all the more abundantly and richly. Full of bitter irony, he points out to the Corinthians how little the rôle of critics over the apostles fits them, the new converts (*cp.* p. 175). But then, as

[1] Gal. iv. 13–20.
[2] Gal. vi. 11–17.
[3] Phil. iv. 10–17.
[4] 2 Cor. xii. 14 *seq.*

if alarmed at his own violence, he continues: "It is with no wish to shame you that I am writing like this, but to train you as my own dear children. For even if you had ten thousand tutors in Christ, you have not many fathers.[1] I became your father through Christ Jesus in the gospel." And then he turns to the idle boasters who were proclaiming aloud that the apostle did not dare to come back again: "What will ye? Am I to come to you with a rod, or in love and the spirit of meekness?"[2] In these proud words we can hear at once a father's love and his authority. After another defence of his conduct, in which he has been obliged to enumerate to the Corinthians all that he has suffered in his ministry, and therefore for them as well (*cp.* p. 174), he says, with no less affection than modesty, "My own Corinthians, I have opened my mouth to you, the gates of my heart are open wide, in me there is abundant room for you. It is in your own affections that you are cramped. Now return my love—I speak to you as to my children—open wide the gates of your hearts and take me in."[3]

On another occasion he greatly terrified them by holding up the terrible example of the Israelites in the wilderness as a warning to them. But he proceeds, "God is faithful, he will not suffer you to be tempted beyond your strength," with many more like words of comfort.[4] Once again, there is a passage in the first Epistle to the Thessalonians which reminds us of one we have already quoted from the Epistle to the Galatians. In both the apostle recalls to his

[1] 1 Cor. iv. 1–15.   [2] 1 Cor. iv. 16–21.
[3] 2 Cor. vi. 11 *seq.*   [4] 1 Cor. x. 1–13.

converts their own affection for him. Both are instances of that charm and delicacy which won so many souls. "Timothy has come to me from you, and has brought me glad tidings of your faith and love; and that ye have good remembrance of me always, longing to see me as I long to see you. For this cause, brothers, I was comforted over you in all my distress and affliction through your faith, for now I live, if ye stand fast in the Lord. Yea, how can I thank God enough for you in all the joy that you are giving me in the sight of our God: night and day I pray most earnestly that I may see your face again, and may perfect that which is lacking in your faith. Now may our God and Father and our Lord Jesus Christ direct our way unto you. And as for you, may the Lord make you to increase and abound in love one toward another and to all men, even as we also do toward you, so that your hearts may be strengthened unblamable in holiness before our God and Father at the coming of our Lord Jesus with all his saints."[1]

As for the letter to the Philippians, we might almost copy every verse if we wished to leave a full impression of the tender and gentle charm of this strong heroic character.

This letter is the most beautiful of all the Pauline Epistles. Even here indeed there are traces of his bitter controversy with the Judaisers, but still it is, on the whole, a precious picture of the deep gratitude which this great heart harboured for all kindness and love that befell him on the way. This short letter should be read more frequently in the upper forms of our public schools. There could be no better intro-

[1] 1 Thess. iii. 6–13.

THE APOSTLE'S WINNING LOVE

duction to the study of the Pauline Epistles. It is far preferable for this purpose to the Epistle to the Romans, or to the first to the Corinthians. In any case, selections of passages—which are never properly understood—should be avoided. If our older boys were to get to know Paul through the letter to the Philippians—which contains the pattern of the perfect Christian gentleman—they would certainly get to love him. The Epistle to the Romans, with its description of the sins of the Gentile world, the first Epistle to the Corinthians with its "dry" account of the "factions," the case of incest, the questions about marriage and meat offered to idols, will never be able to awaken much enthusiasm or even interest. As it is, no one becomes acquainted, or cares to become acquainted, with the wonderful charm of the personality of the great apostle, and scarcely any educated man or woman in our country turns in later life to these letters in order really to get to know the man for the full knowledge of whose character the riper experience of life is needed.

THE MAN.

CHAPTER XXIV.

THE FRIEND. CONTRASTS. IN PRESENCE OF DEATH.

IT is only an occasional glimpse here and there which St Paul's letters afford us of his relation with those who, in the true fellowship of work, were not merely fellow-labourers but friends. It is really only of Titus and Timothy, two comparatively young men, that we catch an occasional phrase. But what a heart-ring there is in the words about Timothy, "My dear, faithful child in the Lord,"[1] when he begs his converts so to behave to the young man "that he may be with you without fear,"[2] and when he gives him the simple praise, "He does his Master's work as I do."[3] The most beautiful expression of his love towards him, however, is to be found in the Epistle to the Philippians,[4] where he speaks of Timothy as the one of all his companions best able to enter into his feelings, and says that none showed such an unselfish interest in their welfare. "The credentials of Timothy are before you. You know how as a son his father, so he has laboured with me in the service

---

[1] 1 Cor. iv. 17. [2] 1 Cor. xvi. 10.
[3] 1 Cor. xvi. 10. [4] Phil. ii. 19 *seq*.

of the gospel." The exact form of the sentence was not decided when the apostle began it. What a delicate touch there is in the turn of the phrase. He first wanted to say, As a son serves his father, so he served me while I preached the Gospel. But he quickly alters the expression so as to place Timothy by his side and thus incidentally testify to his love and esteem for him.

His references to Titus are no less characteristic. He calls the young man "his brother," not in the usual Christian, but in an especial personal sense.[1] Again and again he commends him to the Corinthians, and gains their confidence in him by employing him as his trusted messenger. "In addition to my encouragement, I was made exceedingly happy by the happiness of Titus, for his heart has been cheered by you all. Although I have been boasting a little to him about you, you have not made me feel ashamed: but just as we have spoken the truth to you in everything else, so our boasting to Titus about you has proved also to be the truth. And his affection for you is all the greater, as he remembers the deference that you all showed him, and recalls how you received him with reverence and awe. So I am glad, because I can feel complete confidence in you."[2] He is never weary of commending to their sympathies this young friend[3] in whose heart God has awakened such a lively interest for Corinth that he needed no urging to undertake a new journey thither.[4] He is always careful to speak of him as his equal, "My intimate companion and fellow-labourer."[5]

[1] 2 Cor. ii. 13. [2] 2 Cor. vii. 13–16. [3] 2 Cor. viii. 6; xii. 18.
[4] 2 Cor. viii. 16 *seq*. [5] 2 Cor. viii. 23.

One last example we may give of this combination of deep feeling with outward charm of manner. It is expressed in especially beautiful words to one who stood in a less intimate relation to him than either Titus or Timothy. The Philippians had despatched Epaphroditus to the apostle with their gift of money. Unfortunately he fell sick while at Rome, and was unable to return at once. It is only now that he sets out as the apostle's messenger, bringing them his letter. This is how St Paul speaks of him: "Meanwhile I have thought it necessary to send Epaphroditus to you, whom you commissioned as your delegate to minister to my needs. In him I have found a brother and a fellow-labourer and a comrade-in-arms. I sent him because he was home-sick, and troubled at the thought of your having heard of his illness. He was indeed at death's door. But God had mercy on him, and not on him only, but on me, that I might not have sorrow on sorrow. For this reason I have been the more eager to send him, that your cheerfulness may be restored by seeing him again, and that my sorrow may be lessened. Receive him therefore in the Lord with all gladness, and hold such men in honour, for in order to serve the work he was brought to death's door, having hazarded his life that he might make up by his own exertions the lack of your personal services to supplement your charitable gift."[1] Everyone feels that the man who can write such words truly and from his heart wins the affections of his fellows. It is scarcely possible to write with greater consideration, love, and tenderness. There are no parallels in all epistolary literature to

[1] Phil. ii. 25–30.

the passages in which Paul speaks of his friends and fellow-labourers to his converts. It is only when we place Ignatius's clumsy imitations side by side with them, that we notice what strength of character and what warmth of human affection are reflected in the nervous vigour of that style which is peculiar to the clothworker of Tarsus.

CONTRASTS.

That which lends such a human attractiveness to the apostle's personality are the great contrasts which it contains within itself. The greatest of these we have just examined. This heroic man was ashamed neither of his tender love nor of his tears.[1] He did not include—and rightly so—among the maxims of Christian morality the stoic virtue of clenched teeth and unruffled impassivity—but he said in the spirit of Jesus: "Weep with them that weep, and rejoice with them that do rejoice."[2] He too shares the great hope of all mankind that God will one day wipe away all tears from their eyes,[3] though he has expressed it differently.[4]

In him above all men the truth of Schiller's words is realised: "Religion of the Cross, Thou alone dost interweave in one garland the two strands of humility and of strength."

From the feeling of strength that renders him capable of unexampled achievements, inspiring him with the conviction that the maintenance of his life and health under the pressure of anxiety, sickness, hardship, and hunger[5] must be ascribed to some super-

---
[1] 2 Cor. ii. 4; Phil. iii. 18.   [2] Rom. xii. 15.
[3] Rev. vii. 17.   [4] 1 Cor. vii. 30.   [5] 2 Cor. iv. 10–16.

natural cause, the apostle derives that noble self-esteem and lofty self-consciousness which breathe through every page of his letters, and repulse every attack with a proud confidence. The first chapter of the Epistle to the Galatians and the two letters to the Corinthians are lively illustrations of the truth of the apostle's words, "To me it is a very small thing that I should be judged by you or by any human court."[1] At times this pride becomes somewhat imperious and wounds others, especially when he gives ironical expression to it.[2] Yet the effect is never unsympathetic, for it never degenerates into arrogance — with what kindness St Paul always speaks of Apollos,[3] whose followers embittered his life—and because the apostle is always filled with the grateful conviction that all is of God, who makes him strong;[4] he can do nothing of himself. "I am the least of the apostles, that am not meet to be called an apostle, because I persecuted the church of God. But by the grace of God I am what I am: and his grace which was bestowed upon me was not found vain: but I laboured more abundantly than they all; yet not I, but the grace of God which was with me."[5] Thus his pride being a genuine expression of the fulness of his character, never endangers his true humility, but is always united with it by the closest of ties. You can see the apostle actually blushing when his opponents force him "to boast like a fool"[6] and "to speak not after the Lord," or

---

[1] 1 Cor. iv. 3, cp. ix. 1 ; 2 Cor. i. 15, 21.
[2] E.g. 1 Cor. iv. 8–13.   [3] 1 Cor. iii.
[4] Phil. iv. 13 ; 2 Cor. xii. 9 seq.
[5] 1 Cor. xv. 9 seq.   [6] 2 Cor. xi. 17.

when he has to "open his mouth"[1] to his converts. The best kind of self-criticism is lowly humility such as this, combined with genuine pride when it is derived from the vigorous vitality of a strenuous life. Truly admirable is the downright manliness with which Paul refuses to allow any criticism of his own person, admirable too those brave words of his: "My 'glorying' is this, the testimony of my conscience, that in holiness and sincerity of God, not in fleshly wisdom, but in the grace of God, we behaved ourselves in the world, especially to you-ward."[2]

IN THE PRESENCE OF DEATH.

Paul wrote down these proud words with the memory of the valley of the shadow of death still upon him. They are certainly the result of a self-scrutiny which the apostle imposed upon himself in the sure expectation of death.[3] It is not too bold a conjecture to imagine that thoughts such as these agitated the apostle at this time, for the excitement of that hour still throbs and thrills throughout the whole letter, and above all the apostle's words we can hear the rustling of the wings of the angel of death.

It is often supposed—and the supposition is counted as specifically Christian—that the excellence of a religion, nay, more, even the correctness of a theology, can be measured by the courage with which its adherents face death. That is not true. To look death fearlessly in the face is the brave man's privilege whatever his creed. We may go so far as to say,

[1] 2 Cor. vi. 11.   [2] 2 Cor. i. 12; *cp.* iii. 18, iv. 7.
[3] 2 Cor. i. 9; *cp.* i. 8–14.

that it was only the exaggerated conceptions of heaven and hell, as they were gradually formed in the Orphic guilds and other mysteries, before being taken over by Christianity and fully developed, that produced that peculiar fear of death with which the Middle Ages were familiar, and which we have in part inherited. Courage in presence of death may be due to many causes. And we must never forget on the other hand that He, who was more sure of His Father in heaven and of a life "in Abraham's bosom" than any man, passed from this world, according to the oldest record, with a loud cry after He had exclaimed, "My God, my God, why hast thou forsaken me?" and after that He had striven that this cup might pass from Him. It was not death that Jesus feared: to a brave man death is nothing, it was the terrible question that death presented to Him above all others, that caused the agony in His soul.

The problem therefore does not admit of being stated as simply as this. But if one can read another man's soul, then the question is certainly an important and instructive one, "How did this man face death?"

Until that hour at Ephesus, Paul's belief had been that he would not have to undergo death at all. In the first Epistle to the Corinthians, as in the first to the Thessalonians, he always counts himself amongst those who, when Christ comes for judgment, will be "changed," and will be caught up in the clouds to meet Him. On the road to Damascus he had died in order to rise again to everlasting life, to a life eternal which was to continue deathless after the judgment. But in that hour of the peril of death at Ephesus, the apostle had been obliged to look the possibility of death straight in the face, and in the second Epistle to the Corinthians the prospect of death occupies him very deeply. It has become clearer than ever to him that the treasure which is in his heart, "the light of the knowledge of the glory of God in the face of Jesus Christ," is only contained in an earthen, fragile vessel, that his body is daily decreasing in strength and vigour and will be given over unto death. Sooner or later, death will break this fragile vessel. Paul thinks of this hour of his death with a certain shrinking. It is not so much the thought of physical pain that oppresses him as another conception which was especially awful to a man of the ancient world; it was the idea of losing the body, of having to divest himself of it so that the soul had to go forth "naked," cold, and shuddering to that place where shall be weeping and gnashing of teeth. For one moment the apostle is swayed by the fear of this disembodied, ghost-like state in the depths of the earth. But he overcomes it, "for we know that when our earthly tabernacle (body) is dissolved, we have a building from God, a house not made with hands, eternal in the heavens (the new supernatural body)." That is the old idea which was familiar to the Jews; and now comes a new idea: Christians when they die go to their home, to their Lord. "So we are always of good courage, and know that whilst we are at home in the body, we are absent from the Lord (for we live by faith, not by sight); nevertheless we are of good courage, and are willing rather to be absent from the body and to be at home with the Lord."[1]

This calm and sunny joy also rests upon the Epistle to the Philippians, which Paul wrote during his imprisonment, at a time when the thought of a probable liberation at an early date certainly cheered him, but he had yet to reckon with a possible condemnation and execution. Here we can read deep down in the heart of a good man that has conquered and overcome all fear. We have already noticed in a previous passage how this whole letter echoes with glad joy and the invitation to share therein. No less striking, however, is the simplicity with which Paul weighs against each other the possibility of death and his liberation from captivity. "For to me to live is Christ, and to die is gain. But if to live in the flesh, if this is the fruit of my work, then I know not what I shall choose. I am hemmed in as it were, a wall on this side and a wall on that. I have a desire to depart and to be with Christ, and this is very far better. But to abide in the flesh is more needful for your sake."[2] That which attaches him to life is no longer any selfish wish, it is only his work and his love. "If I am to pour out my life-blood as a libation over the sacrificial offering of your faith, I rejoice, and rejoice with you all."[3]

There were four reasons which Paul might have had for fearing death. Fear of the physical pain, in the hour of agony—as a brave man he does not speak of this at all. Shrinking from that terrible disembodiment in the dark abysses of the nether world—he overcame this shrinking in the victorious certainty

---

[1] 1 Cor. iv. 5–v. 10.   [2] Phil. i. 21–24.   [3] Phil. ii. 17.

that he was going to meet his Lord in His heavenly home. Fear of the judgment—" Who is there that can accuse us ? Jesus Christ is our advocate.[1] Death, where is thy sting ? grave, where is thy victory ? "[2] He was saved and could not be lost again. St Paul is not tortured by that fear for his cause which placed Jesus face to face with the awful question whether God really wished His death, and what could be the meaning of this death. St Paul already stands behind Jesus in the light which is shed forth upon the Church from the cross and from the risen Lord. He stands in the midst of that triumphant progress of the Gospel throughout the world in which he himself had led the way. He can separate his own person from his work, however gladly he would still abide upon earth and continue to live for the sake of his work, in order to bring forth more fruit in his heart. He cherishes a silent longing to depart and be with his Lord. Jesus could not reconcile Himself to His death until He realised it as an integral portion of His work and a necessary condition of His victory. Since that hour at Ephesus, Paul awaited death as the natural termination of life. His work, that, is God's work, continues. And He that has begun the good work will also accomplish it until the great day of judgment.[3]

St Paul never knew what fear was. But a still more remarkable feature in his character, especially for a man of his age, is that his longing for the eternal home did not degenerate into that sickly desire for death which approximates so many martyrs so much nearer to Buddhism than to the Gospel of

[1] Rom. viii. 33 *seq.*   [2] 1 Cor. xv. 55.   [3] Phil. i. 6.

Jesus. Read, for instance, the words with which Ignatius of Antioch protests against the interference of the Roman Church in his trial: " The joys of this earth and the kingdom of this world are of no avail to me. More beautiful to me is death, which will unite me with Jesus Christ, than the kingdom of this world. It is Jesus that 1 seek, Him that died for us; Him would I see who rose again for our sake. . . . Hinder me not from coming to life. Do not wish me to die (by letting me live and be set free), do not give me over again unto the world, since I would be God's very own; let me receive the pure light, then shall I be a true man: grant me to imitate my God in His passion."[1] Paul is entirely free from such a morbid craving for death; he is no saint whose selfishness strives to attain to his own bliss as soon as he possibly can; his love bids him take up the task of this his life in the body. Herein too he gives a proof of the moral excellence of his faith.

One last point: like Jesus, Paul gives us no detailed picture of the world to come and of everlasting life, of heaven and of hell, such as the authors of the Revelation of St John and of Peter and of so many other revelations have painted for us in lurid colours. Neither curiosity nor fear turned the apostle's eyes in spite of himself to that which is behind the veil, that dark gate which is at the end of this life. Whatever may have been the thoughts and beliefs which Paul shared on this subject with the religious minds of his own people and the mystic Orphic guilds, his true life is not lived here, nor does his fancy stray in this direction. It is only here and

[1] Ign., Ad Rom. vi.

there that we have an allusion to this subject in the letters, and least of all in those letters in which he himself looks death straight in the face; calmly and firmly he turns his look away to meet his present tasks, the loving service of his life: "Let us therefore make it our aim, whether we are in the heavenly home, or sojourners here in a strange country, to be well pleasing to the Lord."[1]

And so we take leave of Paul. We look, as it were, upon a wonderful sunny autumn day. High overhead tiny white clouds are sailing in the deep blue vault of heaven, ghostly harbingers of that white mantle which is soon to descend from thence upon the champaign beneath. In the fields stand the last sheaves, witnesses of the year's hot toil and its rich blessing. The sun is beginning to play less fiercely round the wild vine's red leaves, and, as though in silent joy, it is pouring floods of gold upon the bright-gleaming fruit which bows down the branches in rich abundance. The summer heat has passed away; there is, as it were, an anticipation of death in the tender, cool air; but there is no sadness about it, for does it not scatter blessings far and wide among men? And yet something else there is, something mysterious; it speaks to us in a scarce audible whisper. Nor can we tell wherein it lies. We can only feel it, we can only suspect it. Is it the mild soft air that gently caresses our cheeks as though with the touch of a comforting hand? Is it the bright colours of the leaves when a breath of wind stirs them? Is it the pale green of the meadows? In these autumn days there is an anticipation of

[1] 2 Cor. v. 9.

spring, a soft mystic murmur of resurrection and a return of new life which shall be born again from the old when the death and desolation of winter shall have passed.

It is a wonderful golden autumn day, full of blessing, of thoughts of death and of hopes of life.

INDEX

ABRAHAM—
  Christians, the true children of, 294–298.
  Faith of, 295–296.
  Promise to, 60.
  St Paul's faith in descent from, 290.
Achaia, 165, 169, 211.
Acts, the—
  Concordat at Jerusalem, 226.
  Imprisonment of St Paul, 170.
  Lord's Supper, the, 257.
  Missions of St Paul, 164, 166–168, 220.
  Organisation of St Paul's mission, 200.
  References to the, 15, 20, 33, 50, 81, 114, 124, 148, 156, 164, 165, 167–170, 175, 177, 200, 201, 220, 226, 230, 233–235, 250, 257, 361, 362, 363.
  St Paul at Jerusalem, 235—
  sufferings of, 175.
Adam and original sin, 37–41.
Africa, Punic, 159.
Agabus, 114.
Alexander the Great, 7, 158.
Alexandrines, the, 61.
Allegory, method of interpretation, 59–61.
Aloysius, St, 6.
Amos, 290.
Ananias, healing of St Paul, 82.
Anarchy, characteristics, 265–6.

Angels—
  St Paul's conception, 31–33.
  The three categories, 32.
Anglicanism, 116.
Anselm, 311.
Anthony, St, 6.
Antichrist and Belial, 29.
Antioch, 157, 164—
  St Paul's quarrel with St Peter at, 233.
  St Peter's visit to, 227–230.
Apocalypse—
  of Baruch, 37.
  of Elijah, 56.
  of Ezra, 37.
  of Moses, 56.
Apocalypses, the Jewish, 55–56.
Apocrypha transmitted by Jews of the Dispersion, 54.
Apollos, 175—
  Parties after name of, 252.
  St Paul's attitude towards, 367–368, 378.
Apostles, the twelve—
  Acts of, the. See Acts, the.
  Concordat at Jerusalem. See that title.
  Decree annulling the Concordat, 234, 246.
  Early work of the, 220–221.
  St Paul's relations with, 231 et seq.
Aquila saves St Paul, 169, 176.
Aquilas and Priscilla, 277.
Aramaic, 159.
Aretas, King, 175–176.

Asceticism—
　Antiquity of, 239-240.
　Buddhistic, 338.
　Early Christian, 240-242.
　St Paul's, 177-182, 338.
Asia Minor, 165.
Asia, Roman, 168.
Associates. *See* Pharisees.
Associations, early Roman, 160.
Athene, 28.
Athens, 165, 169.

Babylon, 159.
Baptism—
　Institution of the Sacrament, 118.
　Preached by St Paul, 189.
　Vicarious, at Corinth, 120.
Barnabas—
　Epistle to, 124.
　Jerusalem, reception in, 226.
　Journeys with St Paul, 164, 200, 224.
　Lystra, stoned at, 167.
　St Paul, quarrel with, 230.
　St Peter supported by, at Antioch, 228.
Baruch, Apocalypse of, 37.
Bauer, Bruno, vii.
Belial, St Paul's use of name, 29.
Benjamin, St Paul of the tribe of, 15.
Berœa, 165.
Bible, "The Law and the Prophets," 54.
Bishop, origin of the office, 160, 213.
"Blood," meaning "sacrifice," 123.
Buddha, 92.
Buddhistic asceticism, 338.
Burial unions, 160.
Bythnia, 168.

Cæsarea, 165, 233.
Canticles, Book of, added to the Scriptures, 54.

Carlyle cited, xi., 101.
Catholicism—
　Ethics of, 139.
　Evangelical counsels, 178.
　Liturgies, 260.
　Nature of, 122.
Celsus, 85.
Celtic races, 167.
Cenchreæ, 201, 212.
Cephas, 78.
Chastity, law of, St Paul's substantiation, 346-348.
Christ. *See* Jesus Christ.
Christian ethics, 234; problems neglected in, 348-349.
Christian perfection, 98.
Christianity, early—
　A Jewish sect under the Apostles, 7-8, 156.
　Asceticism in, 240-248, 252.
　Characteristics, 180, 263-265.
　Evangelical poverty of, 280-281.
　Jewish laws, rejection of, 227, 228.
　Morality under, 135 *et seq.*
　Nietzsche's attacks on, 85 *et seq.*, 91.
　Origin of, 140 *et seq.*
　Reason and, 11-12.
　Resurrection, the foundation of, 140.
　Roman opposition, 264-265, 278.
　Sacrifice, 123.
　Sacraments, institution of the, 118.
　Services, 249 *et seq.*
　Social equality, 161, 274-275.
　Town religion in the West, 166.
Christians—
　Children of Abraham, 41, 294-298.
　First persecutions by Saul, 66.
　Lawsuits between the early, 272-274.

INDEX 389

Church, the—
  Individual right to admonish, 213-214.
  Marriage and divorce, law of, 271 et seq.
  Organisation of the early—
    Bishops, 213.
    Congregations, 214.
    Deacons, 212.
    Family churches, 214.
    Helpers, 210-212.
    Missionaries, 215.
    Monks, 217.
    Sects, 216-217.
  Parties at Corinth, 252.
  St Paul's conception, 133, 209.
  St Paul's organisation, 160.
Cilicia, St Paul's work in, 154, 161, 165.
Circumcision—
  Galatia, in, 231.
  Imposition of, by Jewish-Christians, 216.
  St Paul's preaching, 154.
  "Seal" of, 48.
  Titus before the Council, 225.
Clemen on authenticity of the Pauline Epistles, x.
Clements, St, letter to, 171, 173, 278.
Commandments of St Paul, 137-139.
Concordat, the—
  Arranged at Jerusalem, 200, 225-227.
  Annulled, 234.
Congregations, the Pauline, 214, 222.
Corinth—
  Asceticism in, 242.
  Congregations at, 251-252.
  Parties formed at, 252.
  St Paul's work in, 165, 169, 170, 187, 197, 201.
  Vicarious baptism at, 120.
Corinthians, Epistle to the, reference to, 15, 17-19, 22-26, 28-33, 36-38, 41, 44-51, 53, 54, 56, 59, 60, 64, 67, 78, 79, 81, 84 87, 91, 95, 96, 98-100, 108, 110, 111, 114, 115, 117, 119-121, 123, 126-129, 132, 136, 137, 143, 149, 151, 152, 153, 155, 162-164, 169, 173-183, 185-187, 189, 191, 192, 195, 197, 199, 201-204, 206, 207, 210-212, 214, 215, 220, 231, 233, 235, 236, 239, 240, 244-246, 250-255, 258, 260, 263, 265, 267-271, 273-277, 279, 282, 292, 301, 303, 308, 309, 314, 315, 317-320, 323, 324, 327, 328, 340, 344-346, 348, 350, 351, 354, 356, 358, 359, 365-368, 370, 371, 373-375, 377-379, 382, 383, 385.
Crispus, 100, 209.
Cross, death on the, explanation of, 307-308.
Cyprus, 157, 164, 167.

Damascus—
  St Paul's escape from, 175.
  St Paul's vision, 79-84.
Daniel, Book of, 27, 29.
David, Psalms, 44, 155, 294.
Day of Judgment, picture of the, 47-50.
Deacon, origin of the office, 212.
Death, courage in presence of, 379-380.
Derbe, 167.
Deuteronomy, Book of, reference to, 67, 219.
Deutsche Schriften cited, 2.
Devils, St Paul's conception, 29-32.
Divine Fatherhood, St Paul on the, 298-299.
Divine nature of Jesus Christ, 313.

INDEX

Divorce. *See* Marriage, St Paul on.
Dogma, St Paul's knowledge, 99.
Dramas, 163.

EARTH, St Paul's conception of the, 25.
Ecclesiastes, Book of—
    Added to the Scriptures, 54.
    Reference to, 39.
Eleusis, 117.
Elijah, Apocalypse of, 56.
Elisha, 361.
Elymas the sorcerer, 167.
Enoch—
    Spirits, 27, 29.
    Translation of, 31.
Epaphroditus, mission to St Paul, 376.
Ephesians, Epistle to the, 195.
Ephesus, 163, 165, 168, 380–381.
Esau, 105, 108.
Esther, Book ot, added to the Scriptures, 54.
Eternal life, 51.
Ethics—
    Christian, 334; problems neglected in, 348–349.
    Nietzsche on, cited, 339.
    Pauline, 329–335—
        Foundation of, 339–352.
        Limitations of, 335–339.
Europe—
    Christianity introduced into, 157, 165, 237.
    Hellenistic culture, effect in, 159.
Eusebius, 223.
Evangelical poverty, practice of, 280–281.
Evangelicalism, 116.
Exegesis—
    Theological, difficulties of, 304.
    Three methods of, 57–61.
Exodus, Book of, 60.
Ezechiel, Book of, 37.
Ezra, Apocalypse of, 37, 38.

FAITH—
    Abraham's, 295–296.
    Humanity and, 104–106.
    Justification by, St Paul's theology, 289–299.
Fall, the. *See* Original Sin.
Family churches, 214.
Fatherhood, the Divine, 140.
Fornication, Apostles' law regarding, 234.
Frederick the Great, 286.

GAIUS, 209.
Galatia—
    Circumcision in, 231.
    St Paul's preaching in, 165, 168, 186, 197.
Galatians, Epistle to the, reference to, 19, 24, 31–33, 36, 41, 45, 48–50, 56, 57, 60, 64, 67, 72, 78, 81, 82, 84, 94, 99, 103, 125, 130, 135, 152, 153, 163, 165, 166–168, 186, 188, 195, 198, 200, 205, 212, 219, 222–226, 230, 231, 236, 274, 279, 292, 296–299, 301, 308, 315, 317, 319, 320, 324, 325, 332, 333, 336, 340, 342–345, 356, 368–370, 378.
Gallic races, 167.
Gamaliel, 15.
Genesis, Book of, 295, 297, 323, 326.
Gentiles—
    Ambiguity of term at concordat, 226.
    Jewish Christians and, condition to regulate, 234.
    Jesus' treatment of question, 218–220.
    St Paul, the Apostle of, 108–109, 153, 200.
Gerhard, hymns of, 197.
God—
    Early Jewish conception, 103.
    Justice of, 306.
    Mercy of, 107–108, 305.

INDEX

God—
  St Paul's conception, 23–24, 102–104.
  St Paul's preaching on, 187.
Goethe, visions of, 355.
Gospel, the, intellectualised by St Paul, 99.
Grace—
  Free bestowal, 293.
  St Paul's doctrine of, attacked, 340.
Greece, 38, 159.
Greek—
  Element in Roman Empire, 158.
  Language, common medium of intercourse, 159.
Greeks—
  Idols of the, 183–184.
  Jesus' words to the, 220–221.
Guyon, Mme. de, compared with St Paul, 142.

HAGAR, the allegorical Sinai, 60.
Hausrath, *The Apostle Paul*, vii.
Heaven, St Paul's conception, 24.
Hebrew, Greek adopted in place of, 159.
Hebrews, Epistle to, 46, 124, 193, 256.
Hegesippus, 223 n., 242.
"Heil," 47.
Hermas, 215.
Herod, 28.
Herodotus, 7.
Holy Ghost, the, 95, 102, 114, 115, 128, 132, 164—
  Divine Fatherhood and the, 325.
  Early faith in, 213.
  Fruits of, 135.
  Preached by St Paul, 207, 216.
  St Paul's faith in, 211.
  "Spirit of God," 326.
Hosea, prophet, 58.

Humility, virtue of—
  Religion a result of true, 146–148.
  St Paul on, 350–351.
Hymn—
  on Love (Cor. xiii.), 199.
  Rom. viii., 28–39, 196.

ICONIUM, 157, 167.
Idols—
  Greek, 183–184.
  Meat offered to, abstention from, 238–239; Jewish law regarding, 241; St Paul's decree regarding, 246–248.
  Thessalonian, 183.
Ignatius of Antioch, cited, 207, 214, 377—
  Death of, 384.
Illyricum, 169.
India, 158.
Inspiration—
  General claim to, 100.
  St Paul's acceptation of, 56–57.
  Interpretation of the Scriptures, three methods, 57–61.
Isaiah, 57.
Israelites, sins of the, 121.

JACOB, 105.
James (brother of Jesus), missionary work, 222.
James, Epistle to, 319.
James, the Apostle—
  Antioch, sends messengers to, 228.
  Appearance of Jesus to, 78.
  Paul, attitude towards, 226, 231.
James the Just, 242.
Jehovah, 155.
Jesus Christ—
  Appearances of, 78.
  Death of—
    A Sacrifice, 301–307.
    Justification for all, 308–310.
    Necessity for, 300–301.
    "Propitiation," 307.

Jesus Christ—
  Divine nature of, 140, 313.
  Gentiles, question of mission to, 218, 219-220.
  Gospel of, characteristics compared with St Paul's, 16-19.
  Greeks, address to the, 220-221.
  " Heiland," the, 47.
  Imitation of, the incentive to pure life, 349-352.
  Judge, the, 49.
  Law, position in regard to the, 218-219.
  Pascal Lamb, 123.
  Passion preached by St Paul, 185-186.
  Preaching of, 187.
  "Second coming of," St Paul's conception, 45-47.
  Son of God, title of, 323-326.
  "Son of Man," title of, 45.
  Supremacy preached by St Paul, 252-253.
Jerusalem—
  Concordat at, 225-227; annulled, 234.
  Decree of the twelve Apostles at, 234, 246.
  St Paul's collection for the poor, 366-367.
  St Paul's home in, 15-16.
  St Paul's return to, 164, 167, 170.
Jewish Christians. *See also* Judaisers—
  Condition regulating Gentiles and, 234.
  Congregations, 227.
  Opposition to St Paul, 231.
Jewish customs, 241.
Jews—
  Dispersion, of the, and the Apocrypha, 54.
  Greek adopted in place of Hebrew, 159.
  Law regarding eating, etc., 241.

Jews—
  St Paul on the, 232.
  St Paul's method with the, 200.
Joan d'Arc, 80.
Job, Book of, added to the Scriptures, 54.
Johannine writings, reference to, 49.
John the Baptist, St—
  Baptism of, meaning, 118.
  Cited, 290.
  Description in St Luke's Gospel, 241-242.
  Last of the prophets, 114.
John the Evangelist, St—
  Attitude towards St Paul, 226.
  Gospel, 221, 303, 322, 327.
  Revelations, 47, 48, 264, 377, 384.
Jonas, sign of the Prophet, 84.
Joseph, St, 6.
Judaisers—
  Attacks on St Paul, 236.
  Opposition to St Paul, 369.
  St Paul's attitude towards, 238-239.
  St Paul's comdemnation, 232.
Judaism—
  Converts to, 201.
  Customs rejected by Christians, 227, 228.
  Doctrine of original sin, 38.
  Eating and drinking, laws regarding, 156.
  Gentiles, mission to, 155.
  Public worship, diminution of, 43-44.
  Sacrifice, decline of, 124.
  Spirits, belief in, 27.
  Traces in St Paul, 138.
  Worship of a will in God, 144.
Judgment. *See* Day of Judgment.
Jülicher, *New Testament*, x.

INDEX

Justification—
  Doctrine of, St Paul's inference, 345.
  Meaning of word, 290.
Justin Martyr, 260.

KALTHOFF, vii., viii.
Kephas, 252.
Kerner cited, 142.
Kings, Book of, 53, 361.
Kirchbach, Wolfgang, allegorical treatment of New Testament, 61.
Knowledge, St Paul on, 245.

LAGARDE, cited on St Paul, 2–3.
Lamentations, Book of, added to the Scriptures, 54.
Last days, St Paul's preaching, 187.
Last Supper, institution of the Sacrament at the, 118.
Latin element in Roman Empire, 158.
Law, ecclesiastical, 272.
Law, the—
  Dangers of, 73–75.
  Jesus' position in regard to, 218–219.
  Quarrel between St Peter and St Paul at Antioch regarding, 227–230.
  St Paul and, 42, 72–76, 86–87.
  St Paul's condemnation of, 101–102.
  System of, 68 et seq.
Lessing, 338.
Leviticus, Book of, 234.
Libations, 163.
Life insurance societies, 160.
Liturgies—
  Catholic, 260.
  St Paul's, 255, 260.
Loman, vii.
Lord's Supper, the—
  Institution, 119.
  Licence at, 256–257.

Lord's Supper, the—
  St Paul's words, 257–258.
  Unworthy reception, 259.
Love, St Paul's preaching on, 131, 137, 245, 253.
Luke, St, Gospel of, 220, 221, 241, 242, 323, 357.
Luther—
  And morality, 92.
  And St Paul compared, 9, 87, 97, 192, 345.
  And the peasants, 279.
  Belief of, 343.
  Early training, 20.
  "Heil," 47.
  "Justification," 49.
  Years of work, 170.
Lutheranism, 115.
Lystra, 167.

MACEDONIA, 165, 168, 170.
Malta, St Paul at, 361.
Mark, St, Gospel of, 118, 119, 146, 211, 219, 220, 271, 302, 318, 334.
Marriage—
  Church and, 271 et seq.
  St Paul on, 179, 267–271.
Matthew, St—
  Gospel of, 136, 149, 220, 221, 278, 319, 323, 356–358.
  On divorce, 271.
Meat. See Idols.
Melanchthon, 103.
Methodists, 116, 140, 190.
Miletus, St Paul's speech to the elders, 170.
Miracles, St Paul's, 360–363.
Missionaries, Pharisaic, 155.
Mithras, 117.
Monasticism, first foundation, 217, 242.
Morality—
  A new, preached by St Paul, 188.
  Second nature, under Christianity, 135 et seq.
Morgenröte, the, 4, 86, 90.

Moses—
　Apocalypse of, 56.
　St Paul on, 1.
　Striking of the rock, 46.
Mount Sinai, 297.
Mysia, 168.
Mysticism—
　Christian, 141.
　St Paul's, 131, 132, 140.

NATURE, St Paul's conception, 25.
Nazarite vow of St Paul, 235.
Nero, persecution of, 171.
New Testament—
　Allegorical treatment of, 61.
　Nietzsche's attacks on, 92.
Nicene Creed, 313.
Nietzsche—
　"Conversion" of, 146-147.
　Ethics, cited on, 339.
　New Testament, attacks on, 92.
　St Paul's conversion, representation of, 88-93.
　St Paul's moral character, accusation against, 45, 85-88.
　St Paul's personal religion, criticism of, 4-5, 140-150.
Numbers, Book of, 235.

ORIENTAL element in Roman Empire, 158.
Oriental religions, 158.
Original sin, doctrine of, St Paul's conception, 37-41.
Orphic Guilds, 380, 384.

PAMPHYLIA, 164.
Parousia, the, 210.
Parties formed at Corinth, 252.
Pascal, influence on Nietzsche, 90.
Pascal Lamb, Jesus the, 123.
Paul, St—
　Asceticism, 177-182, 240-244, 267-271, 338.

Paul, St—
　Acts, account of journeys, 164.
　Allegory and typology used by, 58-59.
　Apocalypses, the Jewish, acquaintance with, 55.
　Apostles and, relations between, 231 et seq.
　Apostleship of, 151 et seq.
　Barnabas, St—
　　Journeys with, 164.
　　Quarrel with, 230.
　Blindness, 82.
　Character, contrasts in, 63, 377-379; moral, Nietzsche's accusation against, 85-87; joy in work, 180-182; temperament, 356-360; human greatness, 360-364; winning love, 364-373; as a friend, 374-377; death, in presence of, 379-386.
　Christians, first, persecutions of the, 66 et seq.
　Church, conception of the, 133.
　Church, organisation of the new, 160.
　Commandments of, 137-139.
　Concessions of, 282.
　Contrast to Christ, 356-359.
　Controversial powers, 359-360.
　Conversion, accounts of, 77-78; passages cited, 78; Nietzsche's representation, 88-93.
　Damascus, conversion at, 152 et seq.; escape from, 175.
　Day of Judgment, conception of, 47-51.
　Death, attitude towards, 171, 379-384.
　Devil, power over the, 96.
　Diplomacy, 366 et seq.
　Doxology of, 322.
　Early training, 21 et seq.

INDEX

Paul, St—
Epistles, authenticity of, viii., ix., x.; relation to preaching, 183.
Eschatology of, agreement with the Jewish Apocalypses, 55-56.
Ethics, 329-335; limitations of, 335-339; foundations of, 339-352.
Faith for humanity, objections, 105-106.
Faith of, nature of, 92 et seq.
Food, decree concerning, 246-247.
Friendship of, 374-376.
God, belief in, 22-24; conception of, 102-104.
Greek language, use of, 159.
Holy Ghost, faith in the, 216; distinction from the Son, 326.
Home and parentage, 14-20.
Humility in his conversion, 145.
Hymn on Love (Cor. xiii.), 199.
Hymn (Rom. viii.), 28-39, 196.
Imprisonment at Rome, 170.
Inspiration, 56-57, 100.
"Intoxication of the soul," 147-148.
James, opposition of, 231.
Jerusalem, prisoner at, 165; return to, 167, 233-237; visit to, 244 et seq.; before the Council at, 225; collection for the poor of, 233.
Jewish traits of, 40-41, 138, 143, 189.
Journeys, 66, 164 et seq.
Judaisers, opposition of, 231-232, 238-239.
"Justification," 49.
Lagarde cited on, 2-3.

Paul, St—
Law, struggle with the, 54, 72-76, 101-102; effect on character of, 69-70; freed from, through conversion, 89.
Legal disputes on, 272-274.
Lord's Supper, words regarding, 257-261.
Love, preaching on, 137, 203, 253, 331-332.
Macedonia, call to, 167-168.
Marriage, on, 267-271.
Meats, eating of unclean, attitude towards, 243-248.
Messianic ideas, 45-47.
Miracles of, 96, 360-363.
Mission—
Call to, 108-9, 151 et seq., 166 et seq.
Organisation of, 200-207.
The field, 156 et seq., 164 et seq.
Threefold aim, 187-191.
Mme. de Guyon compared with, 142-143.
Morality, development of, 135 et seq.
Mysticism of, 140; reasons for, 148-150.
Nature, conception of, 25.
Nazarite vow of, 235-236.
Nietzsche (see also Religion, Personal) cited on, 4-5.
Original sin, doctrine of, 37-41.
Patriotism, 63-68.
Peace efforts, 270-271.
Personality, 192-199, 354-355, 363.
Prayers of, 124-130.
Preaching—
Characteristics compared with Christ's, 17-19.
God, 187.
Holy Ghost, 207.
Idolatry, 183-184.
Imitation of Christ, 349-352.
Last days, 187.

INDEX

Paul, St—
  Preaching—
    Love, 137, 203, 253, 331–332.
    Passion of our Lord, 185–186.
    Resurrection of our Lord, 185.
    Style, etc., 183, 193–200.
    Supremacy of Christ, 252–253.
    Predestinarian theory, 106–109.
    Promise to Abraham, and the, 41–42, 44.
    Public worship, mention of, 43; regulations for, 255–262.
    Punishments of the wicked, 51.
    Refusal of support, 319, 351.
    Religion, personal, 115–121; ethical retribution in, 121–122; social character of, 132; Nietzsche's criticism, 140–150; one with that of Christ, 149–150.
    Roman Catholic veneration of, 6.
    Sacraments, 118–125.
    Sacrifice, practice of, 123–125.
    St Peter and, quarrel at Antioch, 166, 227–230, 233.
    Schell cited on, 5–6.
    Spain, mission to, 171.
    Spiritual world, conception of, 26–35.
    Stoned at Lystra, 167.
    Sufferings of, 174–175.
    Teaching, reasons for influence, 287.
    The man, 353.
    The new man, 94 *et seq.*
    Theology, 288–289—
      Divine nature of Jesus, 313.
      Justification by faith, 289–299.
      Significance of the death of Christ, 300–312.
    Troubles of, 176–177.

Paul, St—
  Universe, conception of, 24–25.
  Vision of, 79–84.
  Weaver of goats'-hair cloth, 161.
  Years of his labours, 170.
" Paulinism," 22, 189.
Pentateuch, compilation of the, 53–54.
Perfectionists, 252.
Perga, 157.
Persian religion, idea of spiritual kingdom, 27.
Peter St—
  Antioch, visit to, 227–230.
  Circumcision of Titus, decision, 225.
  Death of, 171.
  Parties after name of, 252.
  Speech of, 159.
  Revelations, 384.
  St Paul and, 226–230, 233.
  Wife of, 177.
Pfleiderer, *Das Urchristentum*, x.
Pharaoh, 108.
Pharisees—
  Community of the, 71.
  Doctrine of original sin, 37, 38.
  Spirits, belief in, 27.
Philippi, 165, 169, 178, 198, 360.
Philippians—
  Epistle to, reference to, 15, 20, 24, 37, 45, 47, 67, 79, 97, 98, 125, 128, 129, 139, 152, 169, 179–181, 212, 232, 289, 315, 316, 321, 338, 339, 350, 351, 358, 370, 372, 375–378, 382, 383.
  Gift of money to St Paul, 128, 376.
  St Paul's prayer for, 127.
Philistines, 147.
Phœbe of Cenchreæ, 201, 212.
Phrygia, 165, 168.
Pietists, the, 92, 116, 140.
Pilate, 28.

Pillars of Hercules, 158.
Pisidia, 164, 165.
Polytheism, 123-124.
Powers of angels, 32.
Prayer—
  Law, under the, 68-69.
  Man's means of reaching God, 112.
  St Paul's, 124-130.
Predestination, St Paul's theory, 106-109.
Presidents, 212.
Priest, the, opposed to the prophet, 261.
Principalities of angels, 32.
Prisca saves St Paul, 169, 176.
Priscilla and Aquilas, 277.
Promises, the, 44.
Prophets, power of, 113-115.
" Propitiation " in death of Christ, 307.
Protestantism, 139.
Proverbs, Book of, added to the Scriptures, 54.
Psalms, the—
  Added to the Scriptures, 54.
  Reference to, 44, 54, 155, 294.
Public worship—
  Aims determined by St Paul, 254.
  Diminution of, 43-44.
  Women's right to speak at, 276-277.
Punishment, St Paul and, 51.

QUAKERS, 116.
Quietists, 142, 143.

REBECCA, 105.
Redemption, theory of, St Paul's inference, 345.
Reformation, social, 161-162.
Reformers, the—
  Allegorical interpretation crushed out by, 60.
  Churches of, 283.
  Historical research and, 61.
  Teaching of, 311.

Religion—
  Effect of true, 146-148.
  What it is, 112, 115.
Renan, vii.
Resurrection, the—
  Christianity, foundation of, 140.
  Preached by St Paul, 99, 185.
Revelation, God's means of reaching man, 112.
Revelation, the. *See under* St John the Evangelist.
Revivalism, assertions of, 90.
Rewards—
  Jewish religion of, 342.
  St Paul's teaching, 339.
Roman Catholics' veneration of St Paul, 6.
Roman empire—
  Age of, and asceticism, 240.
  Extent at time of St Paul, 158.
  Government, nature of, 160.
  Opposition to Christianity, 264-265, 278.
  St Paul's attitude towards the State, 278-280.
Romans—
  Condemnation of Christ, 66.
  Compendium of Christian teaching in Epistle to, 287.
  Epistle to, reference to, 15, 17, 18, 23-25, 29, 32, 36 37, 40-42, 45, 47-49, 51, 54, 56-58, 64, 67, 74-76, 95-99, 103-111, 120, 123, 127, 128, 130, 132, 136, 137, 148, 151, 155, 169, 173, 176, 177, 181, 184, 185, 189, 194, 195, 201, 212, 214, 226, 232, 236, 239, 244, 245, 278, 279, 289-297, 299, 301, 304, 306-310, 314, 315, 317, 319, 320, 322, 324, 325, 331-333, 335-337, 341, 342, 344-346, 349, 350, 358, 365, 373, 377, 383.

INDEX

Rome—
  Asceticism in, 242.
  Churches, 156.
  St Paul's intention to visit, 168.
Rousseau, 173.
Ruth, Book of, added to the Scriptures, 54.

SACERDOTALISM, 261.
Sacraments, the—
  Catholic definition, 122.
  Efficaciousness, 120–121.
  God's means of reaching man, 112.
  Meaning of, 116–118.
Sacrifice—
  Christ's death as a, 301.
  Man's means of reaching God, 112.
Sacrifices, the Jewish—
  Communion through, 119.
  Decay of, 122.
Salvation Army, 161.
Sanhedrim, condemnation of the Messiah, 66.
Sarah and Hagar, allegory of, 60, 297–298.
Satan, power of, 28.
Schell, 5–6.
Schiller cited, 34, 377.
Schleiermacher, 287.
Schneller, L., *In Alle Welt*, vii.
Scriptures—
  Compilation, 54.
  Interpretation, methods of, 57–61.
Senaca cited, 144.
Services, early Christian—
  Enthusiasm, 249–254.
  Holy Communion, 256–257.
  St Paul's regulations, 255–256.
Shekinah, the, 41.
Silesius, Angelus, cited, 135.
Slaves, question of emancipation, 274–275.
Solomon, Proverbs, 138.
"Son of God," title of, 323–326.

Sosthenes, 100.
Spain, St Paul's journey to, 168, 169, 171.
Spirit of God. *See* Holy Ghost.
Spiritual world, St Paul's conception, 26–35.
State, the, responsibilities, 349.
Steck, vii.
Stephanas of Corinth, 201, 211.
Stephen, St, martyrdom of, 67–68.
Synoptists, 320.
Syria, 154, 159, 165.

TARSUS in Cilicia, 15, 19, 66.
Tatian, 265.
Tempter, the, in the Epistles, 30.
Theosophists, allegorical treatment of New Testament, 61.
Thessalonians, Epistle to, reference to, 24, 29, 30, 32, 36, 44, 45, 47, 49, 51, 98, 99, 111, 114, 125, 129, 152, 169, 180, 183, 187, 189, 198, 205, 207, 212–214, 281, 289, 336, 345, 358, 371, 372.
Thessalonica—
  St Paul's preaching in, 30, 165, 169, 183, 187, 198.
  Social question in, 280–281.
Thrace, 159.
Timothy—
  Epistle to, 29, 171, 195, 277.
  Mission of, 215.
  St Paul's recommendation of, 374.
Titius Justus, 201.
Titus—
  Council at Jerusalem, before the, 224–225.
  Epistle to, 171, 195.
  Mission of, 366–367.
  St Paul's references to, 374, 375.
Tolstoi, 61, 265.
Tongues—
  Gift of, 250.
  St Paul's regulations, 255, 256.

INDEX

Tora, 54.
Trinity, doctrine of the, 327–328.
Troas, 168, 361—
St Paul's vision at, 81.
Typology, method of interpretation, 58–59.
Tyre, 233.

UNIVERSE, the, St Paul's conception, 24–25.

VEGETARIANISM, reason for, 241.
Vices, habitual, of St Paul's day, 336.
Virgin Mary, veneration of, 6.
Virtues preached by St Paul, 335–336, 337.

Visions, theories regarding, 80–81.
Vocation of St Paul, 151 *et seq.*

WAGNER, Richard, allegorical treatment of New Testament, 61.
Weiss, B., St Paul's letter to Timothy and Titus, authenticity, viii.–ix.
Weizäcker, C., x.
Wernle, *Die Anfänge der Religion*, x.
Wine, Jewish ideas regarding, 241.
Women, question of emancipation, 274, 276–277.

ZARATHUSTRA, 147.